A WASTED LIFE

BY
DYKE WILKINSON

LONDON
GRANT RICHARDS
1902

PREFACE

MANY readers will recognise old friends in some of the chapters which make up this volume; as, with here and there slight alteration, they appeared, a few years ago, in the columns of the *Licensed Victuallers' Gazette*, under my pen name, "The Old Guv'nor."

I make no pretension in these fragmentary bits—dove-tailed together, as it were—to produce a faithful record of my life. That would mean a much more serious business. There is, however, enough of it here to show the ordinary reader what a strange, rough road I have travelled. To the thoughtful one, reading between the lines, intent on getting at the heart of the matter, many things will be clear.

As far as these pages apply to myself, I know clever people will stigmatise me as fool, or worse; and good people will call mine a wasted life. To the clever ones my only answer shall be: I have little care what you call me; I am approaching the allotted span of human life, and very soon shall be beyond the reach of praise or blame. I would ask the good folk : Is it not possible that such a life as mine even may have had its uses ? Is there any human life, or, for the matter of that, any atom in the economy of nature, utterly wasted ?

My earnest hope is that no person living, of those I have dealt with here, will feel themselves aggrieved; for, although I have felt obliged to treat of some regrettable personal matters, I have tried to do so without hurt to any man's feelings.

DYKE WILKINSON.

SYDNEY HOUSE,
HIGHGATE, N., 1902.

CONTENTS

CHAPTER I

EARLY LIFE

                                                          Page

IMPOUNDING a Horse—My first Race Meeting—How I got there—How I got back again—Apprenticeship—Birmingham Heroes 13

CHAPTER II

YOUNG MANHOOD

Our Parson—Love and Poetry—I become an Actor—Mechanical Inventions—"A Friend Indeed" 20

CHAPTER III

BUSINESS AND BETTING

Birmingham Millionaires—An infallible System—The System fails—"Taking the Knock" 30

CHAPTER IV

IN THE SIXTIES

Betting and Betting Men—Jackson—Henry Steel—John Robinson ... 36

CHAPTER V

NEWMARKET

Headquarters in Olden Times—Newmarket in the Sixties—Backing a Winner after the Number was up—A Struggle for a big Stake ... 42

CONTENTS

CHAPTER VI
PLUNGING

	Page
Credit v. Ready Money Betting—Ready Money Riley	50

CHAPTER VII
EARLY BOOKMAKING

Walsall Races—"Squaring" the Field—A nice Party 56

CHAPTER VIII
OUTSIDE BOOKMAKING

Betting at a "Judy"—Our Village—An old-fashioned Parson—An unfortunate Partnership 61

CHAPTER IX
"SAFE 'UNS"

"Safe 'Uns" which won—Chesterfield Races—Jemmy Barber and his Gang 81

CHAPTER X
AT LEICESTER

A useful Punter—The Bank replenished 90

CHAPTER XI
REMINISCENCES OF BIRMINGHAM

A famous Inn—Notable Brums—A Case of Sudden Death—The Ruling Passion—A short Boxing Bout—"Nibbler" Birch 94

CHAPTER XII
REMINISCENCES OF BIRMINGHAM

Palmer the Poisoner and Bob Brettle 107

CONTENTS

CHAPTER XIII
SQUARE HEADS

A cute Punter—A droll old Bookie 110

CHAPTER XIV
A STRANGE HISTORY

A Retrospect—Dan Lawrence—A wonderful Collier 119

CHAPTER XV
A PENITENTIAL MOOD

The Prayer of the Apostate—A Band of Hope 134

CHAPTER XVI
KINDNESS REWARDED

Warwick Races—A Dust-up with Thieves—What came of It 138

CHAPTER XVII
STOCKBRIDGE MEMORIES

Stockbridge in Old Times—In the Sixties—Mr. Merry and his hot Jobs—A sensational Dead Heat—An expensive Dinner 143

CHAPTER XVIII
GOODWOOD MEMORIES

Edmund Tattersall—Shannon's strange Win—Short Prices—Ten Broeck and his Jockeys—A short odds Bookmaker—Sharping George Payne 153

CHAPTER XIX
GAMBLERS AND GAMBLING

Hazards—Charley Chappell—Durden and the Parson—Inveterate Gamblers—Frank Lelen—Charles Head 163

CONTENTS

CHAPTER XX

GAMBLERS AND GAMBLING   Page

"Farmer" Quartley—Hazards at Sea—The Ladies' Hair-pins—Diamond cut Diamond 175

CHAPTER XXI

OLD-FASHIONED WELSHERS

My early Experience—Joe Manning—Johnny Quinn—The "Captain"   190

CHAPTER XXII

THE BRUTAL SCHOOL OF WELSHERS

How I came by a Limp—The Battle of Ewell—"Punch" and his History   212

CHAPTER XXIII

WELSHERS AND WELSHING

How he became a Welsher—Welshers Abroad—Punch and the Pigs ... 229

CHAPTER XXIV

NOBBLING

In at a good Thing—Going for the Gloves—How the Favourite was "got at" 251

CHAPTER XXV

ON TRAINERS AND JOCKEYS

The Reward of Civility—A Horse in the Bog—Jockeys and Owners—George Fordham—Tom Cannon—A Jockey "caught Napping"   260

CHAPTER XXVI

A TRAINER'S STORY

How he was broken—How mended 272

CONTENTS

CHAPTER XXVII

A JOCKEY'S YARN

A queer Judge—Racing in the West Country—George Ingram—The Weymouth Sharp ... 288

CHAPTER XXVIII

SHARPERS

The new Firm—A Sheffield Blade—"Cut and Put" Timson and the Trainer—The Swell who fed his Dog on Chicken—Angling for Flats—The Stroud M.P.—A near Thing ... 296

CHAPTER XXIX

WONDERFUL DREAMS

La Mervielle's Cambridgeshire—Archer and Master Kildare—Band Or's Derby—Common's Two Thousand Guineas ... 312

CHAPTER XXX

PUTTING THE "DOUBLE" ON

A remarkable Bookmaker—A false Friend—The Bookie's Revenge ... 321

CHAPTER XXXI

"RINGING IN" "A WRONG 'UN"

How Maurice Felton became a Punter—What came of It ... 329

CHAPTER XXXII

CASES OF MISTAKEN IDENTITY

Sir John Astley's Claim—Lord Marcus Beresford—A Fistic Preacher—Taking a Liberty ... 339

CONTENTS

CHAPTER XXXIII

SETTLING ACCOUNTS

How some Noblemen settle—"A Lady on Horseback"—A Trifle overlooked—Sharping a Sharper—Trying it on—Welshing a Lady 348

CHAPTER XXXIV

PLUNGERS

The Marquis of Hastings—Old Will Roberts—George Gomm—Little Hill—An American Plunger—The Jubilee Plunger 364

CHAPTER XXXV

LAYING AGAINST "SAFE 'UNS"

Pilgrimage's One Thousand—O'Connor and his Safe 'Uns—The true Story of the Fraulein Case—The Disqualification of Pattern ... 376

A HUMAN DOCUMENT

CHAPTER I

EARLY LIFE

"Pounding" a Horse—My first Race Meeting—How I got there—How I got back again—Apprenticeship—Birmingham Heroes.

I WAS born in the good old town of Birmingham, in a cottage then in its suburbs. It is sixty years ago, and more, since I gathered buttercups and daisies, and chased butterflies in Hickenbotham's fields—off Newtown Road. Where Hickenbotham's fields were, to-day is a wilderness of dingy houses and huge manufactories, begrimed and smutty as of age, and unwholesome ugliness of all sorts; and the nearest buttercups and daisies are miles and miles away.

What would the genteel youth of Birmingham now think of daily ablutions in those awful waters of the canal between Snowhill and Walmer Lane? It was there, nevertheless, where I, and thousands like me, learned to swim.

I had a good father, perhaps a little too careless and easy for the head of an unusually large family, composed mostly of unrulable boys. Of my mother it will be enough to say every one of us loved her tenderly during her life; and the few of us who are left revere her memory as the memory of a saint. My parents being of the respectable hard-working artisan class, with a very large family, as I have said, education for any of us was out of the question.

I remember going to a dame's school somewhere up a dark court in Lower Brearley Street and, for a little time, to a Church of England day-school; but at no time did the outlay on my education exceed twopence a week; and whatever of useful knowledge I managed to get was got by myself, after I became a working lad as a buttons "cobber" when about eight years old.

So early as this in my life I developed a passion for horses which, like other human passions,

"Ofttimes led me wrong."

Horses have afforded me a great deal of pleasure and occasionally some profit; but what with broken ribs, legs, arms, and pocket, I have not found my love for them "a joy for ever," or my dealings with them an unmixed pleasure. My first experience of the noble animal was in the year—well, never mind the year—it is farther behind me than I like to reflect on. I found a horse straying about the streets of my native town, without bridle, saddle, or halter even, so I drove him into the yard in the rear of my father's house, and it was not long before I had improvised a halter out of an old clothes line, and was on the way with him to the nearest "pound," where they took charge of the horse, handing a ticket to me which was my warrant for a shilling to be received when the horse was claimed. Instead of receiving a shilling for my trouble, I got one of the soundest thrashings I ever remember to have had. The horse was the property of a small tradesman, an intimate friend of my father, and it appeared some mischievous boys had driven him out of a badly-fenced field where he was grazing. The owner explained to my father the circumstances, and assured him I was one of the culprits—in this, however, he was mistaken—so I not only lost my shilling, but I got a thrashing which was undeserved, and induced me to vow that none of my good actions in the future should consist of taking care of other people's stray horses.

It was, also, in these very tender years that I got my first experience of a race meeting, which came about in this way.

One John Dyke was in those days a notable betting man, made a book, owned racers of his own, and was, as George Payne and other ancient turfites have told me, a man of some account on the turf in the thirties and forties. It happened that this same John Dyke was my mother's brother, who, while a young man, was troubled with ambitions to be something other than a journeyman button maker, so had taken to making a book instead, which resulted in his leaving Birmingham and living in style in London.

Once a year this great man of our family came down to Wolverhampton races. And I know that the less fortunate members of the family, whom he had left behind him in Birmingham, looked forward to these annual visits of " Uncle John" with a great deal of pleasure; and I am sure they had substantial reasons for looking back to them with gratitude, for he was a true racing man, and whatever his faults, had a big heart and an open hand.

In those days the facilities for travelling between Birmingham and Wolverhampton were very different to what they are now; so thousands went to the races by road. Many did the thirteen miles on " Shank's pony," while for the others every conceivable sort of vehicle was pressed into service. My father used to hire our vegetable merchant's " spring " cart, and in this stowed away my mother and eight or ten members of the family or friends.

I suppose I should be little more than eight years old when I took it into my head that it was about time I was included in the party; and I remember how I howled when told that my time for that sort of thing was not yet come. They started gaily on their journey; I raced after them, and but for an unoward circumstance should, I believe, have overtaken the lumbering old horse which carried them and the "spring" cart.

A sister, fleet of foot and twice my age, who had been left in charge, pursued me, seized me by the "scuff of the neck," and dragging me back home, shut me up in the bedroom; and to make quite sure I shouldn't make a second attempt, despoiled me of my cap and jacket. This, however, did not stop me; and half an hour after—bare-headed and jacketless—I was trudging along the Wolverhampton Road, which was lively all the way with motley crowds bound for the races. My goal was "Uncle John." By dint of hard walking—stealing an occasional ride, and hanging on to passing traps—I managed to get to Wolverhampton; got down to the crowded race grounds, but, of course, got no glimpse of this miraculous uncle, or of my father and mother.

When the races were over, tired and very hungry—and helped by bigger boys—I found my way back to the highway, intending to trudge back to Birmingham. I had not travelled very far before I got a glimpse of something a hundred yards or so in front of me which gave me more delight than anything I had seen that day. It was a peculiar Cashmere shawl, which my mother was wearing. I knew she was wrapped in that shawl, but I was far too done up to run after her.

"That's my father and mother," I cried to the biggest of my companions, pointing them out to him. "You go and stop them, and you'll get a lift."

He rushed after them, overtook them, and they halted till I arrived on the scene, then I was dragged into the cart, my friend attempting to follow me, but the "lift" he got was from the instrument with which my father was endeavouring to urge on the jaded horse with his already too heavy load. There was no space for me to sit, but I was very glad to lie among their feet at the bottom of the trap, where I soon fell fast asleep.

When and where I learned to read I could not tell, but

very early in life I was a reading lad, greedily absorbing anything and everything that came in my way. The death of a relative brought my father capital to the extent of two or three hundred pounds; with this he bought a small public-house; and here I found my education grow apace, while my opportunities for reading were largely increased, my literature being, I fancy, very much mixed.

I was enchanted with a torn and dirty old Bunyan's "Pilgrim's Progress," and a "Robinson Crusoe," which I found among the rubbish my father had taken to when he bought the "Dog and Pheasant." With these I found "Jack Sheppard," "Three-Fingered Jack," and several and sundry other tales of a like elevating character.

Nothing, however, in the shape of reading came amiss to me, and all were assimilated with equal zest and impartiality. I am, however, quite sure "Bell's Life in London" was my chief delight.

There was no Birmingham daily paper in those days, and none elsewhere which found its way to the "Dog and Pheasant." The famous old *Sporting Weekly*, with *Aris's Birmingham Gazette* and *The Dispatch*, were the first newspapers I became acquainted with. These were "Taken in Here," as a printed card, displayed in the big "bow window" in front of our house, intimated to all concerned. After these papers had been well read by the "indoors" for a day or two after publication, they travelled all over the neighbourhood from one to another of the "outdoors," and toward the end of the week, much the worse for wear and tear, they found their way back home, and were at my service, and then how eagerly I took in their contents. "Bell" was my prime favourite, especially that part of it which told of the mighty deeds of the gentlemen who were immortalising themselves within the magic circle of the P.R. of those times. Birmingham being the birthplace and school of these heroes, I not only saw their names in real print, but I saw them in the flesh; actually saw the great men themselves walking about our pavements of petrified kidneys like ordinary mortals. I have even known some of the lesser among those demi-gods—such as Teddy Mush and Jotter Palmer—visit my father's humble hostelry, and seen them take a turn at "Madam Clark" and "Ring the Bull" for quarts of "fourpenny" in our sawdusted taproom.

When twelve and a half years old I was apprenticed to a rule maker in St. Paul's Square *for eight years and a half.* Oh! the horrible cruelty of that act. An old and hardened man of the world, I shiver, even now, when I recall all that I saw, and suffered, and did,—I was but a child—during the earlier years of that damnable apprenticeship, and my blood boils up hot and fierce.

There were, as far as my memory serves me, about twenty apprentices, and very few men. Where I worked, a shop full of wild young lads and no man. No one to control us, teach us our craft, or show us a way to good of any sort. Knowledge of our trade was, for the most part, acquired of our elder fellow apprentices, or got as best we might. Knowledge of other sort was abundant, and the teachers plentiful. But the sort was bad, and wrought much mischief in the lives of many of these apprentices. Indeed, in my after life, I have wondered how any one of us came through the ordeal of that fatal bondage without being horribly scathed.

Even before my apprenticeship, although my educational opportunities were so few, I suppose I must have equipped myself after a fashion, for I remember that I was soon adding something to my scanty earnings by writing love-letters and epistles of all sorts for fellow-workmen much older than myself, and by telling stories to my fellow-apprentices, all of which were manufactured out of my own head as I went along. Five or six of these lads, foregoing the pleasure of dining at home, would bring their allowance for that meal wrapped in dirty bits of newspapers, or dirtier little cotton handkerchiefs, and sit around me, during the dinner hour, while I regaled them with tales of horror and adventure, which, I have no doubt, were the outcome of my study of the dreadful trash which was almost the only literary food for poor lads of that time. For this service each of my listeners subscribed a halfpenny a week.

When I was bound apprentice, I was too young to see what I was doing, or to understand the enormity of the sin of which I was the victim, in being bound to a trade I thoroughly detested, and which I soon came to know I should follow no longer than I was compelled to do. Soon the irksomeness of it became unbearable. More than once I ran away from it; and on one occasion, footsore, and nearly starved to death, I found my way to London, determined to be a sailor or hero of some sort.

After much wandering about the streets of the great Babylon, I discovered the lodgings of an elder brother somewhere in the neighbourhood of Old Street, St. Luke's. Alas! I did not find him blessed with my romantic nature; hence, a few days after my arrival, I was knocked up, as it seemed to me, in the middle of the night, and was forced to trudge through the dark streets to Euston Station, which we reached in time to catch the six o'clock parliamentary train—the one cheap train in the day. I was commended to the care of the guard, stowed away in a sort of cattle truck, shunted here and there, and stopping at every station on the way, I found myself, sometime in the afternoon, once more in Birmingham. There was then no New Street Station, and I arrived at what is now the goods station, in Curzon Street. My adventures as an apprentice would make a book, but I must resist the temptation to describe them more fully at present, and get on with other matters, which lead towards the turf and a life of strange vicissitudes.

CHAPTER II

YOUNG MANHOOD

Rev. Charles Vince—Love and Poetry—I become an Actor—Mechanical Inventions.

WHEN about seventeen years old I was induced to join a Sunday-school at Mount Zion Chapel, Graham Street, Birmingham, and this was destined to influence my life very strangely for a number of years. A wild boyish Bohemian with dangerous tendencies, I found here something appealing to another side of my nature. I became a member of educational classes, mental improvement societies, literary and debating clubs, and in the latter, especially, I soon took quite a prominent place.

Almost as long as I could remember, I had been in the habit of writing verse; and now I began to fancy myself a poet, because when I sent my effusions in this line to Sunday-school magazines they were generally accepted and printed; and sometimes the man who presided over these periodicals wrote me nice little letters of encouragement, some of which I have preserved to this day, and am even weak enough to cherish them. One of these, I remember, was from Mr. Edward Baines (afterwards Sir Edward), editor and proprietor of the *Leeds Mercury*, and sometime M.P. for that great city. He was also editor of *The Appeal*, a religious little weekly, to which I had contributed my verse.

As I have said, I was always a reading lad, and in these days I devoured all the books I could lay my hands on, especially the poets, Old Chaucer, Spencer, Shakespeare, and Milton. I read mostly in the streets, as I went to and fro between my home and my purgatory of a workshop.

But let it not be supposed that I detested my trade a whit the less since I had been reclaimed from my wilder ways. I now felt, I do believe, more keenly than ever the galling of the chain that bound me, although I had more control of myself, and was no longer in the habit of expressing my abhorrence in the same powerful language.

I shall now relate a little incident which befel me in these days, and one which was to influence a good deal of my after life; and in my old age I am apt to think it might have been better for me if I had allowed it to have influenced my life all through. The incident may have little interest for many of my readers, but to some Midlanders, and old Birmingham men particularly, I am sure it will be interesting.

I was going home to my dinner, my dirty apron rolled round me, and tucked up at the waist, with a book in my hand as usual, had just reached Mount Street, when I literally ran against a ruddy, round-faced, boyish-looking young man, dressed in a country-made suit of black, with the regulation parsonic "white choker" round his neck. He was bigger, and a few years older than myself, and had, I thought, rather a clumsy gait with him. After the collision I looked up into his face; and what a face it was! I remember it—after all these years—as I remember the face of my mother. A broad, beaming, genial,—aye, even jovial—sort of face, and set in it a pair of eyes full of the fire of genius and kindly human nature, and they captivated me from the moment I saw them. I fancy he rather liked my looks, too, for instead of rating me for carelessness, which he might have done, he laughed good-humouredly, chatting pleasantly as we walked up the street together.

"Can you tell me," he asked, "where I shall find Mount Zion Chapel?"

"Oh, yes. I am going past it, and will show you the way," I replied.

Of course, it soon came out that I attended the Sunday-school there. This appeared to please him, and he volunteered sundry pieces of information about himself, which made it clear he was, at that time, a student of Stepney College, a total stranger to Birmingham, not knowing a soul in the place. Also, that he had received an invitation from the good folk at Mount Zion to preach a trial sermon.

"So you will, perhaps, hear me to-morrow," he said, "and if the people like me, I may come to be your minister. If that happens, I would like to know you better and, perhaps, I may be of some service to you."

And then he made me promise, should these hopes of his as to the pastorship come to anything, that I would visit him.

Well, I heard him preach next day to a company of poor people who had been struggling, for several years, to keep the place going, while loaded with debt, and a weekly dwindling congregation. His success was instant and magnetic, and he was thereupon invited to become our pastor; and, although he had not anything like finished his time at Stepney, almost at once entered upon his duties. I kept my promise, and we became great friends; and many an hour, after my work was done at night, and frequently before I went to it in the early morning, have I spent with him at his lodgings, while he tried to cram me with Latin and other things, which he thought—good soul—would be needful in the future he was shaping for me. Work, this, loving and strenuous enough, but, alas! doomed to futility. The rough granite this good man chiselled at—trying to polish—was obdurate, unworkable, and utterly impossible of being wrought into the well-meaning minister's ideal.

Well, this comely, country-bred young parson who, a few years before, was himself a hard-working carpenter lad, was Charles Vince, who, in due course, became one of the most brilliant preachers in England; not only an ornament and a glory to his own sect, but known and revered by all classes and creeds among whom he lived. A power in educational, social, and political work, he finished his public life where he had begun it; and when he died—which is a good many years ago—all Birmingham mourned for him; the best of its citizens, and many thousands of its toilers, followed him sorrowfully to the grave. The jangle of sects and parties, for a day, was silenced. Roman Catholicism, Church of Englandism, Dissent, Atheism, Nothingarianism, and all the other isms and schisms, stood by his grave, knowing that a good man and true had passed from their midst.

As for me, a good many years agone we had come to the parting of the ways, and thenceforth I had seen but little of him. He had won an eminent place in the world; I was one of its hardened sinners, and shocking to relate, a professional betting-man. Nevertheless, I left my business in the midst of it, that I might stand once more, and for the last time, beside my old friend and master; and I feel no shame to say that many bitter tears burnt my face, and many a bitter thought tortured me, as I watched them hide forever from my view all that remained of one of the sweetest and noblest men I have ever known.

Seeking material for "copy" relating to my early life, I had recently occasion to "rummage" through an immense old oaken chest, which has been a cherished treasure from my boyhood, and which contains a marvellous assortment of odds and ends. Among them bundles upon bundles of letters neatly docketed and tied up with faded bits of ribbon, all in the handwriting of young girls, my various early sweethearts, half a score of them, at least. All gone! Whither, I know not. Some, doubtless, long since dead; others, probably, have become wrinkled and disagreeable old grandmothers. Buried in this great chest, along with these early love-letters, are remnants of wool-worked slippers, worn-out worsted mittens, a few *properties* of amateur acting days, endless newspaper and magazine cuttings of my early poetic effusions — in those times I travelled a good deal in that line. Above these, and a heterogeneous mass of other things of more or less interest, is a layer of neat-looking gilt-edged little betting books, such as are used by young beginners. Alas! what a tale these would tell, and what a sermon preach, could they but talk. Among these I found an old empty envelope, bearing a northern postmark, not far from the famous city of York, and of a date—well, farther back than I like to think. The inside of the envelope was blurred and stained; on the outside—written with a pencil, and still legible—were the following verses. Oh! what a dreadful bad time I must have been having.

A VIOLET.

(Sent by Post.)

Thou'rt welcome—welcome, lovely flow'r
  With sweetly-scented breath,
Thou come'st to me in darksome hour,
And to my soul in sad strange pow'r,
  Art preaching life and death.

Thou wert all fresh and fair and gay—
  Thing of beauty and grace—
When yester morn the King of day
A trembl'ng dewdrop kissed away
  From thy heav'nward turning face.

And now, my flower, thy tiny head
  Hangs earthward evermore;
Charm of thy mystic life hath fled,
And thou art soiled and crushed and dead—
  Aye, dead! my bonnie flow'r!

E'en such is this poor life of ours,
  To-day, with flashing eye,
We stand erect as gaudy flow'rs.
Boasting of all our matchless powers,
  To-morrow we fade and die.

'Twixt love and religion, I was pretty busy among the Muses while still in the "teens" of my years. These effusions brought me no money, but they did procure for me some considerable amount of local notice, especially among the young women folk, and I am afraid I fell in love, and out again, much too often. If any of my old sweethearts are still living, and remember these things against me, it will soften them something to know that, looking back through all these years, a sad remorsefulness mingles with many pleasant memories associated with them. Youthful folly, and inconstancy, my dear old ladies, I frankly admit; and like poor Burns, I fall back on Nature for an excuse. She gave me an ardent, impulsive temperament:

> " With passions wild and strong,
> And list'ning to their 'witching voice,
> Hast ofttimes led me wrong."

I was continually, more or less, in a fever of love, and when about twenty, I had a very severe attack. She was a charming little girl, with kissable lips, rosy cheeks, and a merry pair of eyes. Her father's business took him to live in Sheffield, whither, of course, my Pollie also migrated. I was disconsolate, and flinging all good resolutions, my books and classes, my religious pastors and masters, with the hard taskmaster, to whom I was bound, all to the winds, I followed her to Sheffield; and as I could not live entirely on love, became a member of one of the old fashioned stock companies at the Theatre Royal.

I played sundry small parts for some months. Meanwhile, the course of true love was not running smoothly. I had, or fancied, a reason for jealousy, and walking through the darkness and drizzle from the theatre to my lodgings one certain midnight, I saw my figure reflected by the streeet lamps; strange thoughts flashed through my mind, leading to an instant revulsion of feeling.

"The shadow of an actor," I muttered; "to-night a sham

nobleman, in tawdry trappings; a thing of tinsel and make-believe; hollow and unreal—a veritable sham. Why not try to be, in some sort, a real nobleman—or, anyway, a man—a real live man with a purpose, and not a sham?"

Nature had given me eyes which had been of use to me. Had shown me men, in the great town where I was born, who had lifted themselves out of poverty and obscurity into wealth and influence, and high social position; apparently with brains of no better quality than my own. What these had done I would do—why not? And more, even.

Thenceforth the footlights flared on me no more, forever. Forests of painted lath, painted canvas oceans and mountains, with all the "props" and paraphernalia of the playhouse, from that moment were behind me. I would go back to Birmingham and face the consequences, which I knew might be serious. I acted on this resolution, and my reception was better than my deserts. At home, and among the good folk at Mount Zion, I was the prodigal son returned—a strayed sheep once more gathered to the fold. These good friends of mine—for friends they were, meaning me only good—not only interceded with my hard taskmaster that he should spare me the usual punishment of runaway apprentices—a term of imprisonment—but induced him to forego the little remainder of the time which belonged to him, and cancel my indentures.

I was no sooner free than I set to work as only a free man can work, and with an energy which was a part of me at that time. In the first place I set about inventing and making some little matters of machinery for a rule maker; and so successfully that, locked up in a shop by myself, jealously hidden from the sight of other workmen, and with the assistance of a number of small circular saws, and bits of steel, in a steam-driven lathe, I was able to do the work of ten men.

Now, for the first time in my life, I was able to earn more than I wanted to spend; and so it was not long before I had saved what I thought would launch me in business on my own account.

My intimate chum was a journeyman jeweller, whom I induced to leave his situation and join his skill and workmanship to my capital and aptitude for salesman and traveller. And so we started, in a small way, but with high hopes, as manufacturing jewellers. Our reputation as steady young men who meant to go ahead was very helpful to us. My old employer, who had benefited by my inventions, discounted as many accommodation bills as I chose to take to him, out of the goodness of his heart, and at the modest rate of 25 per cent.

These early days of my business career were not only prosperous, but exceedingly happy ones, which I look back to as the happiest of my whole life. Business was so full of promise, and I so full of love for a meek-eyed frail young thing, the gentlest and truest human being I have ever known, I felt justified in getting married, and starting a home on my own account. The bustle of trade, and these tenderer matters, did not wholly divert attention from my literary purposes; but I would get rich first, money was such a power, would get rich quickly, if possible, and make haste back to my early love—the sacred Muse.

Dr. F. R. Lees, of Leeds, originator, I believe, of the Main Law Movement in England, an eminent lecturer, a powerful thinker, and a writer of great ability, had become known to me through some articles I had contributed to a north-country paper with which he was connected. I recall how, in these days, I paid him a few days' visit to his house at Meanwood, where we sat up nearly all one night discussing these literary aspirations of mine, and my "unholy means" of attaining their fruition, for so he stigmatised my burning desire to be rich; and yet he knew that no mere sordid love of wealth moved me, knew that my aims were worthy; but I can never forget how earnestly he pleaded with me that I would throw down this golden idol, whose worship would blur all my beautiful visions, harden my heart, stunt and enfeeble my intellect, and make impossible any return to the pursuit of my ideals. This, and a great deal more, he said, placing before me, in powerful language, the worthiness and beauty of my own ideals, and showing me how much nobler it were to fail in such pursuit, than it would be to succeed by prostrating myself to this base god. I was a very young man, and thought I knew best what was good for myself. Alas! how many times in recent years have I wished I had listened to the advice of wisdom and experience.

In connection with my early literary work, I may here claim that I originated the first halfpenny newspaper that I ever heard of, and possibly it was the very first that ever existed in England. It was named *The Banner*, and was very largely devoted to the interests of the temperance movement in Birmingham, reporting its meetings, and advocating its claims. It was printed on good paper, neatly got up, and had, I think, a very respectable circulation for a local effort of this kind. I had associated with me at its commencement Mr. Fred Johnson, a Birmingham accountant. I, however, did the editing, most of the writing, reported the meetings, and even got the advertisements. After the death of Mr. Johnson, Mr. William White, an influential member of the Society of Friends helped with the work, and his firm, White & Pike, printed the paper, and ultimately they took it over altogether. While on this subject I may say that *The Banner* was not the only newspaper which owed its birth to my initiative. A good many years after, and while deeply engrossed with my turf and other businesses, and in connection with my friend Mr. "Barty" Weekes, a famous Birmingham solicitor, I made a more ambitious attempt in journalism, starting a penny weekly, devoted to general news. This venture cost me a good deal of money, no end of hard work and anxiety during the ten years we kept it afloat. And when on the point of giving it up we had the good fortune to come across a purchaser with a liberality and generosity I have never found equalled in business. This was Mr. George Cadbury, the present head of the great cocoa firm.

"Will you find out what the paper has cost you from the commencement?" that gentleman inquired during one of our interviews regarding its sale. I told him the amount at our next meeting. I thought, of course, he was about to base an offer for the paper on these figures, and that we might, possibly, see a small moiety of the money back again, especially as I was acquainted with Mr. Cadbury's reputation for generous dealings in business matters. Imagine my feelings when he quietly remarked:

"Oh, that's what the paper has cost you. Well, I wouldn't like to feel that anybody was losing by what I bought of them, so that's the amount I'll give you for the paper."

Mr. Cadbury afterwards spent a good deal of money on it, and it is to-day, I believe, a thriving and prosperous journal, known as the *Birmingham News*.

CHAPTER III

BUSINESS AND BETTING

An Infallible System—Birmingham Millionaires—The System Fails—Taking the " Knock."

DEAR old Birmingham is a wonderful place in many ways, and from the nature and variety of her manufactures, offers opportunities for young men who mean to "get on," unequalled by any other city in His Majesty's Dominions. Outside London there is, I suppose, no city where there are so many prosperous, well-to-do men, who have worked their way up from "the bench."

Some of these I have known intimately, and in one way and another have rubbed against many of them in my time. Here is a story which will illustrate my meaning:

While I was busy on the inventions I have referred to, I had occasion to get a matter of turning done, or something of the kind, so found my way down a poor court in Mount Street where a number of young beginners of various trades—too poor to have steam engines of their own—rented small workshops, with the use of steam power from somebody else. The two young engineers I wanted to see, and whom I did see, in their greasy aprons and work-a-day dress, bore the Cornish name of Tangye.

When my engineering business was done with these young men, I passed into another shop in the same court, where I found two other industrious young strugglers, one of them an intimate friend, and the brother-in-law of my own partner, who

BUSINESS AND BETTING 31

were renting power for the purpose of pointing pins, and making small brass rivets, which should shortly supersede the old-fashioned cobbler's waxed thread, to secure the soles to the "uppers" of our boots and shoes. The two young engineers became millionaires, patrons of art, munificent endowers of hospitals, art galleries, and schools; founders and heads of one of the great engineering concerns of the world.

The other two young strugglers founded and built up probably the largest pin works in the world; one of them, William Cook, the brother-in-law of my partner, is now, and has been for many years, an alderman and magistrate of the city, and was for a time M.P. for one of its divisions and is, I suppose, a very wealthy man.

These are not unique examples, but I name them as two among many firms whose origin and history I have watched, and now I am to make sorrowful confession of how I came to miss my chance of being found among this goodly company.

Considering how small was the beginning, our business grew with amazing rapidity. I did the travelling, my "ground" extending southwards to Penzance and northwards to Edinburgh. Mostly manufacturing jewellers sold their goods to factors. I struck out for my little firm a bolder course, and went direct to the shopkeeper. Orders rolled in, with the result that, in a couple of years, we found ourselves considerable employers of labour—the masters of a thriving manufactory. We had in our service a dear old friend, a certain William Collins, as traveller and confidential help. What he helped us to—doubtless with sincerity and good intention—will shortly appear. One Monday morning he came to the works big with fate for the firm, now busy, starting the new week well, preparing a "melt" which, when properly mixed, rolled, cut up, and manipulated, would be a barrow-load of *bright gold* brooches, earrings, and other ornaments. The ingredients which were to produce this display were already in the crucible: a hundred golden sovereigns, fresh from the mint; a parcel of pure silver; and with these, I am obliged to confess, an amount of copper, something more than twice the weight of its co-constituents combined. The whole, when properly fused, shall be known in Houndsditch and elsewhere as "bright gold," in contradistinction to "coloured gold," or gold of any particular carat, warranted by Hall-mark.

At this moment entered Mr. Collins claiming time for instant private talk on a matter of urgency.

"Fire away, Will, and let me hear quickly what's the matter," said I.

"Well, then, to begin with, I'm come to tell you I'm giving up my job with you."

"Oh, indeed! and may I ask wherefore?" inquired I, with a feeling of alarm, knowing it must be a serious matter which could have driven my old friend to such a course.

"Well, the fact of the matter is," began Collins, "I've found a better trade, and one I wish you would join me in."

And then he proceeded to unfold a scheme which had taken many months maturing, a scheme for backing horses on unerring mathematical principles—in fact, he had already given the system a trial on the quiet, for bits of silver only, and even in this modest way it had been good enough to earn a certain sovereign or more weekly. It could be worked just as easily in fivers and tenners, or in hundreds even, with capital behind you, and so a fortune realised almost at once; and our ambitious young jeweller might save himself the years of plodding toil, become rich quickly, and so, while still young, with all the vigour of youth, be enabled to devote himself to those noble aims and pursuits he was ever dreaming of. At first I struggled against the temptation—even thrust it from me with some disdain. Now, while I did want to make a lot of money, and that quickly, I must do myself the justice to say these desires were founded on no mere sordid motives; so I thought

BUSINESS AND BETTING

there could be no great harm in looking into the thing and examining my tempter's evidence, because if there really was anything in it, would not the end justify the means, etc.? So racing calendars, for several seasons past, with copious sheets of foolscap, were instantly produced by our friend Collins; and, after a couple of hours' closest scrutiny, I was obliged to confess there was something in it. The scheme was revealed to me so clearly infallible, that I turned out of the melting pot the hundred bright sovereigns and handed them to my friend, so he might catch the train for a distant race-meeting, where the infallible system should be put into actual practice.

During the four days following, the scheme was in full work in the hands of its author—for the present, however, only on modest dimensions. On Friday night our agent returned, bringing back with him the hundred pounds and some ten pounds profit, which should have been considerably more, only that the first favourite had been missed on two occasions, the second favourite being backed by mistake, which had thrown the machinery a little out of gear. But with practice should we not be able always to find the true favourite? The great thing was, the principle could not fail. You had only to back the favourite in the first event for a given—rather small—sum; if that lost, increasing your stake on a graduating scale drawn out with mathematical precision, no matter how many times you lose—having nerve enough to plank it down—the first time a favourite wins, you get it all back, and a lot besides. Indeed, so good did it appear, we decided to give it a trial the following week. It was glorious Goodwood, and now behold me accompanied with my guide, philosopher, and friend, fairly launched on the Turf in the character of a new punter. On the first day no favourite won either of the first four races, and on the fifth we had to pull out and plank down a larger sum than I relished. However, I did it manfully, posting the clean notes into the hands of a gentleman who was offering liberal odds. "And now," says I, "let us go on to the Stand and see the race." We had scarcely reached the top of the Stand when the horses were on the way, and in less than two minutes we had the unspeakable pleasure of seeing the gee-gee I had backed romp past the post the easiest of winners, and you may be sure it was not long before we descended gleefully to the ring to receive the money, altogether £60, £40 being the winnings and the remainder my own stake. But, alas! the bright little gentleman of liberal odds with whom I had betted was nowhere to be found; we made inquiries in every direction, among all sorts of people, explaining the circumstances; among others, to one of the officials, who told us rather curtly he thought "we were precious green"; a gentleman standing near winked his eye, saying facetiously, "It's all right, my boys, you'll see him again some day." Another bluntly declared we had been "welshed," whatever that might mean; anyway, we saw him no more that week. Some weeks after I saw and accosted a genteel little fellow named Manning, feeling prepared to swear this was the very man, so I demanded the £60. But he swore in choicest English, and in such a positive manner, that he had never been at Goodwood in his life, so you see it could not have been him. However, to return to the ring at Goodwood. While being annoyed at this loss, I was delighted with the soundness of the infallible method, and acted on it during the remainder of the week, only exercising great circumspection as to the men I betted with. At the end of the week we returned home—in spite of the one untoward event—with my capital intact, and a considerable profit. The following week the system was in full operation again at Brighton and Lewes, with equally good results. So was it for several weeks. I now began to find it difficult to hide my light under a bushel, or otherwise. In fact, I was followed about the ring, and became known as the successful new punter. The ring—for the many years I have known it—has, at all times had its successful new punter. I had now no

BUSINESS AND BETTING

longer need to pull out the "*ready*." I had a weekly account, hence I began to try the system on a higher scale. Alas! however infallible our systems, the best of men are, after all, really fallible. Again I made serious blunders, mistaking the true first favourites, which resulted in a couple of losing weeks, wherein went all the previous winnings. So we find ourselves arrived at the famous York meeting. Here it was decided to go in for still larger results, the method having proved itself faultless, and my bungling alone blamable for partial failure. Well, this same York meeting must remain a very memorable one. All the good things were beaten, and, in fact, not one first favourite got home during the four days. Surely an unheard-of calamity, enough to smash up any—the most infallible—system. My readers will be able to picture to themselves what this would mean to a backer of first favourites, on the gradually increasing—or getting back—system. Need I say I found myself on Friday night an utterly ruined man. Not all the bright gold brooches, earrings, and other ornaments in our establishment, stock-in-trade, household effects, with all our worldly belongings, would have sufficed to settle with the bookies on the following Monday. In the vulgar parlance of the Turf, I was obliged to "*take the knock*."

This was an ignominious ending to my grand hope of getting quickly rich, and being so enabled to plant my foot firmly on the ladder of my ambitions without the tedious humdrum processes of trade, which *seemed* to mean so many years of precious time lost.

CHAPTER IV

IN THE SIXTIES

Betting and Betting Men—John Jackson—Henry Steel—John Robinson.

So far, I had managed this betting business with great secrecy. My chapel-going friends, my business connections—including my banker—and even my own family, excepting my brother Sam, who was thick in it with me, were kept in ignorance. But this earthquake of a calamity shook my business to its foundations, damaged my character, and exposed its hollowness to all my little wondering world.

It left me, however, reckless and defiant. I would not admit defeat; that which had broken me should mend me again. So I continued betting, and not being able to go racing myself, others went for me, and the inevitable came. I lost my business, my friends, my beautiful home, and well-nigh broke the heart of one of the gentlest human beings that God ever lent to this earth; and He lent her for so short a time, she did not live to see the prosperous days which were yet in store for me.

How was it possible for any ordinary backer of horses to do other than get broken in the days I am writing of? The way for non-professional backers in these times is thorny enough, and fraught with dangers they know nothing of. But competition has troubled even the bookmaker's profession, as in all others it is overcrowded, hence they are compelled to lay something like fair prices—that is to say, a backer can now get what looks like fifteen shillings for his pound. It would make modern bookmakers ill and green with envy to tell of the prices we poor punters of the early sixties were compelled to take.

If, in addition to being compelled to accept ruinous prices, you happen to be cursed with a credulous disposition and an ever-open ear for "tips," depend upon it your chance of getting rich, as a punter, is very remote indeed. This was my case in those days, and occasionally I come across painful reminders of it.

It is wonderful how just a glimpse of something belonging to the long-buried past will brighten up the memory, and bring before us men and incidents which had been unthought of for many, many years. I have been having another rummage in that same old oak-chest which contains the odds and ends of a lifetime; among the little gilt-edged punter's books, dated 1864, opening one, quite promiscuously, at the Worcester Summer Meeting of that year, I dropped on one race which reproduced before my mind's eye a scene which occurred nearly thirty-five years ago, as vividly as it were a matter of to-day.

I must tell you that I was fairly gone on Jimmy Grimshaw's mounts. And I don't think it worked so very badly at that particular time. I was walking across the pitchcroft half an hour before the first race when I overtook Joe Sadler, of Wolverhampton, a professional backer, and one of the cleverest I have known in the whole of my experience. You will know he was clever when I tell you he was not only able to hold his own at the game, but to retire, ultimately, on a comfortable competency.

"You'll have a fiver on one I'll tell you of for the first race," says he.

"I hope it will be Jimmy's mount, then," I replied, "because I'm backing nothing else now. But what is it?"

"Jimmy's mounts be hanged! Do what I tell you, or I'll never forgive you," said he.

But he wouldn't tell me what the good thing was until I had

given him my word to have a fiver on, which I promised, but with the mental reservation that I would continue my system all the same; and as old Joe parted from me, he said earnestly:

"Now, as soon as the betting opens you get on Count Batthyany's Suburban; Harry Custance has come specially to ride him, and he's meant, and sure to win."

When the numbers went up I found there were only four runners—Count Batthyany's Suburban, Custance up; Lord Coventry's Umpire, Jim Adams up; Lord Bateman's Moulsey, ridden by George Fordham; and a two-year-old of Joe Saxon's named Bonnie Lass, which was the mount of little Grimshaw. I found Grimshaw, for a wonder, was not favourite. According to my system, I had now to put six pounds on his mount, which I did at 5 to 1. I then inquired the price of Suburban, and the best offer being 3 to 1, I planked down a tenner on that. I was booking the bet when Joe Sadler came running up to me.

"What have you done?" was his hurried inquiry.

"Backed your tip for a tenner," I answered, a little alarmed.

"I was afraid you would, and have been hunting after you," said he. "I find it won't do; it's Umpire, the favourite, you *must* be on. Quick! or you won't get on at all. It's a snip." And away he rushed. What was to be done? It appeared certain the tenner on Suburban had gone; my only chance to get it back was to have a dash on the favourite, so I immediately took 25 to 20 Umpire.

By this time the horses were going down to the starting-post.

"What 'av' yer bocked?" inquired big Dan Lawrence, who came up at the moment.

"Umpire," I answered, ashamed to tell him I had backed three horses out of four.

"Thee mak' hearste, then, and get thee a pony on Lord Beartmon's," growled the collier as he passed on.

This I could not possibly do; already I was nearly "round" on my book, and could win nothing one of the three, and very little the other two, and if I backed Moulsey I must make them all losers, so I decided to stop where I was, and proceeded to watch the race. And now they're off; and they hadn't been long off before I saw two of my champions in trouble. Jimmy Grimshaw, on the two-year-old, was clearly beaten, as was Suburban; and Umpire came on in front of Moulsey, and I saw it was going to be a race with these two. And, sure enough, a tremendous race it was. First one and then the other appeared to have the advantage of a nose; but from the angle I stood at I felt certain Umpire's nose was in front when they passed the post. "Thank goodness!" I muttered as I turned away, resolving to have a small bottle by way of settling my nerves after the excitement I had gone through. You can imagine my feelings when, turning to take a look at the number board, I saw Moulsey's number at top and Umpire's under it.

Truly, in those days, a man needed little beyond the proverbial "pencil and a book" to be a bookmaker, and if nature had only added to this capital a lusty voice, with a fair share of "face," a speedy competence was assured. A neglected education, nay, a total absence of it, was no bar. Two of the three elementary "R's" could certainly be dispensed with; so they could manage to scrawl a name and a few figures, or pay a clerk who could do it, a knowledge of figures being quite unnecessary. The bookie laid such prices, it was next to impossible for him to go wrong—6 to 4, each of two horses, and 2 to 1 another, with very gradually lengthening prices half-a-dozen more, in the same field, was a common occurrence, and, as customers were plentiful, there was no need to keep a sharp look-out as to the state of the book, as the bookies are obliged to do in these times.

A member of the one time well-known firm of Keeling & Gibson, hailing from Sheffield, who betted mostly to ready money, or settled on the following morning, once told me they never troubled to look at their book except to see what they had to pay. When they returned home at the end of the week, they simply turned out their pockets and divided the spoil; and there were plenty of firms in their class who did the same.

It was, indeed, then an easy matter to make money fielding, f one only played the game fair and square. How else can one understand so many bookies of the sixties piling up immense fortunes. Rough and unpolished in manners, without education, and of poor mental calibre, they lived up to incomes far beyond that of a Lord High Chancellor or Prime Minister of England, and dying fat and opulent, their offspring may have become the founders of county families. Who knows?

I would not, however, have it assumed that this description applies to all the bookmakers I knew in the sixties. There were notable exceptions; yet even to these a portion of my description will apply. John Jackson, "Jock o' Fairfield," as he was called, is the first exception I should name. When the decade opened, Jackson had been for years the leviathan bettor of the turf, and, quite early in it, his mantle was gradually descending on to the broad shoulders of a more wonderful man.

There is no doubt "Jock" was a bold and ambitious bettor, and withal, an extremely able man. This and a great deal more applies to Henry Steel, who succeeded—if he did not supplant—him as premier fielder and leviathan. Perhaps no man, in any walk of life, ever started to climb the ladder of fortune more heavily handicapped in many respects than Mr. Steel. Despite of this, however, he went rapidly to the front, and ultimately to the very top of his profession.

Nature had endowed him with many of her choicest gifts. He had clear vision and indomitable pluck; knew what he wanted, and meant to have it. A man of enormous energy, with insight and foresight, and the broad grasp of things, denoting your really able man. Such an one as, with educational and other advantages, might have been fitted to hold the highest places in the State. So one is not surprised that he should become not only a millionaire, but a great commercial magnate.

John Robinson, who must also be named among these exceptions, was not, I believe, in the circumstances of his early life, so unfortunate as Steel; but I remember him well when he first appeared on Newmarket Heath in the character of a fielder. His small face, clear cut, and full of character; his eyes keen as those of a hawk, and his small round head topped with a funny little cap. This was the day of his small beginnings. Observant men, and those who knew him, never doubted he, too, would rise in the world. What he did rise to, and what he is now, with his vast commercial undertakings, are matters of history.

These, then, are the three most notable exceptions to my description of the betting men of the sixties which occur to me at the moment, but I know there are more of them, among whom Sidney Smith, John Foy, and perhaps half-a-dozen others might be named.

CHAPTER V

AT NEWMARKET

Newmarket in Old Times—Newmarket in the Sixties—Backing a Winner after the Number was Up—A Struggle for a Big Stake.

For more than 250 years Newmarket has been the acknowledged headquarters of horse-racing in this country, and during nearly the whole of that time it has been the resort of all the noblest and best in the land, and more or less under the patronage of Royalty itself. The pedantic Scotchman, James I., whatever his faults, was an earnest supporter of the sport, and must have the credit of being the first kingly patron of Newmarket. The reign of his unfortunate son, the first Charles, was too full of trouble to allow him time for this or any other kind of sport, and of course the Puritans of the Commonwealth could not be expected to have any leaning that way; and yet there is ample evidence that even old "Noll" was a dear lover of good horses, and went so far in encouragement of their breeding as to keep thoroughbreds himself.

That merry gentleman, Charles II., in the matter of horse-racing, made, however, full amends for the shortcomings of the Commonwealth and his father's unhappy reign in this respect; and he not only revived all the glories of Newmarket, but he lifted it to a prouder pre-eminence than it had ever possessed; which position it has held, unchallenged, down to the present day. Charles built stables there, the remains of which have been visible in our time; he kept an important stud of racers, attended most of the meetings, and, in fact, lived no inconsiderable portion of his time in the quaint little Cambridgeshire town. The most important races hitherto had been run over what was known as "The Bell Courses," and the most valuable prizes had been bells. These he discontinued, and introduced cups, or bowls, on which were engraved the pedigree and exploits of the winners. And all over the country he did his best to foster and encourage the popular sport; but it was Newmarket that chiefly benefited by his patronage, and there its influence remained a power for generations. William III. was extremely fond of racing, founding an academy for riding, and gave a number of plates to be run for. Queen Anne followed in the footsteps of our Dutch king, and, by her constant presence and encouragement, did much to strengthen the hold which racing had obtained on the habits and affections of the English people. George I. was not behind either of his immediate predecessors in this respect. He abolished plates, and gave instead what was then considered of much more value and importance—prizes of 100 guineas each.

George II. also patronised horse-racing, and in the thirteenth year of his reign secured the passing of a Bill in Parliament for its better regulation. In the first place, he suppressed pony-racing, and, in fact, forbade all weak and undersized horses of all sorts engaging in the sport; and no race was to be of less value than £50, a penalty of £200 being imposed on the owner of every horse competing in such race, and £100 for anybody guilty of publicly advertising it. Another drastic change was that no person should enter more than one horse for any stake, nor run any horse not *bonâ-fide* his own property; and the penalty for breach of this part of the new law was the forfeiture of the horses entered or running contrary to the Act.

Of course, no such thing as handicapping was known in those times, and in the light of our experience our ancestors' notions of weight-for-age conditions appear simply ludicrous. The

Act says that five-year-olds shall carry 10 st., six-year-olds 11 st., and seven-year-olds 12 st. each. They knew nothing in those times of two-year-old five-furlong sprints, which in our time form so large a part of every race programme, and which are, in the opinion of some of the authorities, steadily working a deterioration in the quality of our thoroughbreds.

The two courses at Newmarket in the days of which I have been writing were known as the "Long Course," 4 miles 380 yards, and the "Round Course," which was 6,640 yards, or only 780 yards less than the Long Course. Childers—then supposed to be the fastest horse ever foaled—is said to have done the former in $7\frac{1}{2}$ min. and the latter in 6 min. 40 sec.; but, of course, it is open to question whether our great-grandfathers had the same perfect means of timing races which exist at the present time.

Newmarket and its doings having for so many years engaged my thoughts, and occupied my time beyond every other resort of the racing man, and loving the dear old town and its breezy Heath must be my excuse for this rather long digression into its ancient history. In the times of which I am now to treat, some of the meetings began Monday morning and finished the following Saturday afternoon. It was inconvenient, if not impossible, to get from Birmingham to Newmarket on the Sunday, consequently I and my friends had to get to Cambridge by the first train Monday morning, and from thence, hiring horses and vehicles, drive like mad to catch the first race. Our party, as a rule, consisted of my brother, the two elder Collins's, and myself. Ned Collins, having been a Brummagen butcher boy, had acquired the secret of getting out of the gee-gee all its possibilities in the matter of speed, so on these occasions he used to insist on holding "the ribbons," with a result which, I fear, was by no means agreeable either to the horse or its owner, but he generally managed to get us on to the Heath before the numbers were hoisted for the first race.

AT NEWMARKET

Newmarket, in the days of my earliest recollections of it, retained many of its ancient characteristics, and amongst its *habitués* it was easy to see old English noblemen and squires, whose quaint dress and manners left no doubt about them being survivals of a past age. In the shape of enclosures, grand stands, or shelter of any kind, there was little accommodation on any part of the Heath; nor did we feel very greatly to need them. Numbers of ladies and gentlemen rode about the Heath, while most of the others came in carriages. Even the professional betting men hired carriages of some sort or brought their own, and very largely the betting was done from these carriages, driven to the various finishing posts, and drawn up by the side of the course. This was long anterior to the inventions of "Tattersall's Enclosures," and the one or two small rings then in existence were comparatively little used for betting purposes, for the reason that the winning posts were all over the Heath, and sometimes at a considerable distance from either of these small enclosures; and when it was drawing near the time for the decision of a race, nearly everybody hurried off helter-skelter with carriages, hacks, and on foot, to see the finish, and to bet to the last moment.

As through the vista of nearly forty years all these scenes crowd upon my memory, it is strange how vividly some incidents—trifling enough in themselves—rush into my mind's eye. One of my very early recollections of Newmarket is associated with two old Northerners, who, in their different lines, were among the greatest men the turf has produced. There is at this moment an incident concerning these two men in my mind's eye as vividly impressed as if it were an event of yesterday. On the Heath a great number of carriages are congregated near one of the many winning posts; for, as I have elsewhere observed, in those days there was but scant accommodation for race-seeing, or betting on grand stands and enclosures; hence the tops of these carriages were used for those purposes. I see, standing on the roof of one of these broughams, a man with a pair of field-glasses held to his eyes, eagerly scanning a crowd of gallant horses as they fly across that noble course, while, ever and anon, his stentorian voice is heard above the clamour of the crowd, now shouting for this horse, and then against another. He appears to me a most excitable man, at the moment worked up to the highest pitch. He is stepping backwards and forwards on the top of the carriage, making every moment some tremendous bets. This is John Jackson, the great leviathan bookmaker, who for a second seems perilously near stepping backwards off the top of the carriage, which means probably a broken back or a broken neck.

A genial old gentleman, seated on the driving box of the next carriage, sees the danger, and as the great fielder, forgetting everything in his intense excitement, is stepping back once more, this time on the very outmost edge of the roof, he cries out:

"For God's sake, be careful, John, or you'll break your neck!" and I think it is not unlikely that the old man's timely warning saved Jackson's life. That quaint old gentleman was John Scott.

The practice of rushing away to see the race sometimes resulted in extraordinary *contretemps*, and more than once I have known the few bookies and backers remaining in the ring go on with their betting sometimes after the race was over, quite oblivious of the fact.

There was, I remember, a little betting ring near the spot where some years ago the principal grand stand was erected. From this place there was but scant opportunity of seeing anything of the racing.

At the single entrance stood a movable pay office, something like a sentry-box. Now, it must be remembered I am speaking of my first visit to the classic Heath, my knowledge of racing matters and racing men being of the most primitive description. Along with me was Mr. W Collins, afterwards to become widely and more familiarly known as "Spectacle Collins." He was the eldest of that ilk which has since become tolerably well known on the turf; he was then, however, just as green as myself.

The numbers were hoisted for a match, a regular gambling affair, between Money Spinner and a horse named Catologue, belonging to that hapless young punter, the Marquis of Hastings.

It was a near thing between them "on form," so that the betting was extensive and furious. I had no interest in it, but thought I should like to see the race, which was quite impossible while standing in the ring, the winning-post being nearly a quarter of a mile away, so I mounted the rails and held myself up by the top of the sentry-box. I was scarcely there when I saw the race was actually being run—indeed, was nearly over.

"Why, Catalogue wins," I said to Collins, who stood below me.

"What's that you say?" inquired a sagacious-looking gentleman, who at that very moment was passing into the ring.

"Catalogue has won now," I repeated.

Instantly the sagacious one rushed into the ring, and from my coign of vantage I saw him, book in hand, popping from one to another of the fielders, and I should say he would have made quite a number of bets before it was known the race was over; for before the people in the ring were aware the horses had started the winner's number went up. And this was by no means the first time—or the last—that such a thing has been known to happen at Newmarket.

One of the Newmarket races which has left its impress on my mind belongs to this time, and it was one also in which the Marquis of Hastings was interested. I often think the memories of our old jockeys must be stored with endless pictures of great races which have become historical.

I wonder whether Tom Cannon or Charley Maidment—both jockeys who have played a notable part in the great races of the past, and both happily remaining with us to-day—ever think of that fierce fight of theirs for the Cambridgeshire of 1864. I witnessed it, and can see it now "in the mind's eye." I had been stalled off Ackworth by old Dan Lawrence, and rushed on to Lord Stamford's Brick, who was about second favourite, and I was not long kept in suspense about him, for a long way on the other side of the winning-post there were only two in it; they were the Marquis of Hastings' Ackworth, with Cannon in the saddle, and Baron Rothschild's Tomato, Maidment up. They were both three-year-olds, carrying 7 st. and 7 st. 5 lb. respectively. Ackworth had been beaten less than a length for the Cesarewitch in a tremendous field of twenty-nine, and although there were four or five better favourites for the Cambridgeshire, he had a strong following. On the other hand, Tomato was one of the most despised of the whole party, and really had no price at all. Both jockeys were extremely good lads, just beginning to give promise of the brilliant future that lay before them. I always thought Maidment, as a lad, looked rather delicate, and there is no doubt Cannon was much the stronger of the two, and to this I have no doubt is owing the fact that the layers missed by the merest shave what would have been one of the most perfect "turn ups" ever known in racing. As I have said, a long way from home the well-known scarlet and white hoops of the Marquis and the bonnie blue jacket and yellow cap of the good old Baron were right bang in front, and we knew the final struggle would be with them. And what a struggle it was! As they neared the goal the lads were at it, hammer and tongs, riding as for dear life, and putting in every atom they possessed. The noble animals, inspired, as it seemed, by the same spirit, exerted themselves to the utmost and answered bravely every call. Now the horse seemed having a shade the best of it, and now the mare; head and head together they came along, and, as amid intense excitement, they so passed the post, the bookies screamed loudly for the Baron, and the followers of the Marquis for his horse, while many thought it was a dead heat, and only "the man in the box" could tell that Ackworth had landed by the shortest of heads.

CHAPTER VI

PLUNGING

Credit and Ready Money Betting—"Ready Money Riley."

A GOOD deal of nonsense has been written and spoken on the betting question. From every point of view, perhaps the most silly proposal was that which aimed at putting an end to ready money betting. That there are evils connected with racing and betting it would be worse than useless to deny, but that the evil would be checked in the slightest degree by declaring it illegal to bet for ready money only those with the most superficial knowledge of the question will be prepared to admit. For myself, I unhesitatingly assert that the *legalising* of all forms of betting would tend rather to diminish than to increase the practice.

For many years I have advocated the legalising of betting, especially that for ready money. I am confident it would tend, in a large measure, to purge the turf of some of its most objectionable features. To those without practical knowledge of the subject, and to others who know the turf intimately, but who have not given the matter serious thought, this statement will sound strange, if not paradoxical. Take the occasional cases of reckless plunging as one of the features referred to, than which nothing, perhaps, has conduced more largely to bring discredit upon the turf. Well, I have been in a position to watch attentively many of these cases for nearly forty years, and have been intimately acquainted with some of the victims, and am prepared to assert most emphatically, from my own certain knowledge, that many of them were due, in the first place, to the credit system with its weekly settlings, and then to the fact that there was no law to compel settlement. And it must not be assumed from this statement that I class these plungers—who, after ruining themselves, as a rule finish by becoming defaulters—as intentionally dishonourable; that is not my contention, but the contrary of it, and a case well known to myself will illustrate my meaning.

A young tradesman in a good position goes into the ring, begins to bet, and finds credit thrust upon him. He loses, and, in the parlance of betting men, he "gets the fork"—that is, bets more heavily the more he loses, trying to recover his losses; after glimpses of better fortune, he goes down again and again. He will do anything, make any sacrifice to settle this week, sure that the spell of bad luck cannot continue, and will plunge still more heavily next week to get it all back. So the end is reached. Now, it is morally certain that had this man been compelled to pull out the hard cash and look at it every time he made a bet—ay, or even after every race—he would never have gone to these extremes; neither would he with the certainty of a legal liability before his eyes; for it requires only an elementary knowledge of human nature to assure us that timid men, like rats, will fight anything when in a corner, and even good men, when sorely pressed, will be guilty of deeds they had supposed impossible. Therefore, in my opinion, nothing would do more to lessen gambling and restrain it within reasonable limits than the legalising of all betting; and certainly if any portion of the system ought to be declared illegal, it should not be the ready money betting.

It was not my knowledge of Ready Money Riley, with his short yet strangely chequered career, which induced these reflections, but rather the reflections which gave rise to a desire to say a few words about this notorious character, which will serve to illustrate my contentions regarding the evils of credit betting.

I suppose there are few racing men who have not heard of him and his marvellous plunging, with its briliant run of luck and sudden collapse, and some few of the older members of Tattersall's enclosure will be able to call to mind the figure of the prim and dainty little man—who looked like a sort of cross between a well-to-do young clergyman and the coffee-room waiter of a first-class hotel—as he moved quietly about the ring, handing, now Henry Steel and then Jacob Bayliss, or other of the leviathans of that day, perhaps thousands of pounds in Bank of England notes to cover a bet just made. But I think there are few who know where he came from or what has become of him.

Riley was born and reared in Birmingham, in what is known as the jewellers' quarter; he came of a very respectable family of the superior artisan class, and was himself put early to the jewellery trade, and became an extremely expert and skilful workman.

When he grew up to man's estate, finding his progress toward wealth didn't keep pace with his ambitious designs by means of his trade, he added to it the practice of backing horses. This, at any rate for a time, did not mend matters—indeed, it was very much the other way about; and he went "broke," got somehow mended—people do say by questionable methods—and then went broke again; but, like all great men, he never for a moment lost faith in himself. And I remember hearing him say on one occasion, when in the sorriest plight:

"Never mind! You'll see me win a fortune yet backing horses."

We laughed at him, but the prediction came to pass.

I ran against him one day in Birmingham. I believe it was in the spring of 1865. He appeared—for him—unusually excited.

"Heigho, Fred!" I cried, "where are you off to in such a hurry?" He answered my question by asking another.

PLUNGING

"Don't you know?—it's Northampton races to-day. Aren't you going?"

"I am not. Are you?"

"Yes, I am," he replied, "and I'm going to win a pile of money. I've borrowed a fiver, and if you'll come along you shall see what I'll run it into."

I did not see what he ran it into, because I did not go; but I afterwards knew that it became some hundreds of pounds before the week was over. The following week he was having hundreds of pounds down at a time, and all in ready money. He did not bet on all races; in fact, he bet on few. It was part of his system to wait for the good things, and then dash it down in lumps, and the good things came off so regularly during that part of the season that it was small wonder he very soon began to bet in thousands, and that a crowd of punters was always at his heels to see what the lucky ready money plunger was doing. His method of doing business at times placed the biggest of the fielders in an embarrassing position, as after taking his money for a bet they found it impossible to pay him when he won without borrowing all over the ring, and when he arrived at Ascot he wanted to lay Steel and Peach 3,000 to 2,000 on a horse, and Mr. Steel was obliged to tell him plainly he didn't carry the Bank of England about with him, and that he should decline the bet unless he would settle in the regular way in London. Shortly after that he began to have his bets booked on credit, and fell into the ordinary way of settling. And I have heard him declare that he attributed his downfall to his departure from ready money betting. He continued to bet, with varying fortune, for a month or so longer; but he was no longer invincible, and he had several severe blows; and then toward the end of the summer he got into a groove as unlucky as he had been lucky in the early part of the summer, and then that historic York came to finally settle him, and at the end of the meeting he owed the ring an immense sum of money, and had but little left.

Of course, everybody will be ready to say what a lunatic the man was that he didn't leave off when he had got, say twenty thousand pounds; but the fact was he kept pulling out week after week, and plunging more and more, in the hope that his bad luck would not continue; and instead of it coming to an end, he came to a week which broke better men than he—a week when not only the good things went down, but when not a favourite won.

Some time before this, and while he had many thousands of pounds in the Birmingham Bank, he by some means got a hint that there was a screw loose there, and drew all his money out, and quickly lost it, whereas if he had left it in till the bank stopped payment, almost immediately after, he would not only have saved his money, but would have received it all in full, with interest, after about a year of waiting; but, unfortunately for him, he knew too much. He continued for some time to bet "outside" and away from the post till the remnant of his money had gone, and he was walking about the streets of Birmingham, poor, shabby, and discredited.

It was then he hit upon another and less reputable method of "raising the wind." He began corrupting the honesty of some of his old fellow-workmen and jewellers' lads, and set himself up with a "*hot pot*," becoming well known to the police as a "fence master" of the most dangerous character. But with such cunning and skill did he conduct his business that the police—making repeated attempts—were unable to convict him, although they were perfectly aware of the nature of his "business." At last there was a "plant" prepared for him, but even then, so wary was he and so nimble, when the police rushed him the swag was in the pot and all identity destroyed; but, unfortunately for him, the alloy of the metal was a peculiar one, a trifle of something which, as a rule, was not found with gold, and this settled him. He was tried, convicted, and sent to penal servitude for a long time.

It is a good many years since I saw him, and I don't know whether he is still in the land of the living; but in spite of all I have said of him, I must do his memory the justice to declare that he was not all bad. He possessed some real good qualities, which made him very popular among his friends.

CHAPTER VII

EARLY BOOKMAKING

Walsall Races—"Squaring" the Field—A nice Party.

It was in 1865, I believe, that I began to doubt whether I was not making a mistake in backing horses, and to feel that by this means I should never achieve any great success, or even get back to a tolerable means of living. I still proclaimed, however, that, as the turf had broken me, the turf should mend me, so, with my brother and W. Collins, it was determined to try bookmaking. My friend Collins and his brother Ned had essayed it in a small way a short time before, and with hopeful prospects. So now, behold, I and my brother decided to give it a trial in earnest. Our *début* was to be at Walsall, as being near home, cheaply to get at, and where possibly we might get the patronage of a few people who would know us.

One little difficulty stood in the way—that was the tools to work with. We had pencils and a book, but no money, and even in those days, if you determined to go straight some little capital was necessary. However, with the kindly aid of an avuncular relative, we surmounted the difficulty, and went to the famous saddlery town equipped with a big satchel and a little bank.

I was in Walsall not so long ago, and made diligent search to discover the site of the old race-course, but with little success. I knew where the ancient erection called the Grand Stand was, quite close to the railway station, so it must have been near what is, in these days, about the middle of that prosperous town.

It was long prior to the creation of " Tattersall's Enclosures "; still, there was an enclosure round the Grand Stand wherein most of the betting took place, but the state of our exchequer forbade any aspirations we may have had to figure there. We had to be content with the hire of a little "judy" and a stool, on which my brother stood while holding forth and offering the odds to the assembled multitude of pitmen and artisans from the town and neighbourhood, while I sat beside the "judy" in the capacity of clerk. My brother had a nice, open-looking face and a presence which evidently inspired confidence—ours didn't look like "a joint" which was going to "guy," so we did a great deal more business than might have been expected for young beginners.

In the first race there were six runners, and three of them were backed at about the same price, ranging from a little under to a little over 2 to 1; the other three we laid at *outside prices*, from 5 up to 7 to 1. One of the favourites won, I think it was Volhynia; but if my readers will take the trouble to consider the odds, they will see we couldn't have taken much harm.

Old "Speedy" Payne won the next race on Edinburgh, and he was a 7 to 4 on chance, so we lost a trifle on that, but we ought not to have done so, because there were at least a couple of others backed at 3 to 1.

This brought us to the principal race of the day, and one which marks an epoch in my life. When the numbers went up we found there were five runners, and from what I afterwards came to know about it, I believe it was a nicely " cut and dried " affair.

Poor old Tom Cooper of Birmingham, who died many years ago, was then one of the leading betting men in the Midlands, and he never was so happy as when arranging a job or laying against "a safe 'un," and he it was who had done the squaring in the present case, for, as he himself told me years after, he had arranged either with the jockeys or owners the order of running in this particular race; and what is more, it would have come off exactly as arranged, but for one little mishap.

The only horses arrived for the race, and whose numbers went up, were The Wave, Gamecock, Charming Woman, Volhynia, and Longboat. The Wave was a very hot favourite, even money being taken freely, but as The Wave's form was by no means the best, there was plenty of money for Gamecock at 3 to 1, while the other three were well supported at 4 to 1 each.

This state of things, of course, made us feel quite comfortable; the squaring that had taken place was nothing to us, so long as we were betting against all the horses, and at a fine profit too.

But what is this we behold? A horse-box is on the line quite close to the course, and a horse is being unloaded, and in a minute or so up goes another number, Mr. Wadlow's The Drone. I don't suppose this sort of thing would be allowed now; but strange things happened in those days, and this is an actual fact.

Now, everybody knows Mr. Wadlow was not the sort of man to be squared, and no one would know that better than old Bill Cosby, who owned The Wave, or his friend Cooper, who had done the squaring; beside which, they didn't believe any squaring would be requisite in the case of The Drone—he was such a very execrable performer. Indeed, I am told Mr. Wadlow would have withdrawn him for a very small consideration, and offered to sell him to Cooper & Co. outright for "a pony," which they refused to give. It was not surprising, therefore, that The Drone had not a single backer. The great surprise was supplied when they came to run the race, for the despised Drone won in a trot by three or four lengths, The Wave second, of course!

After this there was a most sensational race, although only a couple went to the post. There are plenty of racing men still living who will remember it, and the stir which it created in the racing world at that time. It resulted in disastrous consequences for some of these actively concerned in it, all of whom have, I believe, gone over to the big majority long ago.

Gamecock and Edinburgh were the runners. The former was a very popular horse in the Midlands, and there most of his triumphs were achieved. But on this occasion it was evident someone had laying orders, and so clumsily was the business done that at the start as much as 4 to 1 was laid on his opponent, which rather exposed the game, as such odds, if all was square, would have been simply absurd. So poor Gamecock smelt worse than "dead meat" of this description usually does. Nevertheless, the knowing ones, who only thought they knew, and had been helping themselves accordingly, had a bit of a scare when they saw the two jockeys, Ward and Payne, putting in all they knew, and each doing the best he could to win. The scare became a veritable fright when, after racing neck and neck to the last stride, it was found that Gamecock had just beaten the favourite. The knowing ones, who had taken liberties without being really in the know, used some strong language.

It turned out, however, that this terrific finish between the two jockeys, which induced a lot of betting while it was in progress, to the discomfiture of those not in the know, was all a part of the play; for when they came to weigh in, it was found that Gamecock had carried wrong weight, and, of course, an objection was immediately laid, which was another part of the play. The takers of the odds were up in arms, and there was no end of a rumpus, and as the people concerned didn't bear the best of characters, the stewards at once suspended the jockeys and reported the case to the Jockey Club, who, after an exhaustive inquiry, let Payne and Ward off with a reprimand for refusing, when called on, to give evidence, considering that the weights had been fraudulently tampered with by Kendal, the trainer, and Bilham, the owner of Gamecock. On the latter they passed the severest punishment in their power, warning him off for ever; but as Kendal was at the time under a life sentence for the Brilliant case at Chester, they could do no more with him.

Now I may say that all this did not affect us. We were betting outside the ring "all in" and "first past the post," so it was rather a good thing for us.

I shall never forget our elated condition as we went home that night. We had won something like fifty pounds, and we were fully impressed with the idea that we had discovered the El Dorado, and would want money no more in this life. Alas! there are thorns among the sweetest roses, and the fairest prospects are ofttimes beclouded, and like many greater people, we were very quickly to find our wealth a burden. The fact is, it consisted almost entirely of silver, and when we left the train at Perry Bar we had a two-mile trudge before we reached home, and we actually quarrelled about who should carry the satchel.

CHAPTER VIII

OUTSIDE BOOKMAKING

Betting at a "Judy"—Our Village Parson—An unfortunate Partnership.

AFTER betting together for some time outside the ring, and, of course, for ready money, my brother began to tire of it, and the brothers Collins having separated, he joined Mr. W. Collins, and in the course of time theirs became one of the most respected and prominent firms in the ring.

As for me, the way was not yet made smooth enough for entrance within that magic circle, and there were many rough-and-tumble days awaiting me outside before it was so. I marred my chances through trying to find winners, instead of steadily laying against everything. The fact is I studied "the book," and too often, when it declared emphatically that a certain horse *must* win, I could not help going a bit for that horse; and, almost as frequently, an occult force to which I, and the like of me, were strangers, was stronger than "the book." I had yet to learn that a horse's book "form," ay, and even his present capabilities, are as nothing when opposed to these forces. Let me confess that I never was, at heart, a genuine bookmaker. The old bad habit of backing horses clung to me, more or less, through all my turf career. This will account for my progress as a bookmaker in these early days being slow, as it will also account for many other things later on, which, in the proper place, I shall have to unbosom myself of.

It was now necessary for me to take a new partner, and the

fates chose one for me with a strange mixture of good and bad qualities; and as the story of his life "points a moral" which may be useful, I propose telling it rather fully.

Fred Jackson was my daily pal, and I had grown to be as fond of him as a brother. There was nothing about Fred very remarkable; nothing in his looks, certainly, to demand one's admiration. He was a little fellow, with a slight cast in one eye, and a nervous, uneasy way with him which made one at times fidgety, and there was no genius or force of character compelling respect, and yet I liked him beyond and above all my friends and acquaintance of those days.

He was a merry little chap, with a good heart, a generous disposition, and one of the sweetest tempers that ever dwelt in a man; and I suppose that's why I was fond of him. These good qualities are desirable possessions for a young fellow; but unless he possesses with them a little judgment, some strength of character and will, he were almost better without them, for these amiable attributes in men—when not mixed with and supported by those of sterner stuff—are apt to lead them astray; to degenerate, indeed, into very vices. For is it not true that all our vices are virtues upside down—our worst faults but the negative side of our good qualities!

Fred came of a good old stock of English yeomen, who had farmed their own land from time immemorable, and nobody could tell how many John Jacksons there had been farming the broad acres of Pentlands in an unbroken succession. He was the youngest of six sons, and when his father died, the oldest of the brothers added another to the long list of John Jacksons who had held Pentlands, with its fine old red brick house, in the Queen Anne style, and its three hundred acres of unencumbered freehold land.

While this was the handsome portion of the eldest son, the others had to be content with very small fortunes, amounting to about £1,500 each.

About a year after his father's death my pal married the

daughter of his father's old friend and neighbour, Moses Fitter, and the event was celebrated amid much rejoicings by the two families, for it was looked upon as a very proper and desirable match, and to merely outside, casual observers it appeared a Heaven-made one, for the young people had been born neighbours within a month of each other, had been playmates and sort of lovers from childhood, and had many things in common. Kitty Fitter, or, as we must now call her, Mrs. Jackson, was at first sight an attractive young lady—she had an almost perfect set of features, which, when illumined by a well-practised smile, captivated all new acquaintances, and sent them away under the impression that they were fortunate in the acquisition of a charming friend. On a more intimate knowledge of the fair Kitty, however, one soon discovered that the sweet smile was not genuine, but a vapid, meaningless thing; that no soul spoke to you through the beautiful eyes, and, indeed, that her loveliness was the loveliness of a picture—

"Insipid as the queen upon a card."

And a still closer acquaintance showed not only these defects, but disclosed also the presence of many of the worst characteristics of human nature.

She had a vanity which exacted homage of men, and made her bitterly jealous of her own sex. She could not endure any other good-looking woman near her. She was an incarnation of selfishness, and therefore cruel. She was capable of the little spites and tantalising manners which are only possible to women—or, I should say, to a woman of this character; while she was incapable of feeling or of understanding the true meaning of love, she was a good hater, especially of those of her own sex who stood in her way, and after that, of such of the other sex as, seeing through her, refused to be captivated by her hollow coquetries.

Fred Jackson saw none of these failings in his wife; with the blindness of love he saw only the attractive outside, and he was proud of the homage and flattery she received from most of their male acquaintance. These considerations, perhaps, influenced him somewhat when he began to look about him for the best means of investing his small fortune. They had been living some months on their principal, and he felt that it was about time he got into a business of some sort; but, like the devoted husband he was, he was anxious to consult the wishes of his pretty wife.

"I have been to Broomwater again to-day, my dear," he said, "trying to find something that would suit us, but I can find nothing that looks such a certain living as the Swan Inn here in our own village. The lease expires in a month or so; it's your dad's property, and he says we can have it. There is a nice little business to it, and fifty acres of good land, which I could look after."

"And you would like to bury me alive in a place like that, would you?" asked the lady; "I'll take care that you don't, though. I should like the public business if you could get a proper sort of a place, but not where I should scarcely ever see the face of gentlemen, but instead, would have to draw quarts of fourpenny and cut hunks of bread and cheese all day for clodhoppers. That's not good enough for me, I can tell you. I want a proper hotel, either at Broomwater or in London."

"But consider, my dear," meekly pleaded her husband, "we have not half enough money for the sort of place you require."

"Well, then, we must get dad to help us," replied she. "One thing is certain, I will never live at the Swan."

"Of course, you won't if you have made up your mind not to do so," replied Fred, with more bitterness in his tone than the young wife was accustomed to hear in these early days of matrimony. "It does not matter about me, of course. What I like or dislike is not of the slightest consequence."

The young wife looked at her husband for the space of a minute with a strangely puzzled expression, as though she rather doubted her sense of hearing. Surely this could not be the meek and subservient young man she had already come to look upon as her abject slave; and when she fully realised the matter, she burst into a fit of tears.

"You are a cruel wretch, Fred," she sobbed, "and I'll go back to my father, and tell him what a brute you are; that's what I'll do!"

"Don't be foolish, Kitty, my dear," said he, wondering what dreadfully cruel deed he had perpetrated to bring all this trouble about his ears. "You know I don't wish you to live anywhere or do anything you don't like. I'll go to Broomwater again to-morrow, and try to find something you would like. I'll do *anything* you wish."

This complete capitulation seemed to satisfy, for the moment, Mrs. Jackson, so they kissed and became friends again, and it was arranged that she should accompany her husband the following day to the great town of Broomwater in quest of a business of some sort, which should be not only profitable but consonant with the wishes and fancies of pretty Kitty. In due course this journey was taken, and, after much parleying on the part of agents and solicitors, the result was that Fred and his sprightly wife became the host and hostess of the Nile Hotel in the pretty little village of Mossleigh, which was the home of several families of sporting men, and was also—considering its size and proximity to its great neighbour, Broomwater—an exceedingly lively little village. And in those days it was a real village. The small ancient church, with its ivy-covered walls—from its age and associations alike sacred—with its low Norman tower, also clad in ivy, was large enough to seat the whole population of the village proper, as well as the squire, his family, and the numerous servants at the neighbouring hall. The parson belonged to a species then fast becoming extinct, and now utterly so. He was a rosy-faced, jolly old fellow, whose most marked characteristic was an intense love of a good horse, and few men knew one—when he saw it—better than our parson; and I have never met with a man with such a profound knowledge of the thoroughbred and all the various strains of blood as Parson Davids.

He was none of your straight-laced sort, was our parson; he entered into all the sports and pastimes of his people. Some of the more unfriendly of his parishioners declared that these matters occupied too much of his attention, to the exclusion of more serious functions. He didn't think himself too good to step into the sanded parlour of the Old Bull—next door to the church—which was an institution only second in importance to the church itself, and there discuss parish matters, or less serious affairs, over a glass of grog. And it was not an uncommon thing—strange as it may seem in these awful pious times—to find him making up a rubber at whist, or, what he loved better still, playing five-card cribbage with old Tom Dickson, the clerk, sexton, bell-ringer, and village carpenter. His people generally liked him all the better for these free-and-easy habits, but the few spiteful villagers before alluded to were terribly scandalised, and I suppose it was one of those who spread the report that the parson, who had dropped into a gentle dose while presiding over a parish meeting, on being rudely awakened, cried out:

"Fifteen two, fifteen four, a pair's six, and one for his nob!"

The Nile was situated some distance from the church, and in appearance and habits was totally unlike the Old Bull Inn. It was a great, big, square modern building, with four stories, having lofty smoke-room, bar-parlour, and billiard saloon, and it disdained the humble inn, and got itself known as the Nile Hotel. It had been built to accommodate a new village, which was no village at all, but a jerry-built stuccoed suburb of the neighbouring big town which was fast arising in its vicinity. A good many of the new-comers, like their new houses, had fine outside appearances—stucco fronts, imitation facings, instead of good, honest brick and stone; and their inside walls all lath and plaster—unsubstantial and unsound.

The new gentry were too respectable to keep the company of the parson and the old-fashioned "knopes," as the villagers were called, whom nothing could allure from the Old Bull, its little rooms of sanded floors, with painted walls and white-washed ceilings, low-roofed and cosy. So such of them as were not afraid of going to any public-house patronised the new hotel, with its fine billiard saloon, its pleasure grounds, gardens, lawns, and rustic arbours, and many a happy afternoon have I spent among these people on the beautiful bowling green, which, alas! has long since been given up to the ruthless hand of the jerry-builder. And it was here also that I first met the hero of my story, and his weak but pretty wife.

For about a year things went on fairly well at the Nile. The charming young landlady had turned the heads of all the youthful swells in the neighbourhood, and some of their elders, who ought to have known better, spent far too much of their time under her fascinating influence in the bar-parlour, this especially being so while Fred was away from home, attending the numerous race-meetings in the locality, for I must sorrowfully confess he would journey with me and my friends to all the races within a reasonable distance of his home. He began to back horses too freely, and I frequently warned him that it was a practice beset with considerable danger for clever men, possessing advantages which he lacked, and I more than hinted that he was not likely to shine in that business—was, indeed, much more likely to come to no boots, and perhaps a bad ending. But inordinate conceit characterises all young beginners at the game; how else can you account for the incredulous and almost pitying smile with which they invariably receive one's warnings? It is clear they believe themselves capable of standing where all others fall, and of doing that which ninety-nine out of every hundred of their fellows fail to do.

When Fred had a good day he was loud in proclaiming it; he told everybody how many winners he had found, and largely discounted his winnings by lavishly treating all comers. When he lost he said little about it, he was quiet and subdued enough; he treated himself then, and drank to keep up his spirits. And so, I fear, he contracted a couple of foolish habits at the same time, either being, singly, likely enough to bring a man to grief, and when combined certain to do so.

Mrs. Jackson did not discourage her husband in his race-going; on the contrary, she rather liked it. She may not have been morally a very bad woman, perhaps not so bad as some of the seemingly modest prudes who made free with her name, and so severely commented upon her conduct in her husband's absence; but she was a married flirt—a most dangerous creature, to be avoided—ay, and even hated—by men who care for their own peace.

"What are you looking so glum about?" I remarked to Jackson, as we walked down the lanes from Lichfield race-course to the City.

"Well, to tell you the truth, I've been making a fool of myself," he replied.

"And is that anything new?" I couldn't help observing, for I had seen enough of what he had been doing in the ring to convince me that he had lost a good deal more than he could afford. "You needn't tell me; I can see you have had a bad day, and you expect me to sympathise with you. Have not I told you over and over again that you are not made of the stuff successful backers are made of? You don't know a race-horse from a donkey, nor a sharp from a juggins. You think you're a sharp, and you are the veriest jay; and I'm telling you once more, if you don't pitch up backing horses, you'll be on your uppers in a few years."

OUTSIDE BOOKMAKING 69

"And yet I can see fellows about who are getting tons of money at the game," he answered, "and some of them, a few years ago, were jockeys' valets, card-sellers and touts, if not worse."

"That is so," I replied, "but you aren't made that way, and you can take my word for it, you will never do as they have done. Don't I tell you that I know lots of swells with opportunities you can never have—not jays, mind you, but clever fellows in their way, having trainers, and jockeys, and horses of their own, and plenty of capital to work the show? and yet nine out of every ten of them go broke at it. Pitch it, Fred, my lad, pitch it before you join the band of brokers."

"I'm afraid I've almost qualified for membership already," he replied dejectedly. "In fact, that's what I wanted to talk about when I asked you to walk down with me; but I'm really ashamed to tell you what a fool I've been, after all the good advice you have given me. I haven't only lost more than I ought, I—I—oh, hang it, I can't tell you!"

"Oh, out with it!" I said, beginning to feel somewhat alarmed, the little man looked so distressed. "You haven't lost more than you will be able to pay, I hope?"

"No, that isn't it exactly. I shall be able to pay all my debts of honour, but I'm afraid the spirit merchant and one or two others must wait; but it's worse than that. I was fool enough to accept a bill three months ago to help poor old Scooper out of a mess; in fact, it was to prevent him being broken up. He told me I should never be troubled about it, for long before it became due he should be receiving a lot of money, and then he would take the bill out of the money-lender's hands. A week ago I got a writ from the money-lender for this bill, and unless it's paid in two or three days, my wife will get to know about it, and there'll be the very devil to pay."

"You idiot!" I couldn't help saying, "to go and put your name to a bill for a lazy shicer like old Ned. Well, you are a fool! How much is it?"

"The bill was a hundred pounds, but the interest and expenses will make it another twenty, I suppose," answered he.

"And what have you lost here to-day?" I asked.

"About forty pounds."

"And what right had you to come here and lose forty pounds?" I asked, quite savagely, for I felt very much annoyed, having helped him out of a similar scrape, on a smaller scale, six months before, when he solemnly promised he would do nothing of the kind again if I would only help him to keep this matter from the knowledge of his wife, of whom he was in mortal fear, and so soon to rush into the same folly was sorely trying to my scanty stock of patience.

"Well, the fact is," he said, "I thought I might have a bit of luck, and run into enough to settle with this infernal money-lender; but that's how it always is, one never does get any luck when it's so badly wanted. The only folks who get luck are those with plenty of stuff."

"Oh, luck be—blowed!" I replied. "Don't twaddle to me about luck; you go and act like a blithering idiot, and when the natural consequences ensue, you begin to whine about your bad luck. Oh, go to the devil!" and in my passion and impatience I went striding on in front of him, and only when I had nearly reached the verge of the city did I turn my head to look for him. He was nowhere to be seen. I was alarmed, for I was sure he was attached to me, and I knew he would take to heart any harshness on my part, for in spite of weakness and vacillation and other bad qualities, he was tender-hearted and sensitive to a degree.

As I have said, I felt alarmed; but I didn't know what to do for the best. I felt I could not go on without him, so I chartered a cab which was returning empty to the course, and went back the way we had come, looking in every direction for him. When we reached the common I caught sight of him walking across it, right away from the course and the people, and in the direction of a wood I could see in the distance. I very quickly came up with him.

"Where do you think you are going?" I asked.

"Where you directed me, I suppose," was his sullen reply, while he never took his eyes off the ground.

"Don't be a fool! Get into the cab."

After a little while I succeeded in getting him to do so, and very soon we were at the Swan, in front of a good dinner and a bottle of Moet's, under the influence of which he became quite cheerful again. I induced my brother to help, and at eleven o'clock that night, when I parted with him at the door of his own house, he shook my hand very warmly.

"You and your brother have made a new man of me," he said. "I'll stick to business, and back no more horses—at any rate till you are paid—and I shall always be grateful for what you have done for me to-night."

Poor old Fred! I am sure he intended to do all he promised, and the tear that he couldn't help my detecting in that queer cross eye of his was the result of as genuine emotion as ever moved a human heart; and yet, so weak was his nature, very soon all his good resolves were thrown to the winds, and he was backing horses as freely as ever. I had another turn with him, and then he confided to me a secret which I already suspected; he was not happy at home. Would I help him to become a bookmaker in ever such a small way, so he might travel to all the meetings, leaving his wife to attend to the hotel, which she had told him she could manage better without him?

In vain I tried to dissuade him from this course; he had made up his mind, and he would give it a trial. It happened that just at the time I was betting outside the ring at what was known as a "judy"; that is, a betting establishment on the course very like a Punch and Judy show. These erections are not allowed in these days, as they were construed into *places* for the purpose of betting many years ago, and abolished; but at the time I am writing of they were common enough, some of the bookies carrying their own shows about with them, while others rented them from men who travelled to all the meetings with a large stock of "judies." These men would pay, at certain important places, large sums to the clerks of the courses for rent of the land on which they erected these small betting boxes. This system gave place to more substantial and commodious offices, which were erected alongside the betting rings, one side fronting to the ring and the other to the outside public, on the course, a man standing on a stool inside the ring doing business with one set of clients, his pal taking on the outsiders in the same way, while a clerk, or sometimes two, sat inside the judy. Some very respectable and substantial men bet to ready money in this way, and made considerable fortunes at the game. I could point to some who, at the present moment, are among the best advertised people on the turf—men of wealth and great respectability, whom I can well remember betting outside these judies, or exercising the humbler office inside. Let me cite as an illustration the one name which most readily occurs to me, that of Robert Topping—the most eminent S. P. man in the world. I remember one year when Steel and Peach, the greatest of all bookmakers at that time, rented the whole of the land at Doncaster or York which was available for this purpose; and setting up a great number of these betting boxes, they let them to bookmakers of good standing, for whom they risked little in guaranteeing, charging £50 and upwards for the use of each of them, and some of the best-known names in the ring—their own among them—were painted above these boxes. Well, it was not at one of these important places that I and my friend, Fred Jackson, proposed to start in partnership as bookies, but at the earlier and humbler sort. Our united capital was not large, but he undertook to raise and be ready with fifty pounds as his contribution to it.

So the capital and stock-in-trade of this new firm was

provided; this consisted of four upright pieces of wood, spiked at the bottom to drive into the ground, brass rods to hold them in their places, five or six yards of green baize to wrap round it, a flaming banner of scarlet cloth, on which was inscribed in large characters this device:

"DYKE AND JACKSON:

All In, Run or Not."

A huge black satchel, with the same device on its face in gilt letters, and with this an orange-coloured leather strap a couple of inches wide, which was to be suspended round my neck and carry the satchel. Then there was a large square book, on the cover of which the name of the firm also appeared, and an immense green gig umbrella formed a roof to the establishment.

For the first week or two business was not very brisk, as we were unknown to the public; still, we managed to win a few pounds over the expenses each week, which was equally divided, and Fred, after the manner of his kind, began to indulge in rosy dreams. It was Liverpool Autumn Meeting, and the new firm, full of the hopes which come from success, even so limited as ours had been, bet through the first day with harmless results, and I had not been obliged to ask Jackson for any money.

On the second day things went badly on the three first races. The favourite won each of them, and we lost about forty pounds, which I paid out of my own stock; but before we began to bet on the next race, I gave Jackson notice that if we lost again he must begin to pull out some money.

In the fourth race there were ten runners, and among them an unnamed colt, Buntline, out of Lassie. In so large a field I thought I might safely lay 6 to 4 anything; so, being anxious to get on with the business, I cried out, "I'll lay fifteen pounds to ten on the field!" Immediately a crafty punter standing by, and who made a living out of young beginners, rushed a ten-pound note into my hand, saying, "I'll have that Buntline colt," and before the bet was booked I found I had been too hasty, for the general offer was even money Buntline. I then laid a number of smaller bets against the same horse at evens to equalise the bad bet, and thinking that, of course, they would be certain to back others among so many runners.

"Here, what price Lassie colt?" asked a square-headed gentleman who stood by with a fiver in his hand.

"Ten pounds to five," I replied, thinking I wouldn't again commit the blunder of opening my mouth too wide to begin with, which blunder had somewhat worried and confused me, and I was rather surprised to see how eagerly the offer was closed with, and also how quickly some of the bystanders followed suit, and it was not until I had laid more than twenty pounds against Lassie colt that it occured to me that it was the same as Buntline; and when we realised that we had laid against this horse something more than fifty pounds, and had only got two or three sovereigns out of the other nine to pay it with, we were in a dreadful state, especially poor me. I broke out into a cold perspiration, trembling in every limb, and became in rapid succession all sorts of colours. I could no longer stand firmly on the high stool; the big satchel, although nearly empty, seemed dragging me down to the earth, so I sat on it, a picture of misery, awaiting events.

"You will be ready with fifty pounds, Fred!" I gasped in whispers; "I feel sure the favourite will win." And the looks of two or three of my clients, who had never lost sight of me, or moved far from me since their bets were made, was by no means reassuring. Fred, however, did not seem to feel our position half so keenly, for his naturally sanguine disposition came to his relief.

"Don't funk," he said; "I don't think he's sure to win; we've nine chances to his one, and we—" but before he could finish his sentence there was a cry "They're off!" and I jumped again on my stool excitedly to watch the race.

At the distance it was seen there were only two in it, and they came away by themselves, locked together, neck and neck. They struggled thus towards the winning-post; now Buntline seeming to get his head in front, and the next stride the outsider, struggling gamely, and helped by the almost superhuman efforts of his jockey, had the best of it; and so they passed the post, everybody crying, "Dead heat! dead heat!"

Looking eagerly towards the number board, where, unfortunately for our young firm and all our rosy dreams, Buntline's number was hoisted as the winner, I sat down again on my stool, feeling at that moment that a brandy and soda would be cheap at half a crown.

"Fred, you must give me fifty; we are dead broke."

No reply came from Fred. I stood up and looked inside the judy. It was empty. Fred had gone. The crowd began to gather around me, awaiting the welcome cry, "*All right!*" before they could draw their winnings.

When I found that Fred had deserted his post, I didn't know what to make of it. I could not for a moment believe that my pal had deserted me and left me to the mercy of an enraged mob; but what could it mean? He had gone, that much was certain, and with him had gone the large, square book in which the bets were entered, so that if any good neighbour would lend me the money, or even if I had it in my pocket, it would be impossible for me to settle with the rough customers already gathering around me, and who, in another two or three minutes, would be clamorously demanding their winnings. There were yet these few minutes of grace left, so I mounted my stool again, looking wildly in every direction for a glimpse of Jackson, with the means of escape from this dangerous situation. There was no sign of him anywhere, and escape for myself, even had I been so disposed, was out of the question—was, indeed, utterly impossible—for I was now surrounded by the enemy. "All right!" being bellowed out by the man employed by the bookies for this purpose, they began at once to discharge their liabilities as their tickets were handed up.

My knees knocked against each other, and every fibre of me trembled with fear as I heard the ominous cry. I knew too well what it meant if I failed to satisfy the demands of this pack of hungry wolves which crowded about me.

"Fifteen pounds," said the sharp who had done me with the unfair 2 to 1 bet, and who was the first to demand payment.

"I must ask you to wait a few minutes till my pal comes back; he's got the book," said I, scarcely knowing what I said, and still standing on my stool looking wildly about me for my pal.

There was a good deal of murmuring, but for the present no hostile movement on the part of the punters. Five minutes passed, the other bookies had finished paying out, and had become interested in the proceedings in front of our shop; and seeing there was something wrong, there gathered around quite a crowd of punters and loafers, who had no interest in the matter apart from the desire to see a row, or to help, maybe, in the baiting of a poor devil standing on the stool, white and trembling, and almost palsied with fear.

As the minutes went the murmurs of the crowd became angry growls, and violence would have been resorted to but for the interference of the owner of the next judy, who told the mob that he believed the young men were respectable, and meant paying. This answered for a few minutes longer; but it was painfully clear to me that the patience of my clients was nearly exhausted, and they were edging closer and closer upon me. I saw fierce eyes intent upon the satchel which hung from the broad strap around my neck; I knew there would be a struggle first for that, and then for me.

Meantime, while this scene was being acted before the betting office of the new firm, Fred was on the course at the side of the principal betting enclosure, whither he had flown the instant he saw the favourite had won, and where he was making frantic efforts to get a glimpse of my brother in the ring. When the race was over my brother had gone to the telegraph office, which in those days was some distance away, so was not to be found. When he returned to the ring he was told of Fred wanting him on the course; he ran down to him, and found him in a pitiable condition.

"For God's sake," said he, "come with me down to the 'joint' at once! We haven't enough to pay, and I'm afraid they'll kill poor Dyke, if they haven't already done it. I'll explain all afterwards."

There was no time for question or explanation; Sam ran out of the ring and made for me as fast as his legs would carry him, Fred running by his side, deadly pale with fear and excitement. Fifty yards from the judy he could see there was a row; when he reached the crowd he saw me in the midst of it, my coat nearly torn off my back, no hat upon my head, and other signs of ill-usage about me; a couple of policemen, who, mercifully for me, happened for once to be where they were wanted, had hold of me, and were valiantly protecting me as well as they could from the violence of the crowd.

My brother pushed his way into the midst of them.

"What the devil are you doing, you cowardly ruffians?" he shouted. I could see he was known by some of the mob. "Couldn't you give the poor fellow a few minutes' grace while his pal came to get some more money?"

Some of them, when they saw the turn things were taking, seemed a bit ashamed, and slunk into the background.

I was glad to find my brother was in time to prevent me being seriously hurt, although I had been roughly handled.

"And now, Jackson," my brother said, "you get into the box and let's have everybody paid; and let me tell you, gentlemen," he said, turning to the crowd, "you needn't be afraid of betting with these men—they won't bet what they can't pay."

In two or three minutes all the claims were satisfied, the satchel had been found and restored, and the numbers were hoisted for the next race.

"Now, then, my lads, bet away and don't be afraid," he said; "I'll be with you the minute the race is over."

With this he ran back to his own business. It was evident the row, and his opportune appearance and promises, had been an advertisement for us, for on his return after the race he found we had been doing a very much larger business than before, and it was also a profitable one. We had laid the winner several times, but had won about a "pony" on the race.

"Dash it at them, Dyke," he said, "give your winnings a chance; this row will do you no harm at finish, I can see."

"But I want to tell you something before I go any farther," replied I.

He had no time to listen to any explanations then, so he asked me to leave it till we could come to his lodgings in the evening.

After he had dined that evening, the new firm went to my brother looking so uncommonly serious that he thought we must have had the bad luck to lay the outsider which had given all such a "skinner" on the last race of the day. His first question was:

"You surely didn't lay the last winner?"

"No, we didn't," I answered, very gravely.

"Well, what did you win?"

"Oh, all we took—about forty-five pounds," was the answer; and without another word I took out a parcel and placed it in his hands. "You'll find there," I said, in the same serious tones, "all I have had from you. I shall never be able to tell you how grateful I am to you for bringing me help at that moment, for I believe you saved my life. But I've done; Jackson must find another pal."

"What does all this mean?" my brother asked, turning to Jackson, who all through the business had never uttered a word.

"I am to blame, I know," he answered; "but I was obliged to use in the business at home the money I had received from Dyke, and I thought perhaps we mightn't want any; and if we did—"

"If *you did* you could come to me for it," Sam interrupted fiercely, and I am afraid he said several things in his passion which would not look well set down here. It was clear to my brother he had acted most dishonourably, and that I was quite justified in pitching him up, and no amount of snivelling and vehement promising on the part of Fred could shake my resolution.

I have often thought how different might have been the after-life and the end of Jackson if he had only had the courage to keep in his new business what belonged to it, or even to confess that his wife had got it from him. And once again his curse was weakness. He had persuaded himself the money wouldn't be wanted; he never for a moment intended working such mischief for himself or his friend.

I was this time so thoroughly annoyed with the conduct of Jackson that I didn't see him or go into the Nile for several months, but I heard some very bad accounts of him. He had got into fresh difficulties of a pecuniary kind, and was constantly quarrelling with his wife and her relatives, and, perhaps driven thitherward by these things, he was now drinking worse than ever. Old Moses Fitter, his father-in-law, who had advanced a good deal of money when they bought the Nile, and since, was threatening to put in force the powers he held over him, and this at last the old man did do, and Jackson had to fly from his angry creditors, for, of course, he was too weak to meet them, and so I lost sight of him, as did also his wife and all his family.

All the remainder of that season went, and the following

winter, and there was no news of him. His friends concluded either he was dead or had gone abroad. When he left there was a pretty little one-year-old daughter, whom he loved with an intensity one could scarcely expect to find in a nature so weak. And Mrs. Jackson was sure if he were alive he would come back for love of that child, if not for its mother's sake.

Now and again I had fancied I saw him flitting about among the crowds on a race-course, and once, when I was being whirled out of a railway station, I thought I got just a glimpse of him through the window of the cab. I pulled up instantly, jumped out, and sought among the throng for him; but if it was him, he had disappeared.

The spring, with its precious promises and all its beautiful budding life, had passed, and the fair face of the earth was bathed in all the glory of midsummer. I was staying at the pretty village of Charlton for the Goodwood week.

It was my custom to walk with my friends from our lodgings up to the races, and on the last day of the meeting we had left soon after breakfast, and were sauntering quietly up the course. We had arrived at that part devoted to the uses of the gipsies and other followers of racing—the Nomads who live—

> "Homeless, ragged, and tann'd,
> Under the changeful sky."

The class one meets with at all the principal races, even when widely apart, and about whom the mystery has always been what they live on, and how they get from place to place.

The gipsies were busy pegging up the sheets for Aunt Sallies, arranging the cocoanuts, empty bottles, and other contrivances for turning an honest penny, and affording the rustics sport. The vagabond tribe, unwashed and ragged, lay in every direction, where I suppose they had lain through the night.

OUTSIDE BOOKMAKING

Passing one of the gipsies' caravans, I was struck by the appearance of something lying under it, something which looked at first sight like a heap of filthy rags: yet from the rag-heap there gleamed a pair of human eyes strangely familiar. After we had passed, I couldn't help remarking to one of my friends: "If Mrs. Jackson hadn't told me they had good reasons for believing her husband dead long ago, I should certainly think those eyes we saw under yon gipsy's van belonged to poor old Fred." My friends pooh-poohed the idea. The eyes haunted me when I was in the ring, and as there was an hour before racing began, I made my way back to the caravan. When about thirty yards from it I saw the bundle of rags pull itself up and scuttle away. I felt sure the being which dwelt in that mass of rags had seen me making directly for it, and had flown to avoid me. Swiftly as possible I rushed on to the ground; there was no sign of him. I went round every vehicle, and shed, and booth without finding him, and yet I knew he could not be far away. Suddenly a happy thought struck me. He would have had just time to run up the bank, get over the fence, and hide himself in the adjacent wood; whither I went on the instant, and the moment I reached the top of the bank I saw the object I was in pursuit of lying in a heap on the other side of the fence. In a moment I was by his side. He was exhausted by the effort he had made, and lay with his eyes closed and breathing heavily. I was afraid he was dying. I saw a decent-looking old gipsy woman sitting on the top of the bank nursing a tiny member of her tribe. I called to her and got her to fetch me some brandy. Before she returned he opened his eyes, and whatever doubts I may have had on the subject vanished. I knew it was Fred Jackson.

"Why, whatever has brought you to this condition?" I asked gently; and seeing he was struggling with some strong emotion, I added: "But don't try to talk yet. You shall have a drop of brandy and something to eat, and then you can tell me all about it."

In a few minutes the old gipsy returned, and with her a powerful but good-natured fellow, her son. After he had tasted the brandy he seemed revived a little, then, turning his hungry eyes upon me, his pent-up feelings gave way, and bursting into a passion of tears, his first words were:

"My child, my little child, how is she?"

I was myself almost choking with emotion, but I gave him such soothing answer as I could.

I arranged with the good gipsy to get a fly and drive him down to Chichester at once, getting him there a lodging, medical attendance, and whatever he might have instant need of, and after the races were over I hurried down to him. He had been comfortably cared for, was now clean and wholesome, and in a good bed, which was a luxury he had not enjoyed for a long time. Between fits of terrible coughing he told me the part of his sad story I was unacquainted with. It appeared he had dodged me on race-courses and at railway stations many times, and till now had always succeeded in avoiding detection. As long as he was strong enough he had earned a scanty living by fetching and carrying for the judy-builders on the course, and doing odd jobs at the stations. How he had lived and crawled about during the last few months he couldn't tell.

I told him I should write at once to his family and let them know where he was. This he strongly opposed, and begged me with tears not to do so.

"Let it be a few days at least. I couldn't bear to see her or any of them just at present." And he pleaded so earnestly, I yielded. I have always thought he knew more than the doctor who had been called in, and more than I suspected, for in four days after, when his friends did see him, he slept calmly, his face had lost its careworn look, there were no wrinkles on his pale, cold forehead; his queer odd eyes were closed for ever.

CHAPTER IX

"SAFE 'UNS"

"Safe 'Uns" which won—Chesterfield Races—Jimmy Barber and his Gang.

SEE me now, then, fairly launched as a professional layer of the odds, or, as it is more frequently termed, a bookmaker—I who had dreamed in my boyhood of being, indeed, a bookmaker, but, oh! with what a different meaning.

I was betting to small money, my operations, except at a few insignificant meetings, being confined to the Judy and Stool business, outside the ring; and but for a too frequent deviation into my old course of punting, I should have done fairly well. But I was not even satisfied with the foolish conceit that I could find winners, I must needs find "safe 'uns" to lay against, a weakness fatal to a bookmaker in my position.

My readers generally will perfectly understand what is implied by the term "safe 'uns." For the benefit, however, of the unsophisticated, I may explain that it is applied to horses—and sometimes to men also—who, for some reason, are supposed to have no chance of winning the contests they are engaged in. Therefore the few who are the fortunate possessors of this information think themselves at liberty to lay against them as far as they possibly can. I have known men—a sort of wholesome merchants in the "dead meat market," as it has been called—who have amassed considerable fortunes in this business, upon which they have lived at ease in honourable retirement for many years. Whatever squeamish people may say, there is no doubt about it being a very profitable business, especially when it comes off all right. I have in my mind at the present moment a case where a dear friend of mine made a little fortune in one transaction of this kind.

That "safe 'un" was one of the right sort. It was one which didn't win; in fact, it didn't even run. This was one of the most sensational episodes in the history of the turf, but that little tale will be told later on.

But I am concerned now with quite another sort of "safe 'uns," for it happens, unfortunately, that

> "The best laid schemes o' mice, o' men,
>   Gang aft a-gley."

And I have known clever men come to grief through knowing too much, for laying against "safe 'uns" has not always been attended with the happy results I have referred to.

It was when I made my first visit to Chesterfield Racecourse; and so little was I satisfied with it that I never ventured on a second. I went with a couple of friends, and our joint resources formed the capital which was to fructify and grow into three colossal fortunes by means of that wonderful system of which our friend was the author. During the first day the system didn't work well, so we lost a considerable amount, and we lost on the four first races on the second day; hence matters began to look gloomy, for we hadn't a Rothschild sort of bank behind us. It became, therefore, a question whether we should pursue the system to the end, and risk all, or be content to lose what was gone, and make a new beginning on the system. There was just one other alternative which we discussed; that was an idea of one of my chums, who suggested we should pitch up the system altogether, and commence making a book with what of the capital remained. This suggestion was favourably received, and I fancy would have been acted upon if I had not, at that very moment, caught sight of three notorious men in earnest conference.

Oh, Fate! what a world of difference that simple incident may have made in the shaping of several mortal lives!

One of these gentlemen was a dapper sort of fellow, with a round face, and a pair of eyes set in it keen as a hawk's, a closely-cropped head, with a silk chimney-pot hat on the top of it. He wore a large stand-up linen collar and a black silk neckerchief, a whole suit of black cloth, the coat being the cut-away, leg-o'-mutton fashion. He was a singular-looking being to find in a betting ring, and until he opened his broad Lancashire mouth you would never have taken him for a betting man, but you might have taken him for a prosperous undertaker, a waiter at a first-class hotel, or even for a Methodist parson, the latter, however, only being possible so long as he kept his capacious mouth closed. This "gentleman in black" was the once rich and celebrated Jimmy Barber, a turf character about whom much may yet be written. One of his companions was a much bigger man, with a large face, heavy hanging jaws—indeed, a heavy, clumsy-looking man altogether, in breeches and gaiters, and a "get-up" something between a stableman and a country squire. This was old Joe Saxon, owner, trainer, and bookmaker. The other was a little, sharp-looking fellow, with an even more pronounced horsy appearance than Saxon himself, and you would have sworn at once he had been a jockey in his time and was now a trainer, and you would have made no mistake, for this was Joe Kendal.

It was a nice little trio, and were it possible to narrate some of the jobs they had been in together, an entertaining volume would result. I looked at them and then instinctively at the card, and found the entrants for the next race were largely composed of horses owned or controlled by them.

"Look at that gang," said I to my friends; "there's something brewing for the next race, let us watch them." Barber quietly slipped away from his pals, and asking my friends to keep their eyes on the other two, I determined to watch the movements of the wily old James. I got pretty close to him, and without exciting his suspicion I managed to keep my eyes upon him. I suddenly became aware of another fellow, who was evidently at the same game, watching Barber; this was a simple-looking but well-dressed and respectable sort of farmer chap. Barber passed this young fellow almost without looking at him, and yet I could see that some silent communication had passed between them, which was clear enough, for when Jimmy passed leisurely to a place at the back of the stand, I saw the young farmer at a distance follow him there, and you may be sure I was not far behind the young man when he entered this place. In not more than a minute after I also entered, but I came very near being too late; they were near together and alone, and the farmer was in the act of thrusting a bundle of bank-notes into his pocket, which I concluded Jimmy had handed to him. Not a word was spoken that I heard, and they separated without any sign of recognition, Jimmy going in one direction and the farmer in another. I followed the young one, and before he had gone many yards I saw him take a slip of notepaper out of his pocket, and after carefully perusing it, replace it there. At this moment my friends came up.

"You see yon farmer-looking chap?" said I to one of my friends. "You follow him instantly, see what he does, and five minutes before the fall of the flag we'll meet here." And turning to the other, I told him to find Saxon with the same purpose. For myself, it was not long before I was on the track of old Jimmy. The ring was a very small one, so it was not a difficult task—not nearly so difficult as it was in such a limited market to get any amount of money on a good thing. Consequently, owners of the class I am describing often had to resort to all sorts of ruses to get a little money on their horses, for it must be remembered that in those days there were no starting-price people to help them in their difficulties.

Well, the numbers were hoisted, and there were three

runners only; they were Barber's own horse, Cutler, ridden by Jem Snowden, Gamecock by Thorpe, and Nothing More, with Clarkson up. I felt certain this was a job, and that it was only a question of " finding the pea." I found Barber industriously *asking after* Gamecock of nearly every bookie in the ring, but only backing him with two men, whom I knew to be his friends, and so adroitly did he manage the business, there was quite a rush on the part of the public to be on that horse, which had the effect of driving Mr. Barber's own horse to 4 or 5 to 1. The readiness of a certain couple of layers to accommodate all comers with as much as they wanted Gamecock, coupled with the fact that Barber, in addition to backing, or appearing to back Gamecock, quietly appropriated several large bets which were offered against his own horse, let the cat out of the bag. It was evident Cutler was the pea. I rushed off to meet my friends with this information, only to have it abundantly confirmed.

One of my friends discovered that Saxon had been all over the ring, backing Cutler wherever he could get a decent offer; occasionally, however, having a tenner on Nothing More; while the other had found the young farmer, quietly disposing of his roll of notes, supporting Mr. Barber's horse. Gamecock clearly was the " safe 'un "; and we could trouble no more about systems or bookmaking, but must have a dash on Cutler, with a little on Nothing More, for a saver. And in pursuit of this object we laid out the whole of our capital to the last sovereign, although we felt sure that, with fair play, neither of them had the slightest chance with Gamecock; and so, feeling we had done a good day's work, we went on to the Grand Stand to see the race. Now, it chanced that when there I found myself standing shoulder to shoulder with Joe Kendal. I had my field-glasses up, and could see the three horses as they came up the straight, all abreast. Then I saw Gamecock forge half a length in front of the other two, who at the close of the betting had been backed at about evens against each other, almost as if it had been a match, with no such horse as Gamecock in the race; while, the truth being apparent, he had retired to any price.

"Why, what does this mean?" I cried. "Gamecock is going to win."

"Then be d——d!" almost screamed the trainer at my elbow; "he *can't* win."

However, he did win, and Cutler was second. I took one look at Kendal, whose face was a picture of dismay, and all sorts of colours, and I have no doubt I and my friends very much resembled him. We were "stony," and had to get home as we could. I afterwards heard on very good authority that Gamecock had been allowed to drink a bucket of water just before the start, and it was thought that would suffice to stop him without trusting the man on his back.

It took me some time to get over this blow, and I vowed to myself that no more would I have anything to do with "safe 'uns." I found myself soon after, however, making a boot at Hungerford Races. I had managed to get together again a decent little bank, and I had for my partner and clerk poor old Ted Horsley, who died a few years ago. We were now betting at a judy with an opening into the ring, so that I could bet with people in the enclosure as well as the outside public. Just before the numbers went up, a gentleman, who since those days has made a considerable figure in the racing world, came to me with the information that old Reindeer would be a hot favourite, but wouldn't win.

"Don't ask any questions," said he, "and don't miss a shilling Reindeer." Of course, I was very much obliged to him, because I was absolutely certain his purpose was to do me good, and I know, moreover, that he even then occupied a position to command information beyond my reach. When the numbers went up we found there were four or five runners in addition to Mr. Henry Fisher's old horse, but beyond him and Discretion, at about 4 to 1, there was nothing else backed. Naturally enough, I concluded that Discretion was the right one, and wouldn't lay against him, content to confine my efforts to getting all I could out out of the favourite, who started at 6 to 4; and I succeeded so well that I had, when the flag fell, nearly a satchel full of gold and silver, besides notes, and a sense of gratitude to my kind friend possessed me as I felt the weight of the bag that hung from my shoulders, and wondered what it would total up to, thinking the while that l should certainly never want money again. I was awakened from this momentary reverie and these pleasant feelings by the familiar cry "They're off!" and so they were, and so was I—off the top of the stool almost in a fit. The old horse had won easily, and I was once more "a broker." All I and poor old Horsley had in the world was not nearly enough to settle with, and the kind friend who gave me the information came forward just in time to save us from an awkward dilemma, and possibly the judy, from serious consequences. Up to the time of his death my dear old friend Horsley would feel ill at the very mention of the word "Reindeer."

CHAPTER X

AT LEICESTER

A useful Punter—The Bank replenished.

SOME of the events of one's life get themselves imprinted so indelibly on the memory that they are there for ever, and this applies not only to the startling and fateful occurrences, but to some quite trivial matters; and what a veritable puff of smoke this human life of ours is when one comes to think of it. I look back thirty years or more; it seems nothing. It seems yesterday I stood, in pouring torrents of rain, on a Yorkshire moor to see a white-faced chestnut horse win the Leger, and come the Leger day again it is thirty-eight years ago—bah! it is nothing. Another thirty-eight years will slip by just as quickly, and then!—and yet some of us swell with pride, like the poor, simple cropper pigeon, because we have more of certain metals, and skins, and papers than our neighbours, and thereby are tempted to look with contempt on our poor neighbours. And others of us fume and fret because we have none of these things, or because, having had them, somebody has stolen them from us; and so, swelling or fretting, we slip into old age without thinking of it.

What trifles will at times stir old memories and induce reveries like that I have just been guily of. My eye caught three words of printed matter, which in an instant carries me back more than thirty years. "*Mr. Bletsoe's Tribune*" are the words I see. They mean nothing to millions of people; to me they suggest an experience I had at Leicester thirty-six years ago. I was making a book then, and was in low water, as frequently happened to me in those days, because, as you know, I was a bookmaker with a backer's heart under my waistcoat. I was betting in a small way, and very cautiously, when I had the good fortune to run against a punter of a sort common enough in those times; but present-day fielders tell me they are an extinct species, and known only in the writings of such old fogies as myself.

Well, I was betting on the principal race of the meeting, the Leicestershire Stakes. There were four runners, and among them an old horse, owned by people from my own neighbourhood, and trained, I believe, by James Hopwood at Hednesford, and this horse's name was Edinburgh, who was ridden by George Sopp. He ran in the name of Mr. Eskrett; but I think there was quite a small syndicate in him, among them being James Lowe, the well-known auctioneer of Birmingham, who lives still and flourishes there, and old Tom Hidson, the sporting printer and sometime bookmaker of the same town, who will be remembered only by the older racing men, as he has been dead many years.

In addition to Edinburgh, the runners were James Dover's Liqurian, ridden by Sammy Kenyon, Tribune, and Success. Just as the numbers were going up, my old townsman, Mr. Hidson, came by me, and I took the opportunity to ask him for a tip; and he told me he thought Edinburgh would win.

Almost as soon as the betting opened, a young swell came up and inquired what price I would lay the favourite. At the time I was not certain which was favourite, but thought I could do no harm by offering 6 to 4 on the field, especially as I could hear that price offered very freely, and here and there a point more.

"I'll take you fifteen to ten Success," said the swell, producing a neatly-folded new ten-pound note, with the "ten" outside.

This staggered me a little, because it would have better

suited my humble means at the time to have laid fifteen shillings to ten, as I don't think the bank was at the moment fifteen pounds strong. However, as I thought there could be no difficulty in getting some of it back at a better price if I required it, I laid him the bet, and as I had made up my mind to field against all the other three and go for Mr. Hidson's tip, I did all I could to lay Tribune and Liqurian. I soon discovered that the swell's choice was not really favourite, for Tribune seemed in much more demand. In a few minutes up comes my swell again.

"I find I have made a mistake," said he. "They tell me Tribune is favourite."

"I'm afraid that is so," I replied; "and he looks like being very hot."

"What will you lay me Tribune?" he asked.

"Fifteen pounds to ten," was my unblushing answer.

"Oh, no, that *won't* do; I have been offered more, and as I have the worst of the other, you ought to lay me twenty to ten."

This, as a favour, I agreed to do, and again he pulled out a clean and crisp fellow tenner to the one in my satchel. I went on with my betting, and soon found that Liqurian was becoming all the rage, and looked like settling into a good favourite, and, in fact, 2 to 1 was being freely taken Dover's horse, while 5 to 2 was offered the other two, when up rolled, once more, my young exquisite.

"I find I've made another mistake," he began, "and as I'm backing first favourites on a system, I must be on Liqurian. What's the price?"

I hadn't the heart to offer him 6 to 4, so I laid him 20 to 10, and another clean tenner was added to my little bank.

"I know I'm a fool," he said, as he turned to go away, "because I can't win on either of them, but then I can't lose."

The fact was, of course, he was standing to lose five pounds Success, thirty pounds Edinburgh, and quits on the other two.

I thought it only right to remind him there was a fourth horse running, and asked if he wouldn't have a bit on Edinburgh.

"Oh, blow Edinburgh!" he replied, as he walked away.

The young swell's thirty pounds had made a good foundation for the book, and I could have been nicely "over round," and had all the four winning a fair amount, as things were going then with me, if I had laid Edinburgh, for I had many opportunities of doing so, as some of the cleverest "heads" in the ring were quietly backing him. As it was, I had only one loser, and that was the favourite, Liqurian, and I had not laid a shilling against my townsman's horse. Well, the race was run, and it was one of those which leave a vivid impression on the mind. As they neared home they were all at it, and in a cluster. Sam Kenyon was just in his day, and I feared him, for it seemed to me Sopp was having to make a most determined effort to keep with him, and Tribune was so close you could scarcely say which was leading as they tore away for the winning-post. From the angle where I saw the finish, I thought my only loser, Liqurian, had just won, and that it was a near thing with Edinburgh and Tribune for second place; but I awaited the hoisting of the numbers with breathless anxiety, for although what was in the balance at that moment would have been looked upon in after years as the merest trifle, it was then of almost vital importance, and my feelings may be imagined when the numbers went up, and I found old Edinburgh had won, and my poor little bank of ten or fifteen pounds had become nearly seventy. "Surely," I said once more, "I should never look back after that or want money any more." Alas!

CHAPTER XI

REMINISCENCES OF BIRMINGHAM

A Famous Inn—Notable "Brums"—A Case of Sudden Death—The Ruling Passion—A Short Boxing Bout—"Nibbler" Birch.

AT length the way had been made smooth, and I had risen above the "judy" style of betting, and was, although as yet in a humble way, a regular member of the ring, and betting to considerably more money. I had left all my old associations of chapel and class-room a long way behind me, and mingled instead, even when not racing, with the sporting men, "peds," and boxers of my native town, and, of course, spent a good part of my time at their resorts, where I became acquainted with many men notable in their way, among whom were some very eccentric, droll characters; others clever and unscrupulous, who became, in after years, conspicuous on the turf; and if they reflected small honour on the good old town of Birmingham, they afforded interesting subjects for the student of human nature, and this shall be my excuse for giving them a place here.

The house I mostly frequented was perhaps the most respectable amongst these haunts of card-players and gamblers; it was known as the "Coach and Horses," in Bell Street, demolished years ago to make way for market extensions. Nearly a century earlier this was the most celebrated tavern in Birmingham. Poet Freeth, a great local celebrity, was the host, and a very clever man, too. Nightly, we are told, he gathered about him a good deal of the intellect of the town, discussing not only Birmingham matters but high affairs of State; diversifying these controversies with literary discourse, wherein, naturally, the poet's own works figured largely.

Freeth's works were well read in his day, were typical of the times, and thought much of, many of them being really very clever. I fancy, however, if you wanted to read them now you would have to do as I have done for that purpose—pay a visit to the British Museum.

In the days which concern us the old house was kept by as honourable a man as ever conducted "a pub," or any other business, although he added to this occupation the making of books on the Derby, and other big future events in racing. Unlike too many of his trade, he discouraged excessive drinking, and although his tavern was frequented by all the big gamblers of the town, he would be no party to sharp or shady practices of any kind; and woe to the man, were he the best customer he had, who attempted such. A good, all-round, honest sport was old Bill Wills, straight and true as the bore of a gun-barrel, if not as smooth; an upright, sound-headed, kind-hearted man.

Among the nightly visitors at the Coach and Horses was a big fat man named Kemp, in his way a character. He possessed a great lion-like head, and a strong, intellectual face.

Coming, I believe, of a highly respectable family, Kemp started life with a good education and brilliant prospects, and with these had natural abilities which might have helped him to any goal he chose to aim at. Unfortunately for him, cards enslaved him; he became infatuated with whist—in fact, nothing less than a devotee; and as was natural with a man of such mental capacity, he was great at this one game, or science, as he would have it. He was the subtle master of all its traps and intricacies, and his memory was even more wonderful than his perfect knowledge of the art. To say that, during the progress of a game, he never forgot a single card that was played, and who played it, is a small matter. I have known him, when a dispute had arisen over a particular game, perhaps a day afterwards, on being appealed to, go through that particular game, playing, card by card, all the thirteen tricks. He was pre-eminently the greatest whist player I have ever met; but alas! what a price he had paid for his pre-eminence!

Whist had absorbed all his faculties, ruined his business, and made him what he was at the time of which I am writing —a poor, broken-down, semi-professional card-player, sitting night after night waiting for the means to live next day. He was the fairest player in the world, and never gambled to any extent at the game, and often gentlemen of means came to play with him, and for the pleasure of being his partner guaranteed him against loss, while the half-crowns won were his own. I learnt my whist off him, and while I admit having spent many happy hours by its means, I must confess that I have at times regretted that I ever came under its fascinating influence, it is such a murderer of time.

Among the old Birmingham sports of the better kind who were found occasionally at the Coach and Horses, and whom I saw a good deal of there and elsewhere, was old William Aston, the great button-maker, and one of the most eccentric men I have ever met. He was not a heavy bettor at anything, and I never knew him do much at horse-racing or cards, yet he was in his way an inveterate gambler. His delight was tossing the coin—heads or tails—for a sovereign, and occasionally for larger stakes, and so much had this habit become a passion with him, he indulged it at all sorts of incongruous times and places.

I remember on one occasion when an eminent lawyer in Birmingham, known as a good sportsman and a shining light in legal circles, was in the middle of an eloquent speech before the Judge of the County Court. Suddenly a bit of paper was put into his hand, containing these words in Mr. A.'s well-known scrawl:

"I am waiting below for you; come at once."

The lawyer paused in his speech, while he glanced at the paper, then turning to the judge, without the slightest hesitation he said:

"Will your honour kindly excuse me for two minutes while I speak just one word with a person outside; it is, I understand, a case of '*sudden death*,' but I will not keep the Court more than a minute or two." Then rushing into the street in wig and gown, he found Mr. A. in his brougham ready for him, and in the familiar position, with a sovereign on the back of his hand.

"Head!" cried the lawyer.

"Take it," replied A., uncovering the coin, which, it seemed, the lawyer had won. "Drive on, coachman." This was all that passed, and in one minute the lawyer had resumed his speech.

Mr. A. was not what you would call a practical joker, yet for many years he indulged in a joke which seemed to afford him immense pleasure, and among those who knew him it could do no harm. Although he really bet little or nothing on horse-racing, he would turn up occasionally at the resorts of the men who do, and start knocking the favourites out, or perhaps backing them for tremendous amounts, both sides apparently booking the bets in all seriousness, while, as it was well understood among them, it was all chaff. This old joke of his, however, on one occasion resulted in most painful consequences, which effectually prevented its repetition. One night, during the Birmingham races, while the town was full of betting men from all parts, he entered a public place and commenced what appeared, to the strangers, a savage onslaught of the favourite for the Derby, finishing by laying some very big bets at about twice the market odds. So the strange betting men who were present—thinking it was his brother Charles, the biggest bettor in the town—rushed off to the telegraph office, wiring to their friends in Manchester and elsewhere that Aston, the great Birmingham bookmaker, was knocking out the Derby favourite, and before the error could be corrected a good deal of damage was done.

Aston was the friend and patron of the hosts of all the famous hostelries in the good old town. He subscribed liberally for the benefit of everything and everybody, and never declined to become a member of sick societies, beanfeasts, money clubs, or, indeed, any kind of club or association. At the termination of a money club, where he had £50 coming to him, the worthy host, Dick Parsons, went to his house to take him the money. He was at the time very ill; in fact, it was shortly before he died. Parsons, putting the £50 in sovereigns on a table by the old man's bed, said:

"I've brought you £50, your chance in the money club, Mr. Aston; but I'm very sorry to find you so ill."

"You'll oblige me, Dick, if you'll go 'sudden death,' double or quits, the lot."

The great button-maker and his daily companion and chum, Richard Walker, one of the largest percussion cap-makers in the world, throughout many years indulged in a very curious practice. Every day, at their first meeting, instead of the usual meaningless conventionalities of words and deeds, one silently took a sovereign out of his pocket, placed it on the back of his hand, and the other named head or tail, for its value. This was their manner of daily greeting.

There came a time when good old Dick was stricken with a mortal sickness. Just before he died he was seized by the desire to see his old friend. When, awe-stricken and on tiptoes, he entered the chamber, the sick man was dozing, or unconscious, but Aston couldn't help observing that a bright sovereign shone on the little table by the side of the bed. By-and-by Dick opened his dulled eyes, and recognising his visitor, with some effort he reached for the sovereign, and without a word placed it on the back of his hand in the usual manner, and, only with these strangely dim eyes, asking his friend to name it.

"Not now, not now! I can't, Dick, I can't!" sobbed the tender-hearted old man.

"You *must*, Bill, for the last time," murmured the dying man, and seeing that it would comfort him, Bill called and lost —and poor old Dick smiled faintly, having demonstrated how strong was his ruling passion, even in death.

Excepting Kemp, there was perhaps not a more frequent visitor at this old "pub" than my poor old friend and sometime partner in the bookmaking business, Billy Thornton. He was a great card-player in almost all its branches, and a born gambler, who would bet on anything at any time or place. A one-eyed, dry old stick was Billy, and very clever. We were playing whist late one night, or perhaps it would be safer to say it was early in the morning, for it was anterior to Mr. Bruce's Early Closing Bill. Thornton was losing his money, so was in no humour to brook the sneers and interference of a big bully who was present—a bully and blackguard at best when sober, but when half drunk a terror to everybody. We were all amazed to see Billy suddenly rise from his seat and challenge the bully to turn out of the house and fight; for although we knew he had been able to "put them up" in his early days, and was reputed quick as lightning, we felt certain he could have no chance against his burly opponent, for he had but indifferent light in his one eye, was double the other's age, and not much more than half his weight, and certainly had the appearance of a consumptive. So we did all we could to keep him in the house, but without avail, for fight he would.

The big bully was not manly enough to decline the unequal contest, but readily went out and stripped for the fray. The instant they faced each other Billy flew at the big 'un like a wild cat, and was all over him in an instant; and before he knew where he was, or had thought of beginning to fight, he was pasted all over his face. It didn't last more than two minutes, and then we saw the old man putting his coat on as he walked into the house, out of puff, and half dead with the terrible effort.

"Come out of that!" shouted the bully; "come out and finish the fight!"

"No, I shan't fight any more," replied Billy. "I'll give you best."

My old friend's racing career, like his fighting, was of the spasmodic order—fitful, uncertain, and unbusiness-like. In the whole course of my experience I never met with a man who was so continually "a broker." He never appeared, from start to finish, to make any headway. I don't know how many times in each of all the many years I knew him poor Billy was "a broker." In fact, his was a case of chronic brokerage. For the sake of his many good qualities, somebody was always ready to help him to a start again. He was a notable example of how bad luck—as he called it—will stick to a man. I will give one illustration of the many which occur to me.

The day before Royal Ascot commenced, all his neighbours and friends who had business there made their way to their quarters, Sunning Hill, Sunning Dale, or other of the delightful villages adjacent to the course, so as to be ready when the ball was set rolling on the following day. Not so Billy; a good friend had provided him with a really nice little "bank," and a clerk to book for him; but he must needs stop in Birmingham to play cards on Monday night, and even into the early hours of Tuesday morning, hence he was late for the 7.30 train. He managed, after bad luck or otherwise, to arrive on the course when three races had been run, and three hot favourites beaten. Was ever such provoking luck known? Now mark the folly and superstition of this clever man. He had got too late to take advantage of betting against these three beaten favourites, therefore he would not bet against any other favourites that day. After three such "turn-ups" it would be like his luck for every favourite to win if he started to lay, so he thought he would dodge Fate, turn round, and back favourites for the remainder of the day. This he did, and the "turn-ups" continued. Not one single favourite won on the day; so instead of making a substantial addition to his friend's bank, he sadly diminished it, which was very far from his friend's thoughts as he gleefully perused the newspaper the following morning. And Thornton maintained to the day of his death that this was the most unlucky week of his life, for a good many favourites did win later in the week when he had settled down to "field" against them, and his weakened bank would not hold out. When the end of the week came, there came with it his usual condition of stony-brokenness, and once more he carried back to his friend in Birmingham the same old story of his persistent bad luck; as though luck had anything in the remotest degree to do with the matter.

This betting bout of Thornton's reminds me of a story in which I am not sure he was not one of the actors, although he told the story as a disinterested third party. It concerned his intimate friend, the well-known old Birmingham bruiser, "Fance" Evans, who will be remembered by many of my readers.

After Fance had finished with the ring he became a professional teacher of the "noble art," and as probably no cleverer artiste in his line ever existed, he got about him quite a large school, composed of the young swelldom of the place, and I remember he was at the time the principal professor of fistics at the University of Oxford. Among his pupils in Birmingham was a young fellow, the son of a tradesman. Unfortunately, the youth had rowdy tendencies, and nothing pleased him so well—especially when he had his mentor with him—as picking a quarrel with some strapping big fellow, and showing off his superior skill. On one occasion, after spending a jolly night together, the professor and pupil were passing through St. Philip's Churchyard homeward, very late at night, when an opportunity such as the young spark loved arose. It was a huge fellow belonging to the Corporation Night-soil Department on the way to his work. At it they went, hammer and tongs, and it was not long before the swell found he had, for once in a way, taken his tools to the wrong shop. The big labourer was knocking him all to smithereens. After the third round he picked himself up with the assistance of Fance, who was acting as his second, while his opponent was waiting quietly at a little distance to see if he required any more.

While Fance was mopping his friend's face, the young man whispered faintly:

"I've called the wrong man up, Fance. You'll have to lend me one."

Fance got his man up to the scratch for the fourth bout, sticking very closely behind him, apparently to encourage him. Scarcely had they got to work when the labourer caught a terrific blow on the eye, which put the shutter up, and sent him to the earth like a stricken ox.

"Take that!" said the swell, with a chuckle.

"I've got it," said the man, as he slowly raised himself from the ground. "It's too dark to see where it came from; but it wasn't from the same place as the others, and I don't want any more."

The most widely-known member of our company was, without a doubt, George Luckett, otherwise known as "the Dodger." At that time he was "living on his wits," and a fairly good living they provided him; he dressed well, ate and drank of the best, and was never short of money. He was a professional cribbage player, and, I am afraid, knew more of that particular game than any honest man would care to learn. He was one of a sort who did not depend upon such trivialities as luck, or on honest skill even, for success. I have often heard him protest that he did not believe in such a thing as luck. "If you haven't any," he would say, "do as I do, make some. I believe in making my own luck, I do."

But sharp as he was, the Dodger occasionally got taken down. I remember him meeting with an amusing little rebuff at our old tavern. He had found what appeared a very soft thing, a young man who fancied himself at cribbage, and who was, moreover, willing to play for big stakes. You may be sure it was not long before he was owing Dodger a considerable amount. By-and-by the seeming "flat" had occasion to leave the room for a minute, and a well-meaning but officious fellow followed him out, and contrived to convey the information to him that he was being done.

"Can't you see," said the informer, "that he's got a pull on you? and don't you know he is the famous card-sharper, Dodger Luckett?"

"I don't know, and I don't care. I'm sure my pull is quite as strong as his," was the reply.

"What pull have you?" asked the other.

"Well, I've got no money, and it's all on the nod."

Mr. Luckett lived to become a big figure on the turf, and as his doings there will aptly illustrate some of the queer, and I may say crooked, phases of turf life, I shall have occasion to make him and my readers better acquainted later on.

I must say this for Dodger Luckett: after he had given up cribbage as a profession, and had transferred his remarkable abilities to the betting ring, no temptation of an ordinary kind was powerful enough to get him back to the old game; still, there were times when he was unable to resist a temptation.

I recall a very amusing occasion when he was persuaded to do so—was, in fact, almost bullied into it. We were staying for the Ascot Meeting at a hotel near the course. One evening after dinner an elderly gentleman—an immense swell, evidently, by his bearing a military man—entered our room. As he stood just inside the door, bolt upright, I should say six foot three in height, with great grey moustache and coloured spectacles, he made a singularly imposing figure.

"Do either of you sporting gentlemen play cribbage?" he inquired bluntly.

One or two admitted they could play, but all were indisposed to do so just then.

He was standing near Dodger's chair, and laying his hand on his shoulder, he asked if *he* played. Luckett admitted he did, but he also declined. However, he worried and almost taunted him at last into accepting his challenge. Turning to one of his friends, Dodger whispered:

"It's a nice thing to live to be challenged at my own game by a cove wearing gig-lamps; ain't it?"

He played, and, of course, won every game. The military man declared it was a mere matter of luck; nothing would convince him he wasn't the better player, and, as a military man ought to be, he was brave, and would have played for heavy stakes if Luckett would have humoured him. As it was, he lost a tenner before he could be induced to give in. It is only fair to the Dodger to say he wouldn't touch a penny of the winnings, but left it towards the hotel bill at the end of the week.

Another member of the motley crew was "Nibbler" Birch. This strange character will only be remembered by the elder race of sportsmen, and among those in the Midlands chiefly, for I think the Nibbler seldom travelled far from Birmingham, where he was a very familiar figure from thirty to forty years ago. He has been so long dead, my impressions of him have become weakened, but I distinctly remember there was a good deal of mystery about him and his movements; nobody seemed to know how he came to or went away from anywhere. Was there a little mill on, a rat killing, a main of cocks to be fought, or a cribbage match to be played, you would always find the Nibbler there. How he got there, or where he went when it was over, nobody ever knew. Nobody knew whether he was a married man or single, had a home of his own, or was in lodgings; in fact, how Nibbler Birch lived, and where he lived, were the two great mysteries of Birmingham in those days. Billy Thornton once declared he had come nearer to solving them than anybody else, for he had seen him one night emerge from the dark vaults underneath the Market Hall; perhaps there were stores of hidden treasure there. Another night, or rather early in the morning, after a cribbage match, he had caught sight of Birch flitting like a ghost in the dark, and he determined to find out where he lived, so he tracked him through sundry streets and passages, and finally saw him get over a wall; and that was the nearest anybody ever got to where the Nibbler lived.

Birch generally attended the Newmarket meetings; but it always appeared to me not so much for the racing as for the sake of playing at hazard. All through the night you could see him sit there right opposite Arthur, the clever old croupier, the mention of whose name will awaken unpleasant memories in some of my readers. I dare say Birch played on a system; most of the frequenters of the table did so. Perhaps that was how he got his money.

Among his other accomplishments, he was a famous bagatelle player, and he used to back himself to hole every ball; and occasionally he had for playfellow Dodger Luckett. On one occasion a friend was betting against Birch doing his great feat of filling all the cups. It happened that the player this afternoon had extraordinary bad luck. He failed in his feat five or six times in succession, and it was not until he had lost his last half-sovereign that it occurred to him that it was rather remarkable it was the number 3 hole he had failed at each time. So he rushed quickly to the top of the table, when, lo! the mystery was explained. The Dodger had slipped a small coin in the bottom of number 3.

"Ah! ah! you've found it out, like all the clever folks, when your stuff's gone!" cried Luckett mockingly.

There came a day when we missed the poor old Nibbler. How he died (if he did die), where he died, or when or where he was buried, were also mysteries which, as far as I could learn, nobody ever fathomed.

Neptunas Stagg was not one of our frequent visitors, being himself the host of a sporting "pub" in Birmingham, and, as far as I remember, he never played cards. I think he came amongst us chiefly because it was the resort of the principal bookmakers, and probably he would have a quiet little commission to work for a future event in racing. History, however, will hand down poor old "Nep" as the jockey who steered the winner of the very first Cesarewitch. He was a very keen but much respected man, a peculiar cast in one of his eyes giving a droll effect to his face, and a certain dry humour, with a fund of amusing reminiscences, made up a comical little fellow. After leaving the public business, he became a member of the old Birmingham Club, which in after years became the famous resort of Midland sportsmen, known as the Central Club. Although but a poor player at billiards, he was extremely fond of the game, and many a time have I played with him in the dingy old club-house in Castle Street, which preceded the splendid building which is now the home of sport in Birmingham. "Nep" married, but had no family. He lived in retirement in one of the suburbs of the town, and it was understood he was not entirely happy in all his domestic relations; and towards the latter part of his days he became moody and restless, and, I am afraid, must have got a bit unhinged in his mind. His end was very sad indeed. In the early morning, something more than twenty-three years ago, he was missed from his bed, and his wife, going to seek him, found him head downwards in a rain-water tub, and, of course, dead.

CHAPTER XII

REMINISCENCES OF BIRMINGHAM

Palmer the Poisoner and Bob Brettle.

BOB BRETTLE was a redoubtable Brummagem boxer, and after he had done battle for the championship of England, and had finally retired from the ring, he kept a small public-house very near to the Coach and Horses, where he frequently joined the merry company. Some queer stories were told of Bob, but one which he used to tell of himself will perhaps best deserve repeating. Everybody knows what a lion-hearted fellow the famous bruiser was; he admitted, however, that he was once in a terrible funk, and the only time he was thoroughly frightened was while in training at Hednesford for his big fight with Mace. Palmer the murderer, with his friend and victim Cook, were Brettle's principal backers, and it was for this reason, I think, that the training quarters had been confined within walking distance of Rugeley, so as to enable Palmer to see his man frequently, and it was his habit to walk over to the old-fashioned country "pub," which was Brettle's quarters, nearly every day. On one of these occasions a great burly navvy was in the tap-room terrorising all the company. Among other dirty tricks he took up glasses and cups belonging to the company, drinking the contents with the greatest insolence. Brettle saw his performance, and it got his blood pretty well up to boiling heat.

"I shall slip into this bully just now," says Brettle; "I can't stand it much longer."

"Don't you be a fool, Bob," said Palmer; "you must not risk getting hurt over such a brute as this. Leave him to me. Now you go yourself to the tap and get a quart of ale, and ask him to have the first drink. He won't refuse."

Brettle was coming through the passage carrying the quart of ale, when Palmer met him, and taking a small paper parcel from his waistcoat pocket, he shook a fine powder over the surface of the ale.

"Now, take it to him, and make him drink first."

This Brettle did, and the navvy almost emptied it at the first pull, and, with scarcely a pause, he put it to his lips again, nearly finishing the lot. For about a quarter of an hour he was noisier than ever; then he became suddenly quiet, and lay down on one of those old-fashioned tap-room settles, and in a minute was fast asleep, the company remarking what a very heavy sleep it appeared; but they thought it better not to disturb him, supposing he would sleep off the effects of the drinking. Towards closing time the landlord began to feel anxious to get rid of him, so gave him a good shaking, without however, shaking consciousness into him. Brettle also, becoming now somewhat alarmed, made vigorous but unavailing efforts to arouse him, so they made him a bed of straw in the stable and laid him there.

Brettle had breathed no word of Palmer and the powder incident, but he had a dreadful suspicion, and scarcely slept for thinking of it. His first act next morning was to rush to the stable, where he found the navvy in the same heavy slumber. He administered another dose of shaking, almost pinched a bit out of his ear, and finally gave him a slap on the face with the palm of his hand, which was heard all over the premises, but all without making the slightest impression. As his trainer was waiting for him, Bob was obliged to leave him, but the moment his morning's work was done, full of fear, he rushed to the stable again. The collier lay in the same state he had been in for twenty-four hours. Bob was alarmed now, not only for the life of the brute whom he firmly believed he had been the means of poisoning, but for his own safety. He thought the man was as good as dead—poisoned—and he should be charged with the murder. He wondered whether he had better go to the police station and give himself up at once, confessing his guilt. He decided against that course, as it would necessitate the implication of his friend, Mr. Palmer. Anyway, he wouldn't do so until he had talked over the matter with that gentleman. He wondered when the inquest would be held—whether the verdict would be murder or manslaughter? Would they put the "darbies" on his wrists when they took him to Stafford Goal; and who would be the judge at the next assizes? He ran through all the great criminal lawyers he had ever heard of, and tried to make up his mind to which he should entrust his defence, and so he worked himself up to a pitiable condition of fear and excitement. During the afternoon he paid numerous visits to the stable. Towards the last the man's heavy breathing had ceased and was only just audible, his huge breast rising and falling like that of a little child. These appearances he took for the certain signs of approaching death. He was horrified, and decided to go no more to the stable, but to await in the house, as well as he might, the development of affairs. But the stable had a fascination for him which he was powerless to resist, so once more, before retiring for the night, he took the candle in his trembling hands and again made his way there. One may fancy his amazement when he found the burly form of the navvy had gone. Brettle afterwards said he couldn't at the time make up his mind whether the devil or Palmer had stolen the body. He, however, awarded the credit to the latter, after the tragical result of his intimacy with Mr. Cook became known. Bob used to say that it was this episode in the life of the notorious poisoner which first induced suspicion, and which was therefore the means of hanging him.

CHAPTER XIII

SQUARE HEADS

A cute Punter—A droll old Bookie.

ONE of the quaintest characters that ever frequented the betting ring, or the Coach and Horses was old Billy Humphries, the noted fishmonger of Birmingham, with his sturdy form, rosy, clean-shaven face, square head, topped with a broad-brimmed Quaker's hat, and his singular get-up, which was a sort of cross between that of a Quaker of the old school and John Bull. In his early days there were no Board schools, and, indeed, but few opportunities of any kind for people in his condition to obtain education, so he had to find his way through life without it, and this he managed to do fairly well. For although to the end of his days unable to read or write a line, he contrived to scrape together a pretty little parcel, reputed to be something like £100,000. He was purely and simply a backer, and one of that genus who held his own, and generally a bit of somebody else's also. He didn't believe in weekly, or even daily settlings, but paid or received on every race. He kept no account of his winnings or losings. When he was leaving home for a race-meeting he would go into his immense safe or strong room and take out a handful of money, notes and gold, without counting it, and when he returned he would simply empty the contents of his pockets, much or little, into his coffers, and he once assured me he had done that for years without once taking stock, and he hadn't the slightest idea what amount the safe contained. He had no faith in banks.

If he wanted to buy a pig or a row of houses he fetched the money from his own bank, having been bitten a little by the failure of Attwood & Spooner's. He was at all times delighted to relate stories of his early struggles, some of which were highly amusing, and worth repeating; his very first start in life—commercially—was particularly so.

Born in one of the very lowest parts of Birmingham, his boyhood was passed in extreme poverty. The town in those early days boasted a meat conner, who exercised great power over the purveyors of meat and fish. One Saturday afternoon his sense of duty—or some other reason—called upon the conner to condemn a great quantity of oysters belonging to a well-known lady in the trade. These oysters, young Humphries observed, were being carted on to some waste land, and immediately a brilliant idea flashed through his mind—he saw great possibilities in this simple incident. His first move was to borrow a wheelbarrow, an old window shutter, and a couple of barrels; these he wheeled into High Street, and in the gutter, right opposite the worthy conner's shop, he fitted up this primitive establishment for the sale of oysters. In the gloaming this industrious youth took his wheelbarrow down to the waste land and carted back to High Street as many of the condemned oysters as he could convey. He did not attempt to sell any until he had put in operation this brilliant stratagem. He opened a score of the fattest of the bivalves, and marching into the conner's butcher's shop, he addressed that terrible gentleman.

"I want you, Mr. Tutin, to accept a few of my fine oysters; some old 'uns in the trade are jealous of a youngster like me starting, because I'm satisfied with less profit than they get. Now I want you to just try my oysters, sir, and if you don't say they're as good as theirs, I'll throw them all away."

"All right, my lad," said Mr. Tutin, when he had examined the oysters, "you go on with your business, and if anyone interferes with you I'll make it hot for 'em."

So Humphries, being able to undersell his neighbours, did a roaring trade all Saturday night; indeed, he sold out the whole of the condemned stock, and that was the first clever little trick which gave him a start in life, and was the prelude to many another, equally sharp, on a much more extensive scale. For many years he was known as a man who kept at command a large stock of "ready." This fact enabled him often to effect extremely profitable bargains. If a fellow-tradesman had a heavy bill to meet, or, under stress of any other kind of emergency, desired to sell his house or property expeditiously and quietly, and for cash on the nail, here was the man, always, of course, providing that transaction was on Mr. Humphries' own terms, and from his—and the policeman's—point of view, honest.

I remember him telling me with great gusto how he became possessed of one lot of valuable property. A tradesman, for certain delicate reasons which I need not go into, desired to realise very quickly, get possession of the cash, and ship himself off to America. He wormed these particulars out of the man, and also the fact that it was of the utmost importance he should get a certain steamer three days hence. It was a very short time in which to complete so important a matter.

"But," said the old man, "I've got the money by me, and can manage it for you if we can agree about the price; but mind this, my friend, you mustn't open your mouth too wide. If I buy, you will have to name a very low figure."

"That I will do, Mr. Humphries," replied the man. "You know the property is in an improving part, and only requires a bit spent on it to double its present income. It cost me, years ago, seven thousand pounds; under present circumstances, you shall have it for five thousand."

Billy protested that he wouldn't pay any such price; but after a good deal of haggling, four thousand five hundred was agreed upon.

"Well, you be at my lawyer's at ten o'clock to-morrow

morning," said Humphries, "and there we'll settle everything."

The tradesman kept the appointment, but Billy failed to put in an appearance. The lawyer assured the man that Mr. Humphries had been called away on most urgent business, but would be certain to be there at six o'clock in the evening, when the whole thing could be completed. And at that time Mr. Humphries really did meet him, but full of a terrible passion, or one well simulated.

"I've been up to see this beautiful property," he began, "and I find you have deceived me. You said it was in good condition, and I find the owner of the property at the back of it threatening a lawsuit on account of your surface water draining into his premises; I'll have nothing to do with it."

The tradesman tried to mollify him with the assurance that it was a little matter that a hundred pounds would put right.

"A hundred pounds be blowed!" replied Billy. "It won't be done under five hundred, and that's what I'll have if I go on with it."

And it was ultimately settled that the price should be four thousand, and settling time at twelve o'clock the following day, which the tradesman weakly confessed was the latest hour he could agree to. So at that time they met again at the lawyer's office, and the necessary deeds were being completed. Billy had counted out a pile of bank-notes, together with a glittering heap of gold, which the unfortunate tradesman looked eagerly at again and again, longing to get hold of it. The suspense was becoming unbearable. Suddenly a violent knocking is heard at the office door; it is opened, and in rushes Mrs. Humphries, *apparently* overcome with terror and excitement.

"Oh, William, my dear," she gasped; "you haven't bought that dreadful man's property, I hope?"

"Why not? What's the matter now?" asked her husband.

"Oh, I've just heard something dreadful about him," she replied; "and I am sure it will be dangerous to have anything to do with him or his property."

And then the worthy couple played a little farce in the corner of the room, pretending to hold a serious conference in whispers—all this, of course, had been prearranged. After a minute or so Billy came back to the table, and collecting together all the notes and shining gold, he shovelled them into his capacious pockets again.

"It's all off," he said. "I'm sorry for you, sir; but my wife won't hear of me running the risk."

The poor fellow, it was easy to see, was in a fearful condition of funk and consternation; he gave them credit for knowing much more than they really did.

"Oh, dear, Mr. Humphries, whatever shall I do?" asked he; "you have placed me in a most awkward position."

Billy snuffled out what he intended the man should accept for sympathy; then turning to his wife:

"You go down to the Market Hall, my dear," he said; "I promise you I won't buy this property, but I've some more business with the lawyer."

Mrs. Humphries left the room, and the wily old man immediately turned hastily again to the unfortunate tradesman.

"I am awfully sorry for you," he said, "and I really oughtn't to touch it after what my wife tells me; but, dash it! I don't like to see you left in the hole like this, and I'll do it—I will—I'll risk everything if you'll knock off another thousand, and make it three; and here's the money, and you can have it in five minutes."

Pushed into the corner as he was, what was the poor fellow to do? He could only succumb; which he did, and so Humphries became possessed of a really valuable property at a ridiculous price.

On another occasion he proved himself more than a match for one of the shrewdest of his townsmen—an eminent architect. The freehold of some important business premises were to be sold by auction. These premises he very much desired, and determined to have, so he attended the sale, and managed to squeeze himself in next to the architect, whom he knew would be his most dangerous opponent, and he knew also that this man, who owned the adjoining property, had reasons for desiring to buy it stronger even than his own.

"What the devil brings you here, Humphries?" asked the architect, annoyed to see whom he had for next door-neighbour. "You surely don't want this lot?"

"No, I don't particularly," replied the old man; "but I've a bit of money lying idle, and I'd nothing to do to-night, so I thought I'd just step in, because if I don't buy I might perhaps earn a bit."

"Well, it's no use you and I opposing each other," said the architect, "so we had better be in at it together, and arrange after the sale—if we buy—to give or take something, or have a knock out."

This was exactly what Humphries desired, so it was arranged that the architect should open the bidding ridiculously low, and should fall out of it—seemingly in disgust—long before it reached the price he was willing to give, and that at this point Humphries should take it up. The property was at last knocked down to him at a very low figure.

"Well, Humphries," said the architect, "how shall we settle it?"

"Oh, I'll leave you to say how we shall settle it," meekly answered Bill.

"I'll tell you what I'll do, then," said the other, never dreaming that Humphries really wanted the property, and therefore concluding that he would hold out both hands for the handsome payment for the night's work he was offering—"I'll give you a hundred, or you shall give me a hundred."

"That'll do for me," said Billy, coolly pulling out a hundred pounds in notes and handing them to the architect.

"Oh, that be d—d!" screamed the outwitted professional, giving himself away at once; "that's not good enough for me. You said you didn't want the lot."

"I said, not particularly," replied Humphries; "but I can do with it at that price as well as you can."

The architect, seeing he was trapped, went on the cajoling tack. He confessed how badly he wanted the property, offered another hundred, and seeing that wouldn't do, another, and after that several hundreds more. Nothing would move Billy. He afterwards declared that his partner in the deal shouldn't have had it for twice its value, because he considered he was attempting to rob him of his fair share of the profits when he tried to make him take a paltry hundred pounds for it.

Humphries died a few years ago at a ripe old age, and up to the last neither racing nor anything else could induce him to neglect his fish stall in the Market Hall on Saturdays, where he and his wife would be found dabbing in cold water, cutting up cod and serving out mackerel from early morn till late at night—the lady with perhaps five hundred pounds' worth of diamonds on her hands. He left no family to inherit his wealth, his wife succeeded to that, but did not long enjoy it. She died a year or two after the old man.

Among those who found their way to the Coach and Horses seeking customers was Jem Pritchard, of Darlaston, one of the drollest fellows that ever lived. He is the author of many witty and quaint sayings. For forty years, at least, he has been a bookmaker, travelling the meetings all over England, one singularity about him being he was always his own clerk. I fancy if he had a mind to he could give us a sufficient and perhaps curious reason for it; anyway, in the old times of ante-post betting, if one found old Jem very busy laying a Derby—or any other—favourite, one was apt to conclude it was not a healthy sign for that favourite; but it was rarely these movements were detected. He did his business in such a quiet way—he not only employed no clerk, he took no regular "pitch," but wandered about the ring, pencil and book in hand, "seeking whom he could—" well, I'll say, do business with. I am glad to hear that he still lives, and that he is, for an "old 'un," hale and hearty. I suppose he has retired to the salubrious "banks and braes" of his native Darlaston.

Thousands of my readers will remember that among the other things which he managed to do without were beard and moustache. I have sometimes wondered what he would have looked like if he hadn't shaved. Then, again, I've speculated as to whether he found barbers who would shave him at the price they charged ordinary men, because he has not only a thick stubborn growth, but there was such an expanse of face to go over. I recall one occasion when a strange barber was laboriously at work upon it. Perhaps he hadn't a very sharp instrument. Anyway, hearing Pritchard grunt a good deal, he politely inquired if there was anything he could do for the gentleman—did the razor suit him, etc.

"Thee get on wi' thy work, mon," said the old 'un. "An' thou canna mak' me cry, *I'll* tak' —— good care thou dunno mak' me laugh."

One day one of the would-be sharps—who, by the way, are, as a rule, the very flattest of flats—had buttonholed Pritchard, and was holding forth on the merits of some particular horse's performances, and trying to impress Pritchard with his own great knowledge and ability. He finished up with:

"I'm no jay, Mr. Pritchard, I aren't."

"I know that," replied Jem, in an instant; "thee'st as dape as a tay-spoon, thee bist."

Jem's a real good sort of fellow, but a rather rough diamond, and his most partial friends don't claim for him anything out of the common in respect to good looks. He hasn't what you would call a severely classical cast of countenance. A brother bookie once taunted him with this fact, and I think it was generally allowed that Mr. Pritchard, in his retort, scored one.

How he did score, together with a number of highly amusing, if not particularly elevating, stories concerning Mr. Pritchard cannot be told here.

CHAPTER XIV

A STRANGE HISTORY

A Retrospect—Dan Lawrence—A wonderful Collier.

It has been said that "adversity makes us acquainted with strange bedfellows"; it is equally true that an active life on the turf must necessarily make one acquainted with a great variety of characters, and if one goes about with open eyes, having a faculty for observation, there are opportunities of noting many extraordinary events, as well as strange men; indeed, I know of no walk in life so fraught with chances for an observant mind as a life on the turf.

Since I commenced these reminiscences of my racing days, how often have I wished I had been blessed with enough wisdom and industry to have taken notes all through my career, with occasional pen-and-ink sketches of the men I have met, and the events I have witnessed during nearly forty years of turf life. What a mass of valuable material I should have had ready to my hand, and instead of the halting and uncertain efforts of memory, I should have been able to reproduce, with life-like accuracy, the actors and scenes of many now forgotten comedies of real life, which would have been interesting to readers of the present generation.

Indulging in a retrospective glance at the turf in the early sixties, and then observing it to-day, what a tremendous change seems to have come over the scene! The whole of what I may call the most important actors on the turf of those days have wholly disappeared—actors who afforded us so much profit and pleasure, and, alas! occasionally so much pain. I allude, of course, to the equine celebrities; and how few also of the notable men remain. Owners and trainers of horses, as well as those who backed and those who laid against them, have mostly gone, and a fresh race has taken their places. It is all changed, and methods and habits have altered as much as the people. It was always so—it is inevitable; we that are old become slow, dull of sight, and thick-witted. The young ones arise with keener sight, and generally more vigour, sometimes pushing us from our places, and it would have been well for some of us had we been wise enough to know this is in the everlasting nature of things; we should then have retired profitably, and perhaps gracefully, and not have lingered to be ousted from our places.

The large army of noble and gentle backers who were notorious in the sixties I have no space even to mention here. John Jackson, the great bookmaker, was bringing his career to a close, and was succeeded by Henry Steel, who was, "taking him for all in all," one of the most wonderful men the betting ring has known in any time. The struggle of his early life is a lesson worth knowing; his manful fight with adversity, under unfavourable circumstances and surroundings, and how he fought, with pluck and untutored gifts of nature, his way out of them, is a romance. As it was, he and his lifelong friend and partner, William Peach, raised themselves to positions of great wealth and importance, which happily they still maintain. Jacob Bayliss, who came about next after Steel in importance, is also still living. Tom Stones still lives, but is found no longer at the front, laying against favourites. John Robinson and his brother Sam, whose advent in the ring I so well remember, have "wrapped up," as the saying is, only putting in an occasional appearance, and then only to smoke a well-earned cigar and have a modest flutter for pleasure. The same might be said of Mr. Sydney Smith, who for a good many years has ceased to take any active part as a layer. Excepting these few,

A STRANGE HISTORY

I can think of none of the bookmakers of the earlier sixties who have any sort of connection with the ring at the present time. Billy Nicholl, who once bet to a tremendous lot of money, and was accounted a somewhat eccentric individual, lived, I believe, in retirement in Nottingham for upwards of twenty years, and died a year ago. Peggy Collins, a sharp, clever fellow, who made a fortune laying against horses, giving way to drink, lost it all again, and came to hanging about outside Tattersall's and other resorts of his old companions actually begging, and finally finished in the workhouse. Old Billy Marshall, Sam Haughton, Larry Wallace, Bob Coombes, and John Hibbert have been dead many years. Three of these are, however, represented in the ring by sons who play no unimportant part there, and, singularly enough, neither of the three is satisfied with the profession of their sires, but each combines in his own person the characters of owner, layer, and backer of horses. It is many years also since Tom Hornsby, Old Stevie, Harry Batten, Keeling and Gibson, Bart Onley, Joe Saxon, Tom Manning, George Luckett, and Matt Collinson died, and in comparatively recent years Jimmy Barber, Joe Slack, John Foy, Waterhouse, Turner, Wilson, George Silke, and James O'Connor have joined them. These were the well-known fielders of those days. All had done an enormous turn-over, and had been men of wealth and consequence in their time. Many of them retained this position to the end; others, and among these some who in life had been accounted the very keenest and cleverest of all, died in difficulties, nay, in absolute want. If one could only write a faithful biography of each of these men, what an interesting and startling volume it would make, for mostly they were indeed men with histories behind them.

Of all the fielders of this time, the one whom I saw most and knew best, and can best recall, was a very extraordinary character, and his strange life was made up of more striking vicissitudes than was that of any of those names I have run through.

This was Dan Lawrence, the famous collier, who came to the Coach and Horses with Mr. Pritchard, and for the same purpose; and as he was by far the most extraordinary character who frequented the old house, and perhaps because I saw more of him, I propose dealing with him somewhat more fully than I have with the others; and while I am about it, I think it advisable to carry his story to its sad ending.

When I first knew the collier he was a broad, thick-set, powerful black-countryman, who had spent most of his years under ground getting coal; he had book-learning of no sort, nor any kind of school education: he could neither read nor write, yet his natural intelligence was something marvellous. Being at a very tender age taken to work down a pit, he had few opportunities of improvement; but when he became old enough to look about for himself, he soon found out the fact that there was another world beyond the cinder-heaps and pit-banks of his native county, so he found his way on to the turf, and into the betting ring, by what conjunction of strange circumstances I cannot tell; I only know I found him there, a rough, uncouth, ill-dressed, and ill-conditioned being, a great head on his thick square shoulders, with eyes in it black and piercingly bright, which one soon discovered were capable of seeing whatever was visible to other men, and much also that was hidden from the ordinary, and his voice, once heard, could never be forgotten. A friend of mine says it was something between a policeman's rattle and the roar of a lion. It was truly an awful voice; I have heard nothing like it, and never expect—and certainly have no desire—ever again to do so.

Well, the collier had not been a member of the ring long before his daring gambling spirit had been rewarded with considerable success. He was notable for the frequency and good luck with which he played the "doll trick." He, indeed, was the first man whom I can remember practising that dangerous feat; he would think nothing of laying hundreds of pounds against a hot favourite, and then planking it all down on another horse in the same race. Of course, if you can do this sort of thing successfully, you may soon be rich. The black-countryman did manage to do it; indeed, for two or three years it didn't matter what he did, he could never do wrong, consequently he had to carry about with him, or stow away somewhere, an amount of ready money which was becoming quite embarrassing. He confided as much to an intimate friend of mine, who thereupon enlightened him upon the subject of banking accounts, recommending him to open one for his own safety and convenience, which he did forthwith, and my friend went with him to the bank for that purpose. He was shown into the banker's parlour, going through the necessary preliminaries, and making some sort of hieroglyphics in a book which was to be taken as his signature, and then he was shown to the counter to make his first deposit, which the banker naturally supposed was going to be merely a few pounds. Fancy the amazement of the bank people when he began to unwrap himself, producing huge rolls of notes, some of them clean and crisp, on the Bank of England for large amounts, with hundreds of shabby and ragged countrymen, looking uncommonly like bits of dirty tobacco paper, but representing altogether many thousands of pounds. It was wonderful where he kept on hauling them from, back and front and all over him; he seemed to have pockets crammed full with the precious paper. I know that within a year or two of opening that account he had no less than £35,000 lying there to his credit. One would think that was a fair share of the commodity for such a man to possess. Evidently he didn't think so, for I have never met with a man more earnest in pursuit of it than he was now; in fact, the richer he became, the more eager he was for more.

The collier became an owner of racers, had not only horses, but trainers and jockeys, and, who can tell, perhaps also human beings with pencils in their nimble fingers, all in his employ, and conspiring to increase his huge pile. He knew nothing of Shakespeare, but an unerring instinct told him

> "There is a tide in the affairs of men,
> Which, taken at the flood, leads on to fortune,"

and he had availed himself of that tide, and for a man of his origin and quality he had become inordinately rich. The pity of it was that nobody could drive it into his big, clever head the meaning of another passage from the great bard about

> "Vaulting ambition which doth o'erleap itself."

It might have saved him from much evil in after years.

Everybody knows that nature has a knack of compensating blind folk for their loss of sight by abnormally developing the sense of touch, or other of the senses; so it will be found frequently where men cannot write, but are driven to commit to memory what other people commit to paper, that faculty becomes marvellous in its expansion and capability. I have known several cases of this kind, but nothing that equals that of my friend the pitman. His memory was simply wonderful. For several years I shared with him the same private lodgings at the Newmarket meetings and elsewhere, having ample opportunities of proving this statement with regard to his memory. One case I will give my readers illustrative of it, premising, however, that I don't expect everyone will be able to swallow the facts entirely; nevertheless, they are strictly true.

I may say that the collier had occasionally partners, and sometimes clerks, but as a rule he didn't get on well with either; consequently, it was no uncommon occurrence for him to find himself at a race-meeting without either one or the other. Considering he could not write a single line for himself, it might be supposed that his backing and laying would on such occasions be at a standstill. Nothing of the sort; in fact, it seemed to make little difference to him, he would go on with his backing and laying just the same, and when he returned to our lodgings in the evening, and had dined, he would hand his book to me, or to one of the others, calling over every bet he had made during the day entirely from memory, where doubtless he had the names of the men and horses, and amounts, indelibly impressed, and I do not remember him being at any time convicted of an error. One advantage of this method was such an one as he was peculiarly well able to appreciate; it enabled him to dispense with a partner, who would take away some portion of his profits, and to do without a clerk, for whose services he would have to pay.

I will relate one little incident very early in his racing career which will show the utter density of his ignorance regarding the usages of civilised life. Now the pitman's early life, when not underground, had been spent in a dwelling which was more hovel than house, such as was only too common in the pit districts of South Staffordshire fifty or sixty years ago. Such a thing as washing themselves upstairs was, of course, unknown. Mostly this service, and other portions of the toilet, was completed in the little living room, or, as frequently happened, at the pump outside. Fancy, then, our friend's bewilderment the first time he went away from home for a few days, and found himself putting up at a decent hotel. Everything was so strange, so wonderful. Carpets on stairs, carpeted rooms, bedsteads with gorgeous hangings, tables with tops of marble, mirrors half as big as himself, chairs with delicate cane seats, and furniture too costly to touch. Coming off a long and dirty journey, he wants to wash and brush up, so " Boots " has carried up his little carpet bag and shown him his bedroom, where he stands motionless, in a puzzled condition, for a quarter of an hour. There is the marble-topped washstand, with soap-boat and large basin, with jug of water, together with all the usual necessaries for a wash, but to the collier these things are strangers. He sees insurmountable obstacles in the way. He looks at the narrow-necked jug, and then at his immense hands, such as pitmen only own, and it was an indisputable fact that they needed washing. But how? "There's the rub." In his perplexity he looks about the room, and seeing a silken cord with a tassel at the end of it, it dawns upon him that this may mean a bell at the other end of it, and as he is not afflicted, even in these early days, with any large amount of timidity, he snatches at the cord and gives it a tremendous jerk, so bringing off his first double event—he breaks the bell-pull and brings up a rosy, good-looking chambermaid.

"Cum eer, mi wench," said he, "wheer bin I to wash me?"

"There you are, sir," replied the girl, pointing to the jug and basin, and looking at the uncouth figure of the collier with mingled curiosity and alarm. He, in his turn, looked with a puzzled expression of countenance, first at the girl and then at the jug, and then again at his own huge hands. Turning to her, he asked:

"'Ow bin I to get mi honds into that jug, wench?"

This was quite irresistible; the girl burst into a loud laugh, and when it subsided she proceeded to separate the jug from the basin, which the collier had supposed one article, pouring out the water for him, for which he showed his gratitude by amatory language, and sundry delicate attentions of a kind so common on the pit-banks of South Staffordshire forty years ago.

Before the collier had been long in the ring, by sheer force of character and boundless audacity he had pushed himself to the front, and was hobnobbing with dukes, earls, and all sorts of titled folks, and so fearless was he about introducing himself to the great ones of the earth, he didn't draw the line even at Royalty itself. On one occasion a very exalted personage was standing in the Jockey Club enclosure at Newmarket, within a few yards of where the collier stood—of course, in the adjoining enclosure. Royalty intently studying his racing card, as any ordinary mortal might—who knows? perhaps weighing the chances of the runners, and settling it in his own mind which was to carry his bit. The Prince looked up from his card straight into the eyes of the persevering pitman, and the pitman was by no means frightened or abashed; on the contrary, he leant over the rails in a most familiar manner, and with that indescribable voice of his roared out:

"Now then! Wat wun yer Majesty bok."

The genial Prince, with an amused smile, quietly walked away. Doubtless Royalty, as well as humble people, may have a flutter occasionally—and very properly so—but it is opposed to the etiquette of Royalty to do it directly; it is always done through the medium of a middleman, generally one of the Prince's intimate friends.

In dress, manners and language, he never was anything but the big pitman, even in his palmiest days. He arrived in Birmingham one night very late—too late, in fact, to get a train to his home on the pit-banks of South Staffordshire. With him was Jem Pritchard, a black-countryman, as unmistakably as was the collier himself; he proposed they should put up till morning at the Queen's Hotel adjoining the station, whither they proceeded. Jem, who was one of the drollest fellows I have ever met with—a real character—stepped up to the door of the hotel and rang the bell; then turning to his companion, he whispered:

"Yo' stond back i' the dark, Dan. If the hotel mon see thy pretty mug, we'll get no lodgin' here; they'll think we bin cum a-cadgin'."

Whenever the collier made one of a party, staying and boarding together, he always contrived, if possible, to do the settling. I remember an occasion when the party numbered seven, and we had agreed to pay a guinea each for our beds, and at his request we each one paid him our proportion of the bill—including the guineas for beds. The evening we were leaving we left him behind to settle. For some purpose one of the party had to return to the house, and dropped upon the collier haggling with the landlady whether it was guineas or pounds we were to pay for the beds. The poor woman stood but small chance in a bout of words with him, and so we discovered the collier's motive for liking to settle the bills.

The collier was not what is known as "a giver," yet he was not altogether incapable of a generous action; to prove which I may mention an incident arising out of Blue Gown's Derby. He was intimately acquainted with Sir Joseph Hawley, and had large transactions with him. It is a well-known fact that Sir Joseph could never be made to believe that the almost cobby Blue Gown was the equal—much less the superior—of the aristocratic Rosicrucian, and it is also known that this prejudice cost the famous Baronet the trifle of £100,000 or thereabouts. There is no doubt that Sir Joseph had told the collier the whole strength of the business which had influenced him to lay a considerable sum against Blue Gown, which, of course, he lost and paid. Among his Birmingham friends there was a bookmaker in humble circumstances, to whom—doubtless intending to help him—he gave the tip to lay. At the end of the Derby week he went to see the pitman, and told him that he had so far overlaid his book and crippled his means, he should be compelled to pull up lame on the settling day unless he could get help. What was necessary to save him the collier advanced; and more than once, when people have been abusing the collier, I have heard this man stand up for him against all comers, manfully and gratefully defending his absent friend.

In the sixties there was a popular race-meeting in the Isle of Man. It was an agreeable annual outing to Douglas, when a good many of us managed to combine business with pleasure, and it was by no means a little local affair confined to Manxmen and Manx horses, for many of the leading turfites patronised the meeting, and some fairly good horses were sent from England. I recall one occasion when my friend the pitman won a race there, I and my immediate connection being among

A STRANGE HISTORY

his supporters, so we had a jolly time of it; but the return journey took all the jollity out of us.

The Manx boats were not the elegant and comfortable steamers which we see plying between Liverpool and Douglas to-day; the one in which we returned was a wretched old tub, which pitched and rolled about in the most distressing manner. It was bad weather when we started, and we were scarcely clear of the bay when it blew a perfect hurricane, and the face of many a bold betting man was blanched with fear, and I verily believe some among them never expected to see their cosy homes again. It was one of those occasions which show what men are made of, and it served to show up the character of our collier. It proved his natural cuteness and mother-wit was more than a match for his better educated companions. He actually had the audacity to open an insurance office, there and then, aboard the steamer. He began betting £100 to half-a-crown that we got safely back to Liverpool. It may seem incredible, but it is true, that a good many in the panic of the moment handed him their half-crowns for the sake of the long odds, among the takers being several reputed dead sharps. However, when it dawned upon them that the layer was standing all these half-crowns to nothing, in spite of sea-sickness and suffering they were obliged to have a hearty laugh at each other.

No opportunity of getting a bit ever escaped the collier. Sagacious and alert, he was always on the look-out, and nothing missed his keen eyes. There was no rule in those days about newly-named horses, or horses with changed names, being advertised to that effect on the cards. In this respect there was not the wholesome protection for innocent backers and layers which this excellent rule now affords; consequently, at times great injustice was wrought and much scandal caused. I remember one case particularly illustrating this, in which the collier was concerned. A horse, known as the Colt, by Trumpeter, out of Miss Bowser, won in a canter the first day of the meeting at Reading. On the following day there was a

I

horse on the card named Hornblower, and when his number went up for the race he was in nobody knew anything about him, and not until the collier had cleared all the market at fives, fours, threes, and even much shorter prices, did it become known that this strange horse was the identical Miss Bowser Colt, about which a fair price would have been 6 to 4 on, and as he won again, our cute friend must have had a pretty haul.

But cute and clever as he was, there came a day when "vaulting ambition did o'er leap itself," and the collier was as incapable of doing right as he had hitherto been incapable of making mistakes; and it is a fact that when once the tide sets in against a gambler it is all over with him. Having become drunk with success, and full of the egotism born of it, he is sure it will all come right again; so, with a stubborn faith in his own judgment, he fights Fate with a blind valour, and cannot see from whence come the buffets he is getting, and only when he is panting with distress, utterly and irretrievably defeated, is he able to see the strength of his foe. And then he curses himself for a fool that he had not given up the unequal contest long before, when he might have retired with some honour and credit. So fared it with our clever pitman. His horses went wrong, his jockeys went wrong; everything went wrong with him. Even the great "doll trick," which he had played so often and with so much success—that also failed him. The pile he had made went faster than it came. He had a floorer one week, and he came up smiling the next, with strong faith in himself, nothing daunted. But now his pluck availed him nothing, and Fate mocked at his strength and his cunning, and went on to complete his ruin. While this was in progress there were, however, fitful gleams of sunshine for him. I recall with a vivid distinctness one week at Newmarket. When the last day of the meeting arrived, he had lost thousands of pounds on the week, and he was making ready to go home, and I never remember him so completely broken down before.

"I'm dun, lads," he said, "I mun goo hum. Yo'll never see me i' th' ring again."

It was almost pathetic to see the great, strong fellow at last admitting defeat. Somebody present made the remark that he might as well be hanged for a sheep as a lamb, and urged him to give it one more trial. He sat with his head in his hands for several minutes, then jumped up with a look of determination in his eyes; so he went with us on to the Heath again.

For that day he was once again the wonderful collier. Time after time he laid against the favourite and backed the winner. At the end of the day he had recovered all his losses on the week, and had a balance to the good, and so for a little time he was reprieved.

These gleams of sunshine were, however, but transient; the fickle jade Fortune was merely playing with him. Week after week he continued to lose, until he reached the one preceding the St. Leger week, which was a scorcher for him from the first day of it to the last, and those of us who knew him and his concerns intimately were wondering how he would get over the next settling. Of course, the ring generally knew nothing of the straits the collier was in. Months before this he had backed a horse for the coming Leger for a very large amount, and at this time this horse had come to a short price, and seemed to have a fair chance of winning, so placing him on his feet again. These bets were worth a good deal of money; so I felt sure that on this account, if the money could by any means be found, the settling would be done. I happened to be lodging at the time with the young man who was acting as clerk to him. The account was made out accurately on the Saturday and posted to the collier, that he might enclose the requisite cheques and forward them on to the agent in London to settle on Monday, and we were left to speculate as to what would come of it. On Sunday morning, to our surprise, the collier himself turned up, looking restless and unhappy. Producing the account, he said:

"Look 'e 'ere, mi lad, this account wunnor do; I want yo to mak' another."

"What's the matter with it?" asked the clerk. "It's exactly according to the book."

"Never yo moind the book," replied the collier. "Yo'n left out swells that owe me a heap of money, and there's a neame or two on the t'other side yo can leave out till next week."

Fresh sheets of foolscap, with pen and ink, were provided and carried to the little summer-house at the top of the garden, where the new account, which was to provide a week's grace for the poor collier, was made out and forwarded to London, and being made to show a small balance in his favour, of course no cheque was sent with it. It is unnecessary for me to say there was a good deal of grumbling and dissatisfaction at such an unusual number of mistakes being found in the account, but it was settled as well as possible, and it served to get him over the St. Leger week, and as the horse he had backed won, it was all made right on the following Monday. The account was duly settled, but not without sundry shakings of the head and ominous mutterings of discontent.

Nevertheless, the collier once more enjoyed a passing gleam of sunshine, which was, unfortunately, of short duration. The clouds gathered again above him; so after a little time we missed him altogether—he gave up the fight. The enemy had got him down and kept him there. He returned to his old trade of collier, only not now himself handling the pick and the shovel. With the assistance of, and in partnership with, an old racing friend who had had much dealing with him, he became tenant of several small coal-pits. But even here, in his native regions, an evil fate pursued him: instead of a coal-pit, it seemed he had leased an underground reservoir, and in place of coal they hauled up little but water; so the undertaking failed, and the friend who had helped him lost several thousands of pounds by it.

A STRANGE HISTORY

He tried a public-house, and that looked like providing him with a living, and quite as much of luxury as he had allowed himself in his richest days. I cannot tell how it came about, but after a while this also failed him, and he became really very poor. I am told worse than poor—old, and terribly afflicted with an incurable malady; and only a few years ago he passed away, after many years of weakness, and suffering, and poverty. Few would have recognised in the broken and decayed old man the strong, clever, and rich collier of thirty-five years ago.

CHAPTER XV

A PENITENTIAL MOOD

The Prayer of the Apostate—A Band of Hope.

LET no one imagine that in the midst of this whirl of racing, gambling, and drink I was always and entirely happy. At the risk of being laughed at by some of my friends, I am going to confess that was not so. Deep down in my heart were thoughts undreamt of, and perhaps not understandable by my companions—a sense of remorse and unrest, a feeling that I was not meant to go by this way, but by a widely different one.

During what I must call the religious period of my life, I had had lapses which pained my friends, and gave me uncomfortable days and nights. These lapses originated, I believe, in a study of Voltaire, Rousseau, Tom Paine, and others of the like, whom I found Paley and Simpson powerless to counteract; but I had never before gone wholly and openly over to the enemy, and I was troubled with many doubts as to the wisdom of the course I had taken; and at times an overpowering force seemed driving me back to the old ways. The verses inserted here were written in these days, and I beg my critical reader to believe I print them now with no purpose of showing my poetical wares, but with a simple desire to give just a glimpse of my mind during the time I was struggling with influences so opposite.

A PENITENTIAL MOOD

THE PRAYER OF AN APOSTATE.

Friend of the poor and sad! bend low Thine ear;
   A heavy sorrow is upon me now;
My eyes, for ayé, refuse the kindly tear,
   And clouds have chased the sunbeams from my brow,
And human hopes, erstwhile so bright and clear,
   Dear God! are gone—ah, dead for ever now!

Bend, bend Thine ear; come to me once again!
   To-night great sorrow hath crushed all my pride;
I turn to Thee in darkness and in pain;
   The fount of human love for me is dried,
And ev'ry human sympathy is vain,
   And none can help, if Thy help be denied.

Then come, oh, come! my bruiséd heart doth yearn
   To feel Thy Spirit move in me once more;
Rekindle here Thy fires, and let them burn
   But once again, as in the days of yore.
I feel Thou wilt, I know Thou could'st not spurn
   The humbly penitent from Mercy's door.

These verses, and the rather gloomy matter which opens the chapter, having worked me into a penitential mood, I may as well make one or two other confessions, and have done with it.

For years after I became a professional racing man I found it impossible to go into any place of worship. Such a coward was I in these matters, the solemn tones of a church organ heard in the distance, or a familiar hymn-tune on a hurdy-gurdy in the street, would make me run away. And yet at times I yearned with a yearning almost irresistible to go back to the other life, and sit once more among my old friends.

I remember one night when I was making my way to a rendezvous of sport in Birmingham, I had to pass a small meeting-house with which, in other days, I was well acquainted, and where, had I dared to put my head inside, I should have been instantly recognised. The room was lighted up, and a meeting of some sort in progress. The sound of sweet voices singing a glee arrested my footsteps, nor for the life of me could I move from the spot while the sounds continued. When they ceased, I felt impelled to go inside; so crept stealthily into the little vestibule, and listened to a young man pleading with youngsters to avoid the temptations of drink. It was a "Band of Hope" meeting. I heard the whole of the little speech, and then the chairman called upon another young man for the next item on the programme. This was a recitation popular at such meetings in those days, and it may be so now for aught I know; it was called "The Broken Heart." Before the reciter had got through half-a-dozen lines, I rushed half mad from my hiding-place; I could bear it no longer, and quickly as possible I was in the midst of my new friends, with a pack of cards in my hands, trying to forget all about it. "The Broken Heart" was a poem I had written several years before; the teetotallers had it published, and it became popular among them as a recitation. It is not so long ago I received the original MS. of this very poem from Mr. Edward Pickering, Mayor of Durban, and a wealthy colonial merchant, who, as a young man and a teetotaller, had been entrusted with the printing of it in Birmingham more than forty years ago. In the letter which accompanied it, Mr. Pickering hoped that the sight of this soiled and time-worn manuscript would awaken some pleasant memories, assuring me, at the same time, that the piece had been of much service in South Africa. Alas! alas! what pleasant thoughts could it —or anything like it—produce for me?

On another occasion I was with my brother in Liverpool, awaiting the races at Aintree. I had seen an announcement on all the hoardings in the town that the celebrated preacher, Charles Vince of Birmingham, would lecture in some institute or hall there. After dinner, I said to my brother:

"The Reverend Charley is lecturing in Liverpool to-night, and I should so like to hear him again, if one might hear and see him, and not be seen."

"Oh, that is easy enough!" replied Sam; "we will go."

A PENITENTIAL MOOD

In good time, before the lecture commenced, we made for the hall, paid for seats on the floor, and had time to secure them not far from the platform, where we could see and hear our old friend. If I remember rightly, in the shade of a gallery, or screened from his keen eyes by a friendly pillar, we were both interested and delighted with the lecture, and also with the success of our arrangements for avoiding the lecturer. We had turned to leave the hall, when we were stopped by the sound of a well-remembered voice:

"Hi! hi! you chaps there! Are you going to turn your backs on an old friend in that way?" and down from the platform stepped the Rev. Charles, his face still ablaze with the old genial smile.

Well, having unbosomed myself of these confessions of little weaknesses, as my readers maybe will deem them, I must get along with my life on the turf, wherein I shall have to introduce many scenes and characters of quite another sort.

CHAPTER XVI

KINDNESS REWARDED

Warwick Races—A Dust-up with Thieves—What came of It.

WARWICK may be classed among the ancient English race meetings, and, like other of these old-fashioned affairs, it has been the subject of many "ups and downs." In the last century, and during the early years of the present one, it enjoyed great consideration, and was a resort of all the prime old sports among our fathers and grandfathers. Of course, the racing was an altogether different thing to what exists in the present day, when a programme is made up almost entirely of five furlong sprint races, and the majority of the performers are perhaps two-year-old horses. Then the runners were nearly always four-year-olds and upwards, which is natural when we come to consider that such a thing as handicapping was unknown; the courses were generally from two to four miles, and as the races were nearly all run in heats, it was not unusual for a horse, carrying much heavier weights than those allotted at the present time, to have to do sixteen miles before being proclaimed the winner, and generally he would have to travel twelve miles. Hence it happened that, as a rule, the race card—if such a thing was then known—would only contain two or three items. At Warwick it was quite the proper thing for the pauses between the various heats to be occupied by a little cock-fighting or a merry mill between a couple of Brummagem boys.

Coming nearer to our own times, and well within the memory of some among us, I may mention that as far back as the

September Meeting, 1842, there were evident signs of a decadence in this good old meeting, and one sporting writer of the day bewails the fact in most plaintive language, contrasting the miserable acceptance of six for its glorious old Gold Cup—which, by-the-by, was won that year by the famous old jockey, Sam Darling, on Mr. Holme's Vulcan—with that of 1830, when there were thirty-one subscribers, many of them horses of the highest class, and when the trophy was captured by that real good horse, Birmingham, who won the Leger the following week. Through the forties and fifties there was, I am afraid, still a downward tendency. The swells of the county had largely withdrawn their patronage, and at one time there looked like being a collapse. It was Warwick in the sixties, however, that I was most intimately acquainted with, and during that decade I saw some splendid sport there, and meetings which were a credit to the old place. A better spirit pervaded the local gentry, and the swells among owners began again to look with favour upon the meeting, and consequently many of the equine cracks of the time were to be found there. I have a perfect recollection of some of these, and the races they figured in; but perhaps the one race of that time which clings to my memory most tenaciously was a very small and unimportant affair at the September Meeting in 1868. But before I come to this race I must relate a little adventure of the previous week.

I was at Lichfield races, and had remained on the course till after all the people had returned to the city, for the purpose of seeing a horse I was interested in have a "rough up" with one which had been running during the day, and it was after six o'clock when, all alone, I set my face towards the city. Although it was more than a couple of miles to my destination, it was at that time my custom to walk down from the course, as I had many times witnessed the dangers attending the drive down in the wretched old conveyances which were pressed into this service on these occasions. I left the turnpike road and went by the back lanes, and was strolling leisurely along when, suddenly making a bend in the road, I came upon a scene which quickened my movements. A hundred yards in front of me I beheld a couple of powerful young ruffians seize a slim, well-dressed young man with the evident intention of "running the rule over him," and there is no doubt that but for my timely arrival he would have had a rough time of it. The first intimation the ruffians had of the presence of a fourth party was when one of them got a tremendous whack from a strong cudgel I carried in my hand. The first effect of this was to liberate the young man, and then the thieves, seeing there were two to two, and one tolerably well armed, took to their heels and were soon out of sight.

"You had a near shave of being turned up, sir," I said, recognising in the young man a youthful recruit to the turf, who, however, has since become an important figure upon it.

"I had, indeed," he replied, "and I have very much to thank you for your timely assistance."

The upshot of it was that we walked back to the city together, and over a bottle at the Swan he became very confidential about certain horses he was going to buy, and hoped he might be able to repay me for the services I had rendered him.

Just as we were about to part, taking hold of my hand, he said:

"I should like to do you a good turn, old fellow, and I think I know a real cert for a race at Warwick next week. You saw old Wynnstay run second for the Cup to-day?"

"Yes, of course I have seen that."

"Well, take no notice of that," he resumed; "but look out for him in a race at Warwick, and don't speak of it to anybody."

I knew my young friend was in a position to know more about it than I could, and I had the strongest reasons for believing he would do me a turn if he could, so I was on the watch for old Wynnstay the following week. I discovered him

KINDNESS REWARDED 141

in a little handicap—I think only a paltry fifty-pound plate the first day. When the number board was hoisted I found there were only five runners, and I made them out a very bad lot, and although Wynnstay was at that time no flyer, and had not, I believe, won a single race during the season, he appeared to have nothing to beat here. Handley rode him and Fred Webb Muezzin, and I must confess that I would have felt much more easy in my mind if the jockey's had been reversed. Well, the betting was 3 to 1 on the field, and at about this price the two I have named and one called Citron were backed furiously, while Distaff and Rhine Wine were also fancied. I had already backed the old horse for as much as I could well afford, and was about going on to the stand to see the race when I saw my young friend, book and pencil in hand, very busy taking all the 5's to 2 he could get Wynnstay.

"Have you backed him?" he asked quietly.

"I have," I replied.

"Well, don't be afraid," he rejoined; "he will win easily."

At this I returned to my bookies and put down a considerable amount more, and did not reach the stand till the horses were on the way home. I was dreadfully nervous, because I knew I had bet more than I ought on one race, and if it went against me it would pretty well skin me. The first good look I got of the race I could see that Wynnstay and Muezzin had slipped away from the field and were coming on by themselves, and the excited partisans of each all around me were shouting themselves hoarse; I could not shout, the tension of my mind was too great for that. I could only stare straight at these two horses and the two lads on their backs, making superhuman efforts to get in front, and neither seemed able to do it. I felt cold at the heart, and was conscious of turning all sorts of colours; it was quickly over, and I was out of one trouble to be in another. Muezzin, they said, had won by a short head; I could not have known that if I had not seen the fatal number go up. This, then, was the result of that young man's genuine desire to help me, and this the reward of my good action on his behalf in the lonely Lichfield lane. I had lost all my money, and should be a cripple, pecuniarily, for some time to come. But I lived to laugh at my folly in having so many eggs in one basket, and a long life, with perhaps more than a fair share of life's vicissitudes, has taught me that we cannot always tell which are our blessings and which our curses.

CHAPTER XVII

STOCKBRIDGE MEMORIES

Stockbridge in Old Times—In the Sixties—Mr. Merry and his hot Jobs—A sensational Dead Heat—An expensive Dinner.

DURING my early struggles I was so many times reduced to a condition of having to begin the game all over again that I had now got quite used to it. Somehow, however, I always managed to scramble out of my difficulties, and get a new start, as I did on the present occasion. I was a long time reaching anything like a substantial position; but, in spite of my many deviations from the paths of true bookmaking, I did ultimately achieve a considerable success, and for very many years occupied a fair position in the ring, travelling to every part of the country, attending race meetings of every description in pursuit of my business as a bookmaker.

The chapters which follow are reminiscences of those years. Unfortunately, I took no notes as I went along; had I done so, I have no doubt that these rambling stories of an old racing man would have been better worth reading.

A good many of the old race meetings, to which I travelled regularly once a year, have disappeared altogether, and their places have been taken by huge company concerns—race meetings with expensive clubs; gates here and gates there; with rings of all sorts, with charges of admission to them all, ranging from one shilling to fifty times as much for a single day's racing. This will, of course, mean an improvement in some respects, at a tremendously increased cost to the regular race-goer, but with big dividends to the happy holder of shares.

After all, I look back regretfully to those old open race-courses which have gone for ever. I know they had their objectionable features; but had they not compensating qualities?

Of all the lost meetings, none has left such a void as Stockbridge; none was of such antiquity and importance, and to not one of them does memory cling with such strength and tenderness.

Stockbridge, after a long and, taking it altogether, most successful career, has come to an end, and many of the elder members of the racing world will regret the old Hampshire meeting exceedingly. For them there are few race-courses around which gather such pleasant memories; excepting Newmarket, I don't know of any. In the early days of my racing life I remember how eagerly I anticipated the Hampshire week. It was not only the racing was so high-class and enjoyable, but the whole surroundings of the meeting were pervaded by a spirit of quiet orderliness and dignified repose. You got lots of things here which were pleasant to have, and rarely obtainable elsewhere; while many of the most objectionable features of racing at nearly all other places were entirely absent.

I stayed at the pleasant little market town of Andover for many years during the race week, and not the least of its pleasures was the delightful drive every morning over that lovely stretch of country which lies between Andover and the Grand Stand at Stockbridge, enlivened, as the drive invariably was, by puns, and jokes, and racy stories, accompanied by the best of cheer and the presence of dear old friends, who, alas! are dead or scattered—gone beyond the possibility of reviving these happy days here or elsewhere.

A glance through the scanty racing chronicles of the last century, although they fail to tell us much we should like to know, cannot fail to amuse us; but the one thing which impresses us beyond everything else is the tremendous change which has been wrought not only in the appearance, habits, and spirit of sportsmen, and in the surroundings of sport, but in the nature and condition of the sport itself. There were no handicaps such as we know. The only handicaps our forefathers knew anything of was a system of giving horses with the longest legs the most to carry, or what they called "weight for inches," so that anyone possessing a good little one had a fair chance of clearing the board. Then they knew nothing of five furlong races; indeed, there was rarely any under two miles, and most of them were four, and run, be it remembered, in heats; so that it would frequently happen that the winner would have to win four races.

Betting was carried on very differently to what it is in these days, and although there was plenty of it, there were no loud-voiced bookmakers, whose profession it was to lay against all runners. It must not be imagined that because the exigencies of racing had not yet called into existence this professional element, that therefore there was little betting, and no scope for the ingenuity and perseverance of the *sharper*, a creature not peculiar to racing, or indeed to any form of sport, but who will be found in every profession, class, and condition of human life. It has always seemed to me that the old practice of running races in heats lent itself in a remarkable way to "*roping*" and other fraudulent practices, and one can but smile as we read such meagre accounts of the betting as is handed down to us. In 1775, Stockbridge and Bibury Club had three days, and, including a match, they had five races on the three days. But frequently one race was enough for the day, especially where there were four heats of four miles each, with an hour perhaps between the heats, this time being usually occupied with fighting a main or two of cocks, a bout of fisticuffs, or other sport. In one of the races on the last day of the meeting there were four runners. Before the start a very short price was taken about Mignonne, who was the public favourite. She won the first heat very easily, and one would think that should have made her still a better favourite for the race, but that was not so; indeed, she was ousted altogether, and Miss Bell, who could only just manage to get fourth in the first heat, was not only a better favourite, but she improved so much in less than an hour that she very easily disposed of Mignonne and the others in the remaining two heats. It is wonderful how often the winner of the first heat, although meeting his opponents over the same distance and on exactly the same terms, is nowhere in the succeeding heats, and it appears a bit suspicious to we moderns. I notice a race where Mr. Medley's Bacchus was thought real jam, and odds of 6 to 4 was laid on his beating his solitary opponent. He won the first heat so easily that the odds lengthened to 7 to 1 on him; but his opponent, the Duke of Cumberland's Ora, won the second heat just as easily, and for the final heat 7 to 1 was laid on the Duke. So if there had only been anybody knowing enough to systematically take odds, what a good thing they might have made of it.

The Duke of Bolton and His Royal Highness of Cumberland, during the seventies of the eighteenth century, seem to have been great supporters of Stockbridge and Bibury Club. The latter, who kept an immense stud of horses in training, usually had one or more entered in all the races; and he won with a good many of them. Toward the end of the century, and in the early years of the nineteenth, the Prince of Wales had taken the place of the Duke of Cumberland, and kept an even larger stud. And as he was a constant patron, Stockbridge became, at this time, one of the most fashionable meetings in the whole list, and it was doubtless a brave sight to see the meeting of the club, composed not of the swelldom of a county only, but of all the young bloods of the country, with the first gentleman of Europe, the Prince Regent, at their head, in the uniform of this aristocratic club—green coats, buckskin breeches, and top-boots.

For a good many years after the Regency, the meeting,

which had fallen on bad times, remained in low water, and much of the credit of its revival belongs to John Day, who in the early sixties took charge of it, providing special accommodation for the many noble patrons of Danebury, and for the aristocracy generally; and never, perhaps, in its long history had it seen such glorious times as those of the sixties. And these were the times I knew it best, and looking back to them, memory is crowded with faces and forms and stirring incidents which the space at my disposal will not permit me to reproduce. Among the owners I was in the habit of seeing there were the Dukes of Beaufort, St. Albans, and Hamilton; Lords Portsmouth, Uxbridge, Ailesbury, Stamford, Westmoreland, Vivian, Falmouth, and the unfortunate young Hastings; Baron Rothschild, Sir Joseph Hawley, Sir Frederick Johnstone, Sir William Throckmorton, Count Lagrange, Mr. Merry, Mr. Cartwright, Mr. Chaplin, Mr. Ten Broeck, good old George Payne, and a host of others. The most prominent among the gentlemen riders—and this was ever a great meeting for them—were Captains Little, Knox, Scobel, and Coventry; Messrs. W. Bevill, Edwards, and G. S. Thompson. The chief professionals whom I remember there were Fordham, Daley, Wells, A. Day, Custance, Arthur Edwards, Aldcroft, Rogers, Tom French, Chaloner, the two Grimshaws, the three Adams, and Tom Cannon. The latter, destined to become more intimately associated with the place than either of the others, made his first appearance there, Thursday, June 23, 1864, and my old friend Teddy Brayley gave him the first mount, where he was afterwards to achieve so much glory. The horse was a three-year-old called Black Friar, 6 st. 12 lb., which weight, however, he was not quite able to do, and consequently had to put up 1 lb. extra. He was unbacked, and ran nowhere. The following day, in a big field of eighteen, he rode the Star, 6 st. 13 lb., and managed to get a good third to Sam Adams on a colt by Vedette, who beat Fordham on Missionary, after a magnificent race, by a head. These were the only two mounts the future master of Danebury had at the meeting that year. The following year we find him doing better in the matter of mounts—riding for Brayley again, for Lord Hastings, and others, but with no win, and although he rode regularly he won very few races here for several years, and it was not until 1870 that he made any mark at Stockbridge; then he won five out of fourteen mounts.

The greater part of the jockeys and others whom I have named, and whom I knew in connection with the famous old meeting, have gone over to the great majority, many of them long years ago. Harvey Covey we still have with us, and occasionally see in the saddle. As far back as 1860 he won the Amport Stakes on Mr. Merry's Northern Light, three years, 6 st. 4 lb.; F. Robinson's Ariadne (Arthur Edwards up) was second, and Crater third. In the earlier days I have been writing of they thought they had a good field if they mustered six runners, which was not often. Things had improved a bit since then, for in the Amport Stakes there were 123 subscribers, 77 of whom paid £5 each, and 22 started for the post; but Richmond, as usual, became restive and unmanageable, and throwing his jockey over his head, got away and reduced the field by one. This turned out one of Mr. Merry's well-kept good things, and as he started at 10 to 1, there is no doubt he won a large stake; and at no time was the result in doubt, for Covey had only to sit still on the horse and win by three lengths.

After two more races, Mr. Merry provided them with another very warm order, and playing his winnings up, he gave the ring one of those blows he so often inflicted upon it. It was only a £200 plate which he set himself to capture with his two-year-old Dundee, which, it will be remembered, was such a warm favourite for the Derby the following year, when just beaten by Kettledrum; but, of course, he made no mistake in this little race; it was simply an exercise canter for him.

STOCKBRIDGE MEMORIES

The race I have just described was on the first day of the meeting. On the last day Robin Hood confirmed his previous form, and I am afraid he did something more than that. He was certainly never the same horse after the gruelling which he got in the Troy Stakes. In some respects the race was like the one earlier in the week. There were a dozen runners, many of them of real good class, and again the interest and the betting were almost entirely confined to two, only instead of King Hal, Mr. Merry's Student was one of the fancied candidates. King Hal was among the runners, but this time without a friend. Wells again had the mount on Robin Hood, and Covey rode Student. It was for a long way a desperate race between the pair, and Harry Grimshaw, on Lord Stamford's Chibisa, for a moment looked like taking part in the final struggle, but he failed at the pinch; and it rested for the last 200 yards with the other two, and what a struggle it was! For a few strides Harvey got his horse's head in front, and loud cries were raised for the great Scotch ironmaster and his horse; the great horseman, however, was not to be denied, and sticking to it with his dogged determination, and getting every ounce out of his mount, he just managed to make a dead heat of it with Robin Hood. The after-history of these horses—both of them, no doubt, at the time at the very top of the tree—proves that they were both ruined by this race, and we should be surprised if we could only know how frequently good two-year-olds are hopelessly ruined by a terribly severe strain which is put upon them while they are so young.

One of the most brilliant of all the Stockbridge Meetings of my time was that of 1866. It was not only made glorious by a great company of the cream of English aristocracy—male and female—and all our most distinguished professional and gentlemen riders, but also by the presence of an unusual number of equine celebrities.

Two notable youngsters—Hermit and Marksman—first and

second in the Derby of the following year—made their appearance on the scene; but without being in opposition, both ran twice at the meeting, and both were victorious each time.

For the principal two-year-old race there was a grand field, numbering no less than sixteen. In spite of this, however, odds were laid on Mr. Chaplin's gallant little chestnut, Hermit. Pericles and Veridis had lots of admirers. Fordham donned the light blue and white hoops of the Duke of Beaufort on Vauban, and in my mind's eye I can see him and his horse, and the determined face of Harry Custance and the brave little chestnut fighting out the battle between them as vividly and clearly as it were yesterday. Hermit had the best of it by a neck, which, singularly enough, was the exact distance he beat Marksman for the Derby, on which occasion Vauban was third.

What I said of the previous meeting might be repeated respecting that of 1867. I saw Lord Hastings' beautiful two-year-old filly, Lady Elizabeth, one of the best he ever owned, canter away from Ironmaster and The Earl for the Eltham Plate. The Marquis owned The Earl also, and declaring to win with the mare, extremely long odds were laid on her. Fordham rode the winner, Tom Chaloner the second, and Tom Cannon The Earl, who finished a long way in the rear, although, no doubt, Cannon, if he would, could enlighten us a good deal on that matter! For myself, I have not the slightest doubt he could have finished close up with his stable-companion if there had been any need for it, for it is absolutely certain he was a ton in front of Ironmaster, even if he was not better than Lady Elizabeth, which has always been a matter of controversy.

Later on, we saw Lord Lyon, then a four-year-old, with Chaloner in the saddle, give a year and 6 lbs. and a beating to that good old horse, Ostreger, with Fordham up, a two-year-old of Lord Hastings'—Mameluke, Sammy Kenyon—being a bad third.

The Cup of 1868 was not a very exciting affair. The betting indicated the good thing it was for Knight of the Garter—just then at his best—to beat that great mare, Achievement, who had deteriorated very much from her form as a two or a three-year-old. Now she could not even beat Mr. Saville's two-year-old Ryshworth. Much more exciting was that magnificent struggle for the Troy Stakes the following day, when John Daley on Ryshworth, Fordham on Belladrum, and Custance on Mr. Chaplin's Orphan, made one of those sort of finishes which lives in the memory for ever.

They went past the post in the order named, all these three consummate artistes, pulling out every ounce that was in them, and at the finish nobody knew, excepting the judge, that Daley had just pipped them.

But talk about sensational races, that for the Hurstbourne Cup beats all. There were but three runners; and one of those, Mr. J. B. Morris's Birdseeker, I may dismiss at once by saying he had not a million to one chance, and was never able to go the pace with the other two. They were both denizens of one stable, and owned by a most noble duke—their names, in short, were Julius and Gomera. Everybody knew, of course, that Julius was a very long way in front of the mare; so much so, there was no need to make any declaration. It was so good, there was practically no betting. Some clever people did manage to get a few sovereigns on, laying the odds of 50 to 1 and upwards, with foolish bookies who would take odds —on principle—about anything. I have told some time ago how old Billy Marshall came to be among this clever few. It was the last race on the Thursday, and Mr. Marshall was wanting his dinner, so he decided, instead of stopping in the ring to see the race, and being tempted, perhaps, to take odds that he would lay a hundred pounds to two on Julius, and while the race was being run drive down to Stockbridge, get the best dinner that could be provided, and a bottle of the best to wash it down, with the two sovereigns he was going to win on the race. Daley on Julius looked like landing him his dinner everywhere but on the post; and here Tom French came with such a rush that the horse was done by a head, and the dinner cost poor old Billy a hundred pounds. It was an expensive feed, and, what was almost as bad, for a long time it was the cause of his having to stand a good deal of chaff.

CHAPTER XVIII

SOME GOODWOOD MEMORIES

Edmund Tattersall—Shannon's strange Win—Short Prices—Ten Broeck and his Jockeys—A short odds Bookmaker—Sharping George Payne.

GLORIOUS Goodwood, what stirring reminiscences throng the chambers of one's memory at the very mention of it! what troops of dead-and-gone racing men march past—owners, trainers, jockeys, bookmakers and punters. What giants among horses, what sensational races! The day's hot work, with its worry and excitement over, what a pleasure to get down to quiet little Charlton-Singleton, or any one of the numerous little villages which surround the birdless groves. The pleasant after-dinner chat in the big porch of the old cottage, with its clinging honeysuckle and jasmine. The friendly rubber, with a fragrant weed and glass of grog, interrupted, now and again, by the good-tempered discussions of dear old pals, dispersed or gone for ever. How all these memories are revived at the mention of Goodwood!

For very many years I and my set lodged at the tiny village of Charlton, just at the western foot of the hill as you descend from the course. One evening in the week we were in the habit of walking through the cornfields to the adjoining village of Singleton, where innocent frolics and sport were held, the leading spirits being Mr. Bland and Tom French, the jockey. A good deal of money was distributed in prizes among the stable-boys and villagers on these occasions, and great fun was afforded to many ladies and gentlemen—among whom I could name some of the highest in the land. Well-known jockeys didn't think themselves above competing in foot races, jumping, and other exercises; but the pole-climbing and sack-jumping, was, I believe, confined to the native rustics, and rare fun have I seen with them.

Goodwood, in the sixties, was the El Dorado of the bookmakers, and it would make the modern bookie's mouth water, as the saying goes, were I to tell some of the anecdotes I know respecting the sort of clients one had to bet with at Goodwood from thirty to forty years ago, and the sort of prices they took. There died not so long ago a dear old client of mine, owning the most widely-known name of any on the turf in England, and as loved and venerated as he was widely known. I remember having to get a copy of this gentleman's bets out for the four days at Goodwood. He had had so many bets, sometimes backing five, and even more, horses in a race, that he had missed some of them, and when he saw the list occupying a couple of sheets of foolscap he was perfectly appalled.

"Oh, shut it up; take it away, my lad!" said he; "and when old Christy settles with you, for God's sake don't show it to him. I don't want him to see what a d—d fool I've been."

.   .   .   .

Mr. Edmund Tattersall, for that was the gentleman, although he backed so many horses, rarely could be induced to have a sovereign on a favourite; he liked to pick out three or four, or more, according to the size of the field, of such as he thought had chances, and back them at long prices, so I need not say he didn't often back winners; but when he did so, it was a treat to see his handsome old face beaming with the most perfect happiness, as he went from one to another of his many friends with the news that he had backed the winner at 10 to 1. He was no plunger, however, his investments being usually from two to five pounds on each horse, but even at this rate he managed to lose to me between two and three hundred pounds on the week I am speaking of, but on that occasion I think he confined his business pretty much to myself.

I have said he would back a number of horses in the same race, and I have known times when, listening to tips first from one authority and then another, he would back so many that he would find himself almost "round" on a race, and would come back to me with as wry a look as it was possible for such a jolly face to bear.

"Why, dash it all, old Guv'nor," he would say, "I can't win on anything; and if the favourite should win, I lose the lot."

I remember very well on one such occasion I remarked quite jokingly to him:

"Well, you had better have a sovereign or two on Mr. ———'s horse; he'll very likely win."

"Will he now?" said he, taking me in earnest. "What's his price?"

"One hundred to eight," was my reply.

"I'll have a hundred to eight, then," he responded.

I was amazed, because it was an unusually large amount for him to have on any one horse, and I was very much more surprised when this horse won; but I shall never forget the beaming radiance of his face when, after the race, he came back to thank me.

The last time I saw Mr. Tattersall I had strolled into the sale yard of his own famous repository at Knightsbridge, and he was officiating in the rostrum, offering a sturdy-looking hunter. He immediately recognised me in the crowd beneath him.

"A capital horse this," he said; and, from the corner of his eye darting a merry twinkle at me, he added: "Just the horse to carry a fourteen stone merchant to hounds." I little thought then that I should never look upon his robust old form and noble face again.

"*Requiescat in pace.*"

One of this good client's intimate friends was very like himself in this fondness for outsiders, and he once gave me good reason for remembering it; and, although it is so long ago, the circumstance I refer to is as fresh as possible in my memory. I was no leviathan bettor, and if I made a two hundred pounds' book on an ordinary race I thought I was doing pretty well. I had a book of that sort on the Goodwood Cup, and what a wonderful book it was! They took about evens each of two, the Derby winner, Favonius, and the mighty Frenchman, Mortimer. Mr. Henry Saville had one in which was backed on the off-chance of the two cracks cutting one another's throats—at 7 or 8 to 1, so we were well "*over round*" without laying the outsider of the party, a mare called Shannon; indeed, scarcely anyone backed her, and fielders considered it was so much found if, by chance, they could get a sovereign out of her at any price.

The horses were at the post and about to start, when this gentleman came up:

"What will you lay you give me a loser?" said he.

"Fifty to one," I replied, thinking I was going to find a sovereign perhaps.

"Well, I'll have two hundred and fifty to five. What do you give me?"

"I give you Shannon, of course," I answered.

In a few minutes that extraordinary and unexplainable race was over, and the despised Shannon had won. She was my only loser, and instead of a "skinner," which most of my friends enjoyed, I lost about £40 on the race, and I never felt more wild with myself about anything, because I believe I could have got the £250 back for an outlay of three sovereigns

I very well remember once laying a young swell at Goodwood thirty pounds to twenty a certain horse; in a minute or so he came back, having discovered he had backed the second favourite when he meant to be on the favourite.

"I find I have made a mistake, sir," he said. "Now, what will you lay me the favourite?"

"Well, as you've made a mistake," I replied, "I will lay you thirty to twenty that also, which is over the price."

"Put it down," he said, and walked away.

Just before the start he came running up to me with a sovereign in his hand.

"My wife has just had a tip for another in this race," said he. "What will you lay her to this sovereign ready money?"

This horse was the rank outsider of the party.

"Well, as it's for a lady," I replied, "I'll lay her ten to one."

"Oh, thank you so much!" said the swell.

Now it so happened that the outsider won, and immediately after he rushed up, almost frantic with excitement and delight —I may say that all our bets, with the exception of the lady's sovereign, were settled after each race. Handing me four clean ten-pound notes, he cried exultingly:

"And now, sir, I want *ten* pounds for Mrs. Jay!"

It is difficult for anyone whose memory goes back to the Goodwood of those days to realise the fact that the very best of our native jockeys are now obliged to take a back seat among their American brethren, for, as far as I recollect, the first importation of them was anything but successful, and our Fordhams, Oldcrofts, and Kitcheners found no difficulty in holding their own with the best of the Yankees.

Mr. Ten Broeck, who, by the way, commenced his racing career in England, at the Duke of Richmond's beautiful Park, several years before my first appearance there, was among the very first to introduce the foreign jockey among us, and it didn't take that exceedingly cute Yankee long to find out his mistake; and he didn't, mind you, introduce commoners of the pigskin, but the very best America could produce.

He began by running a couple in the Cup, and declaring to win with Prior, a five-year-old, with 8 st. 9 lb., ridden by Littlefield. The other was his good mare Prioress, which was the mount of the Yankee crack, Gilpatrick. There can be very little doubt the latter ought to have won, for she seemed fairly to run away with Gilpatrick, and had a tremendously long lead, when by some means she ran out of the course, and was not set right again until it was too late for her to have any chance, so allowing Count Lagrange's Monarque to get up and win. Still, after all, she finished among the front lot, and old Ten Broeck was so annoyed at the figure his crack jockey had cut, he settled up with him the following day, and had done with him. Some time after that, and for many years, George Fordham was his favourite jockey, and many a time and oft in those days have I seen that great horseman carry to victory those well-known colours.

Talking of Fordham and Goodwood recalls to my memory one of the grandest races and most brilliant finishes I ever remember to have seen, and it was not for any of the great events either; indeed, I think it was merely a fifty-pound plate on the second day of the Goodwood Meeting in 1864. I wonder if any of my elderly readers can call it to mind. I forget how many runners there were, but I know that the struggle between the two horses I am referring to—Crytheia and Voluptus—began in the betting ring, for both were backed by equally determined friends at about 2 to 1 each, and at the finish of the betting it was a dead heat for favouritism; and what a struggle for mastery in the race it was! Fordham rode Crytheia, and Morris, just then in his prime, had the mount on Voluptus. All up the straight these two, neck and neck, were at it hammer and tongs, neither being able to get the slightest advantage, and it was only just on the post that Fordham made one of those superb efforts for which he was noted, seeming to fairly lift his horse in, and secured the verdict by a nose.

I believe it was in the very next race to the one I have described that I saw Fordham on Idler and Tom Oldcroft on Ascham have just such another struggle, Harry Custance being a bad third on Gownsman; and, as in the other case, Fordham secured the verdict by a very short head.

SOME GOODWOOD MEMORIES

There is a wide gulf—indeed, an indescribable difference—between some of the Yankee racing men of this day and some I knew well and did business with years ago, and somehow I don't think the comparison favours the moderns. I may be wrong, of course, and I can only speak for myself. Take poor old Ten Broeck; in spite of a bit of temper and a sharp tongue at times, what a gentleman he was! I remember being told that he was not very popular with his own countrymen while he was over here racing. The fact is, there were many vastly richer men than he amongst his countrymen who would have done anything to have been received by the cream of the English aristocracy, and even by Royalty itself, as he was. So their dislike was probably the result of a miserable little jealousy.

I knew Mr. Ten Broeck as a rich man, respected, and indeed courted, by many of the highest in the land. When he left the scene of so many victories and of so much glory to return to his own country, I am afraid he was a poor man. I never heard the amount of his losses in the Derby of 1860, but it must have been something enormous. Mr. Merry, who was said to have netted altogether about £70,000 by the success of his horse Thormanby, won a good deal of that from Mr. Ten Broeck, who had so many cross bets with him, Umpire over Thormanby. Not satisfied with this, Mr. Ten Broeck laid against Thormanby right out, and very heavily, the same time backing his own horse Umpire to win him a tremendous stake; and Horror, which was the only horse he feared, he backed to save himself.

In the days I am dealing with, one of the best-known men in the ring at Goodwood and elsewhere was Matt Collinson. It is true he did not bet anything like as heavily as Steel and Peach or Jacques Bayliss, or like the leviathans of the present day, Richard Henry Fry, the brothers Millard, or good old Joe Pickersgill. The professional sharps he would have no dealings with, and even the regular frequenters of the ring he didn't desperately struggle after. The young beginners and the occasional comers were the sort he liked, and laid himself out to secure, and among these he had an enormous *clientèle*. It was wonderful how these people found their way to Matt; his suave manner and the peculiar kidment he used charmed them. I have amused myself many a time watching crowds of them flocking around him with their neatly-folded fivers and tenners, eager to take of him 6 to 4 about two different horses, while an equally substantial man next door was shouting himself hoarse with ineffectual effort to lay " 2 to 1 on the field."

But while he was a favourite with the thoughtless youngsters who mostly traded with him, there were, of course, some who didn't like him.

I remember seeing him at Goodwood pay one such personage a rather large bet he had won, and as he counted out the notes to him, he thanked the gentleman with great effusiveness, concluding with his stereotyped phrase :

"Thank you, sir; you are a gentleman."

"I wish I could say the same of you, sir," replied the young fellow, with much curtness, as he turned away.

I saw the real Matt flash up in his angry eyes as, quick as thought, he retorted :

"You could, sir, if you'd tell as great a lie as I have."

It was at this same Goodwood Meeting a young country solicitor was betting with him rather heavily, and to ready money. I heard him say :

"I tell you what it is, Mr. Collinson, if I go on like this, I shall be broken before the end of the week."

"If you are," replied Matt, "you can ask me for fifty."

"Oh, thank you, sir! you are very kind," said the solicitor, and away he went, elated to think he had made a friend of the wealthy bookmaker.

Now it happened—perhaps naturally so—that toward the end of the meeting, on the Friday afternoon, the young man was really cleaned out. Mr. Collinson had captured all his bank; however, he came up again smiling.

"Now, Mr. Collinson, I'm sorry I shall have to trouble you for the loan of that fifty pounds," said he; "I want to have one more dash, and try to get some of my money back."

"I'm sorry I can't oblige you," replied Matt. "I am compelled to make a rule never to lend but one fifty pounds, and that's already out."

"What do you mean, sir? You told me you would lend me fifty pounds if I got broken."

"No, no, sir! there you make a mistake," answered the astute bookie. "I said, if you got broken, you might *ask* me for fifty, which, you will see, is a very different thing."

The young man didn't say many words as he turned and walked away, but just enough to show Collinson that he saw through the shabby subterfuge; but the look of contempt which he gave him as he uttered these few words I shall never forget, and even the thick-skinned one winced under it.

Collinson, in his early days, had his wits sharpened by much practice, for while knocking about in London, before taking to bookmaking as a profession, it was said he had to live by them, and even in prosperous days he didn't neglect his opportunities.

Goodwood was not only a little gold-mine for the bookies, it was the happy hunting ground of the welsher and the sharper, on account of the great number of young gentlemen who were to be found making their entrance into racing life at that favourite meeting; and, of course, their inexperience made them an easy prey to these harpies, who were "got up" elaborately, and without regard to cost, for these occasions. It was little matter of surprise that young beginners should be victimised when one knows that well-seasoned old turfites, with reputations for uncommon cuteness, did occasionally get bitten by the same people.

I remember when the late Mr. George Payne was a victim, under rather amusing circumstances. The genial old sportsman was, among other accomplishments, a first-rate story-teller, and this particular one, although it raised the laugh at his own expense, he told with great zest, and laughed at as heartily as any of his hearers. One day he was in the Victoria Station booking for Chichester among a great crowd of other swells, the day before Goodwood. There was quite a crush at the booking office, and as Mr. Payne struggled up to the window, a heavy fellow who stood head and shoulders above the others, dressed at the top of the fashion, called out, " Take a ticket for me, George!" and not doubting he was one of his numerous casual acquaintance, he immediately took a couple instead of one ticket, one of which he handed over the heads of the crowd to his tall friend. And then he suddenly lost him, and didn't get sight of him again till, leaning on the rails in the royal enclosure talking to old Billy Marshall on the other side, he espied him in the betting ring.

"Who is that tall gentleman, Billy?" he inquired.

"One of the most notorious welshers in the ring, Mr. Payne," was the old bookie's reply.

CHAPTER XIX

GAMBLERS AND GAMBLING

Hazards — Charley Chappell — Durden and the Parson — Inveterate Gamblers—Frank Leleu—Charles Head.

THIRTY years ago, and previous to that, no first-class race-meeting was complete without its company of travelling gamblers, with green baize-covered tables, roulette machinery, and dice for hazard. They usually rented luxuriously furnished rooms in a private house, for which, I suppose, they would have to pay a pretty high figure. Spirits, champagnes of crack brands, and other expensive wines, with high-class cigars, were supplied gratuitously, and *ad libitum* to the young swells who nightly thronged these rooms. They were not always confined to private houses, for at some places—as at Doncaster, for instance—they made arrangements with the owners of the public subscription rooms, and play was permitted in well-arranged chambers on these premises.

That the heavy, and at times ruinous, play could have been carried on in this semi-public manner without the slightest interference on the part of the authorities proves how great is the change which has come over us since those days. What would the Anti-Gambling League say to this state of things?

It must not be supposed that because the managers of those rooms were so lavish in their expenditure upon their clients they were a set of swindlers, playing with loaded dice. I should be sorry to infer anything of the kind. I believe the rooms I am now referring to were conducted fairly as far as the play went, for on many occasions I have known the half-drunken and perfectly reckless young fools play so heavily and so luckily that the owners of the tables, or bankers as they were called, have declared the bank broken, and the play over for the night; which would never be the case if they were playing with loaded dice. The turnover at these establishments was so enormous that the slight advantage of about twenty-one to twenty—which it is admitted they had in honest play—was quite sufficient to account for their lavish expenditure, and also for the large fortunes which have, in some cases, been made at the game.

While I assert that the first-class rooms were conducted fairly, I am bound to admit there were to be found at the same time travellers, in like way of business, most unscrupulous rogues, who would stand at nothing when they got a flat in their net. I was once in my salad days one of these flats, and found myself in one of their traps. On my very first visit to Newmarket I was politely invited, after the first day's racing, to spend a few hours in the evening at the lodgings of a fellow-townsman, about whom I knew nothing, but who would, I was made to understand, afford us an opportunity for a little innocent game. The game was chicken hazard, which was new to me, and, naturally enough, I had to pay for my experience. I knew afterwards that, in this case, I was taking on a man with whom I had not a thousand to one chance.

It is unnecessary I should give the name. He afterwards became a well-known bookmaker, and an owner of race-horses in training at Newmarket.

In subsequent visits to Newmarket I became acquainted with the travelling gamblers of the better sort, and had opportunities of seeing roulette and hazard played under other conditions, and have witnessed thousands—hundreds of thousands; yea, perhaps millions—of pounds change hands, where old Joe Wood bossed the show and the keen and eagle-eyed "Arthur" wielded the croupier's rake. I remember one night at Newmarket, while sitting under the presidency of this able old coupier, the renowned Jem Mace came into the room, accompanied by a brother brusier with whom he had, during that day, made his first attempt at bookmaking. What happened I should like to relate—that is, if I only had the genial ex-champion's permission. This incident is something more than thirty years ago, yet I am bold to say it would be no very severe tax on his memory to recall the occasion. Many have come and gone since that time, and some are decrepit with age who are no older than he; but when I last saw the gallant old boxer he looked but little the worse for wear, and not so very much older than he looked at the termination of the proceedings of that memorable night.

Of course, one occasionally witnessed strange scenes at these gaming-rooms, but I never saw the slightest approach to rowdyism; and any attempts at "besting" a youngster on the part of the old sharps, were promptly stopped by Arthur.

There are probably still living thousands of sporting swells who will remember the rosy-faced, good-looking, and stylishly got-up Charley Chappell. Many of them would perhaps like to forget him; the very mention of him will revive unpleasant recollections. Forty years ago, and more, Chappell's was a well-known figure in racing circles; he attended all the principal race-meetings throughout the country, having well-appointed rooms wherever he went, which were the resort of fast young swells and hardened old gamblers alike. For these people the excitement and betting which the day's racing afforded were not sufficient. So after a good dinner, with a copious supply of champagne, they felt themselves just fit to tackle Mr. Chappell and his clever assistants at the roulette or hazard tables, and the rosy one was always ready to oblige them, not only providing the necessary tools for these games, but as much more champagne, soda, and brandy, or other drinks as they could manage to consume. And there is no doubt that very often old Charley netted some very fine fish. Still, I have often heard him swear that he was a mere jackal for the bookmakers. He provided during his intercourse with the aforesaid swells any quantity—and the very best—of the good things of this life, and straightway delivered them up to the "bloated fielders." Poor old Charley was indeed an inveterate punter, and although he is reported to have made fabulous sums at his own game, I am afraid he was in but poorish circumstances when he died, some sixteen years ago.

Only the most aged of racing men will recollect Chappell's master and predecessor in the same business—Old Durden. He died while the writer was a promising youth, groaning through the dreary years of apprenticeship. Hence I am unable to speak of him from personal acquaintance, and therefore not with that freedom which springs from a consciousness that I am conveying to my readers the truth. I was recently privileged to spend an evening with one of the oldest and most respected betting men in England, who retired on an honourably acquired fortune, before some of the present race of bookies were born; to this gentleman I am indebted for what I know of Durden.

Outside his profession, Old Durden was one of the greatest sharps that ever lived, and at the same time the most perfect "take down," because he didn't look it. On the contrary, he had a sober, old-fashioned look about him which disarmed suspicion, and almost a clerical appearance, which marvellously assisted him in his wily purposes. Many are the stories which are told of him—all of them desperately wicked—but some redeemed by the fact that they afforded amusement to hundreds of his contemporaries, and now I hope they are about to do the like for many thousands belonging to a generation which knew him not.

On one occasion, when he was working the tables at Abergavenny Races, he was pestered by a young fool who, having lost some money to him at roulette, thought himself entitled to hang on to him wherever he went. They were staying at an old-fashioned hotel. Durden had found his way into the spacious kitchen, where, as he bargained for, the youngster followed him. The ceiling was well hung with flitches of home-cured bacon and prime hams, which the young man began to admire.

"Why don't you ask the landlord to give you one of the hams?" asked Durden.

"I'm not fool enough to do that," replied his companion, "and he'd not be fool enough to give me one if I did."

"Oh, yes, he would," replied the crafty old man. "You have no idea how generous these Welsh folks are; they're as generous as they are honest."

Now the young man, while he thought they might be the most honest people in the world, had not been impressed in any very remarkable manner with this fact; and with regard to their generosity, the treatment he had received at the hands of this very landlord had assured him that if it was a national characteristic, the landlord didn't possess it, so he concluded it would be a pretty safe thing to bet about.

"Well, will you back your opinion, Durden?" he asked.

"Yes, I will, for whatever you like," answered the old man.

"Then I'll bet you a pony he won't make me a present of one of those fine hams for merely asking."

"Done!" said Durden; "that's a bet."

The dupe wouldn't allow the old man to leave the kitchen, but insisted that he should go alone to the landlord, who was in the bar-parlour, and put the question in his own way. This was agreed to, and the young man proceeded to test the question. Walking into the parlour in an unconcerned manner, he addressed the landlord:

"Nice lot of hams, Mr. Owen, in the kitchen; shouldn't mind begging one of them, if you are in a giving humour?"

"I'll give *you* one with pleasure, sir," replied the host; "and you'll find it as good as it looks."

Of course, old Durden had readied the landlord, so that

prime ham cost the young fool about eighteen shillings a pound.

Durden was fond of laying traps for unwary friends to fall into. He was walking one afternoon in Hyde Park, and, as was most likely to happen, he chanced to run against one of his numerous playfellows—a young aristocrat. While they stop to speak, a groom comes prancing along on a magnificent hack.

"Look at that lovely chestnut!" exclaims the swell.

"He is a beauty," replied Durden, "but not a chestnut. He's a bay."

"Bay be d—d!" replied the swell. "You've been looking so long on green baize you've gone colour blind. It's a bright chestnut, I tell you."

"No, no, my lord; it's distinctly a bay," replied the wily old man.

"A chestnut for a hundred," said the swell.

Durden protested he didn't want to bet; he wouldn't like to rob his lordship; but rather sneeringly concluded by hinting that the swell knew nothing of horses or their colour.

"Damn it, bet me a hundred, then!" cried the exasperated nobleman.

"Done then, just to oblige your lordship," replied Durden. "But who shall decide the bet?"

"Oh, we'll leave it to the groom who is riding him," answered the victim. "See, he is coming by again."

This was settled, and the groom was stopped. His lordship said:

"That's a charming hack, my man; but what do you call his colour?"

"He's a bright bay, sir," the groom replied.

The swindled nobleman looked dazed for a moment as the beautiful creature began to caracole and caper about, then dashed down the Row at a great pace.

GAMBLERS AND GAMBLING

"Well, that beats cock-fighting," he said. "I think the Park's full of colour-blind folks or infernal idiots this afternoon!"

He agreed, however, that he had fairly lost the hundred pounds; nevertheless, he hung about the Park for a long time in the hope of seeing the groom and his beautiful horse come by again. Of course, having already done a good day's work, he didn't come that way again; and I suppose I needn't tell my readers that Mr. Durden was not wholly unacquainted with that groom.

Durden once found himself *tête-à-tête* in a railway carriage with a simple-looking old clergyman, bound for a long journey to the same town. Durden began talking about horses, and racing, and betting, and, as was natural, it was soon clear they held extremely opposite views on these subjects, and each expressed his own with some warmth.

"I think betting in all forms a crime, and the greatest curse on the earth, and under *no* circumstances would I be guilty of it," said the parson.

"Now, that's very unfortunate," answered Durden, "for I was going to do you a good turn. I wanted you to have a sovereign on a horse of mine at the races to-morrow. It will only be an even money chance, but it's sure to win."

"Oh dear, no! Not a shilling, were it ever such a good thing!" answered the parson.

"Well, but this is an absolute certainty," urged Mr. Durden. "No risk whatever, so there really is no gambling about it. Indeed, so sure is it to win, I wouldn't mind paying you the sovereign to-day which you would be certain to win if you invested it on the race to-morrow."

He made this tempting offer, being curious to know how far the parson's objection to betting was founded on principle, and he was not greatly surprised when he found the good man, after very little more persuasion, willing to bet on these terms. So the bet was made, and the sovereign duly paid over to the parson, whereupon he was favourably impressed with his fellow-traveller's liberality, and he began to think he had been over-harsh in his judgment of these betting men.

Durden, seeing how the land lay, thought it was now time to try to recover his sovereign with a little interest, so he introduced a couple of beautiful scarf-pins, carefully wrapped in cotton wool. They appeared to be of bright gold, with a small dimaond in an enamelled setting.

He pitched a plausible story of getting them at half their value of a friend in the trade who was about to become bankrupt. One he wanted as a present to his nephew; the other he wouldn't mind parting with for what it had cost him —two pounds five. There was no doubt the shopkeeper's price would be three times that amount.

As he had expected, the parson, now full of faith in his generous friend, and full, also, of that weakness for a good bargain inherent in human nature, and from which parsons even are not exempt, eagerly bit, a deal being effected on these terms. Need I say that the diamond was a bit of good French paste mounted in real *Brummagem* gold, worth probably five shillings? Durden often boasted of this swindle, which was perpetrated not for the sake of the sovereign profit, but for the fun of the thing, and to punish the parson for his greed and hypocrisy, knowing also that he could practice on him with impunity after the betting experience.

Most of my readers will remember Frank Leleu, a fish merchant in a very large way of business in London, who attended most of the better sort of race-meetings throughout the year, and who was known, at one time, as one of our heaviest punters. Frank didn't confine himself by any means to betting on horses; he was at heart such a dear lover of a gamble, he would bet on anything. He indulged this propensity at cards; and at his favourite club he would bet very heavily at billiards also; and there was a time when the baize-covered table, and the merry rattle of the little box, had a

GAMBLERS AND GAMBLING 171

wonderful charm for him. The story I am about to relate is perfectly true, and demonstrates, in a marvellous manner, how strong in him was this passion for gambling.

As I have said, about thirty years ago Stockbridge was one of the best attended and most fashionable meetings in the country, and one Leleu never missed. On the occasion to which I allude, he had had a day's racing at Odiham, and at its conclusion he made tracks for the quiet little village of Wallop, which is not very far from the Stockbridge course, and where he was to stay for the races. To his immense annoyance, he found, on his arrival, that he was the only person staying at the inn. So, after a solitary and miserable dinner, he sallied out in the hope of finding company; for him to get through a night without play of some sort seemed an impossibility, if not an uncanny thing; and he was certain he wouldn't rest if he attempted it. He found the village in the same condition as his hotel. At present none of the visitors had arrived. It was a wretched, drizzling sort of night when he made his way back to the inn after his unsuccessful prowl, and he was about turning in when he caught sight of the only human being he had been able to recognise as a sport of any kind. This was a slim young fellow, evidently poor, but not disreputable in appearance, and whom he at once remembered as a sort of runner for the bookies, who varied this employment by occasionally adopting the *rôle* of tipster, if not, sometimes, an even still humbler occupation.

"Hi! ho! What are you doing here, shaver?" asked Frank.

"I've come on from Odiham, Mr. Leleu," said the young man, "to be ready for Stockbridge to-morrow."

Then Lelu invited the sharp young fellow in for a drink, for which he found the young man not at all indisposed. After the dose had been repeated, Mr. Leleu opened up the matter next his heart.

"Look here, young fellow," said he, "did you ever play hazard?"

"Yes, sir, a very little," he replied.

"Well, as there is nothing going on here to-night, we'll play," said Frank, producing the tools.

"Oh no, I can't play, Mr. Leleu! I've got no money to play with," was the answer to this challenge.

"Well, look here, I'll lend you a fiver to start with," replied Frank, and finding the young fellow not slow to accept such an offer, he did actually lend him five pounds, with which he allowed this needy person to play against all he carried about him, and he did this not, as some hasty readers may conclude, because he was a fool. Those who knew Mr. Leleu would never accuse him of being that, but simply because his passion for play was so strong, he would rather play with no possibility of winning than not play at all, and a fiver was of small moment to him; but, fortunately for the young man, in trying to recapture the fiver, Leleu lost a good many fivers; indeed, at the end of the night's diversion one of the players was a richer man than he had ever been before, walking away from the inn with nearly a hundred pounds, after having repaid the fiver. He won also a pressing invitation to return the following night to give Mr. Leleu his revenge; this invitation likewise he availed himself of, and with such result that in a pecuniary sense he never "looked back" after it. He had converted his borrowed fiver into seven or eight hundred pounds, which he immediately invested in what was in those days the extremely lucrative business of bookmaking.

This poor young fellow was endowed with abilities of a very high order. He had great aptitude for figures, a cool head well stocked, immense energy, and a ready and brilliant wit, never equalled or approached among bookmakers of my time. These qualities soon won for him a foremost place in the profession, and in a few years he was a man of large means. He had theatres and music-halls in London, some useful horses on the turf, and one of the very largest and most profitable connections among bookmakers. To old racing men I am sure I need not announce that the great bookmaker to whom Frank Leleu had afforded this singular start in life was none other than the celebrated Charles Head.

There are few games which obtain and exercise such complete mastery over the human will as hazard, and it is really very difficult to understand why this should be so. It calls forth none of the higher qualities of the mind as does chess, cribbage, and whist, and it demands no great power of nerve and skill of hand as at billiards. Yet the rattle of the magic box is sweeter in the ears of its votaries than all Cecilia's charms, and more potent to fascinate poor mortals than any siren who ever bewitched them to destruction.

Bill—or perhaps I had better call him by the name he was best known by, Farmer Quartley—was one of the strange characters whom I have met with on the turf. There was scarcely a game of any kind, or a form of gambling, with which Mr. Quartley was not acquainted—indeed, I may say, at which he was not an adept; but of all games, I think hazard was his favourite. He had gone down West for the races, held near the delightful old city of Exeter, his headquarters being the New London Hotel, where was staying also a fair-faced young betting man, hailing from another West Country cathedral city, but nearer the Midlands, and whom, for this purpose, I will call Mr. Henry. This young man, like Quartley, had a passion for the box and dice, and coming into the hotel about eleven o'clock the first night with the intention of having a turn at hazards with the old man, he was surprised to find he had retired for the night at that unheard-of early hour. The fact was, Quartley was really very unwell.

Henry marched up to the old man's room and quietly knocked. There was no reply; he knocked a little louder; still no reply. Then taking the little box out of his pocket, he slipped the bits of ivory in, giving it the magic rattle, and in a moment Quartley jumped out of bed, the door was flung open, and in another minute, ill as he was, he was calling the main.

After playing for a couple of hours and winning a considerable amount, the old man declared he would not play any longer. This didn't suit Mr. Henry, and after a good deal of wrangling, Quartley bluntly ordered him to leave the room. Henry walked to the door and quietly locked it, and opening the window, threw the key into the yard below.

"You understand that, Master Farmer, I suppose?" said he. "I came here to make a night of it, and I don't intend you to sneak off to bed now you've won a few quids."

So the farmer was almost compelled to play on, much against his wish, as he was really ill; but a friend of Henry's tells me that it would have been much better for that young gentleman had he retired earlier, instead of throwing away the key.

As the author of some funny stories, and chief actor in most of them, I propose devoting a chapter wholly to this remarkable turfite, Mr. William Quartley.

CHAPTER XX

GAMBLERS AND GAMBLING

"Farmer" Quartley—Hazards at Sea—The Ladies' Hair-pins—Diamond cut Diamond.

IN a somewhat chequered journey through life, I have been a keen observer of the many specimens of my fellow-travellers, and I can honestly say I have made earnest effort to see all sides of them, and I can also truthfully say that while I have not been fortunate enough to make the acquaintance of many quite perfect men and women—such as are plentiful in the writings of certain novelists—I have rarely met with humanity so utterly degraded and worthless as not to disclose, on acquaintance, some redeeming qualities. Of course, one would not seek among the *habitués* of the turf for what are known in this world as saints, but I am thankful to say it is not a history of the saints I am writing, nor even a history of perfect men and women. I haven't at hand the material for such work; my characters are all sketches from real life, and do mostly relate to men who are very human, which will account for them being more or less sinners.

Everybody knows that too much of the residue of the rascality of this great and pious country finds its way on to what is known as "the turf"; but what racing men properly object to is that ignorant and unthinking goody-goody folk should persist in looking on this sediment and speaking of *it as "the turf."*

Would it be fair, because *the pious* Jabez Balfour & Co.

were a set of unmitigated scoundrels, to look upon the general body of chapel-goers and professors of religion as a huge mass of canting hypocrisy, intent only on schemes for the plunder of trustful widows and helpless orphans? No, no, my friends, the congregations of betting men are much like your own congregations, composed of all sorts, good and bad. I have in my time seen something of both—have found, I am bound to say, among religionists some of the gentlest and noblest human beings I have known in all my journey; but believe me, my friends, when I declare that in matters of integrity, honour, and goodness of heart, the respectable members of the betting ring are comparable with any profession or class in the country.

In these reminiscences of the turf it is my purpose to make my readers acquainted with the good and bad, and also with some very much-mixed specimens of racing people.

In the course of an acquaintance extending over at least a quarter of a century, I saw a good deal of Mr. Quartley—had, indeed, very many transactions with him, and had ample opportunity of observing his varied characteristics, which I may say I did not neglect.

He was well known to most London sportsmen, because his home was there for many years. His burly figure was a familiar one on race-courses and in betting rings all over England; but as he originally hailed from the West of England, it was at the little west-country meetings he was best known. The farmer was in many respects a remarkable man. He hadn't been blessed in early life with a University education; indeed, in the matter of book-learning, I am afraid he had been sadly neglected. To use a word he was very fond of using, he was no "grammarmatician." For all that, he had a ready wit and strong common sense, and these enabled him to take his own part in such company as he was in the habit of meeting with. It is true he knew but one language, but that he spoke with such forcibleness, that in a war of words he was seldom defeated; but of all his accomplishments, that which he prided himself most about was his knowledge of all gambling games. And he was all his life an inveterate gamester, and as he was not in the habit of over-handicapping himself, or taking on very difficult jobs, he was, as a rule, able to hold his own—and generally a little of his opponents—at any game.

He was a tricky billiard player, but—like a certain eminent fielder who is fond of billiards, and plays fairly well—he wasn't an elegant player; indeed, from the way he held his cue and jerked himself about, innocent strangers picked him up for a jay at the game, and only dropped him when their money was gone, and they had arrived at a different conclusion.

Perhaps the farmer's favourite game was hazard, at which he was an adept, and many are the startling feats he is said to have accomplished with the bits of ivory.

I once heard him declare that if he had never dabbled with keeping and backing horses, but had instead taken care of all the money he had won at hazard, he would have been a rich man. Sometimes he played with people who didn't take their losses kindly, often getting a notion into their heads that the dice were loaded, or some other unfair means employed. On one occasion something of the kind happened under circumstances which upset the farmer's usually strong nerves. He was attending Weymouth races in company with two west-country betting men, both at the present time alive, one of them being now an extensive S. P. merchant. They put up at the Victoria Hotel, and there fell in with the owner of a yacht, which lay out in the bay. Rather late in the evening they began playing hazard, and after watching it for some time, the gentleman began to nibble, and at eleven o'clock, having lost a few pounds, he was pinned down to the table with the hot determination to get it back. It was before Mr. Bruce's Act became law, so eleven o'clock was closing time, and the host could not be prevailed upon to allow the game to continue, or the gentleman whose bed was aboard the yacht to remain any longer in the house.

"Look here, my lads," says he, "my man is opposite the door here with the dingey, waiting for me; come aboard my yacht for an hour and finish the play. I've plenty of good stuff to drink there, and some good cigars."

The two younger men were for accepting at once this pressing invitation; the more cautious old farmer didn't like trusting himself on an element where he didn't feel at home, but after a while he yielded, and all four went over to the dingey, and very soon they were cutting through the sea in dreadful darkness, and Quartley felt very uncomfortable until he was safely aboard the yacht, and even then he was not particularly easy in his mind.

Play commenced with the accompaniment of good cigars and drinks, and they were all very jolly till about two o'clock in the morning, when the farmer declared they had played and drunk enough, and he would be going back to shore. The yachtsman's bad luck had followed him aboard, and he had by this time lost a considerable sum. He was a powerful man, and under the influence of the drink looked fierce, and capable of executing any threat he might make.

"I'll tell you what it is, gentlemen," said he, "I'll blow out the bottom of the damned dingey rather than she shall take you back before I have had another hour's play." So he compelled them to go on with the game, and as his bad luck continued, or his bad play, or for some other reason, he kept on losing; at the end of the hour he had lost all the money the yacht contained, and was a considerable sum in debt.

The farmer, happening to raise his eyes, saw what made him very uneasy; this was another pair of eyes looking straight into his, bright and keen as his own. Looking from the strange eyes to the owner of them, he saw a strongly-built middle-aged sailor fellow, with a sinister look about him, threatening trouble.

"Don't be alarmed, stranger," said the sailor, when he found he was discovered, "I've been here a-watching of you gents a good time.'"

"And what the devil business had you doing anything of the kind?" asked the gentleman. "It's no part of my steward's business to be watching me or my friends. What do you mean, sir?"

"You know me, master," replied the man; "and you ought to know I wouldn't do sich wi'out good reason. Come into my cabin, sir, and I"ll tell what'll surprise you!"

The gentleman rose to follow his steward, and while addressing himself to his servant, fixed his eyes on his guests.

"No foul play, I hope, Jack? By God, if there is I'll scuttle the damned ship but I'll pay somebody for it!"

The condition of the farmer and his friends may be imagined while the couple were shut up in the adjoining cabin. Either of them would have given their winnings two or three times told to have been safely bedded down in the Victoria Hotel at that moment. They were perfectly aware how much they should be overmatched by the yachtsman and his hands if it came to strife. Still, the old man in the frightful anxiety and suspense of the time never lost his wits. It was lucky for them all he didn't. The first thing he did was to wrap some little matters in paper, and then throw the parcel through the open cabin window into the sea. He could hear the loud and angry voice of the yachtsman in the steward's cabin, but he couldn't make out what was said. When at last the door was opened, he heard the master roar out:

"Shake up every man aboard, Jack, and bring them into my cabin!"

This order boded no good to Quartley and his friends; but whatever they may have felt, when the gentleman re-entered the cabin they put on a bold front, and the farmer, knowing how useful it is to get in the first good knock, started at once with well-affected indignation.

"What does this treatment mean, sir?" he inquired. "I thought we were playing with a gentleman."

"You'll soon discover, sir, that you have been *playing* with a gentleman," answered the yachtsman, emphasising the word "playing"; "and a funny devil you'll find you've been playing with before I have done with you, if you can't disprove what my steward charges against you."

"Charges against me, sir?" said the old man, in a voice almost choked between simulated rage and injured innocence.

"Yes, against you, sir!" cried Jack, coming forward at the moment with four strapping young fellows at his heels. "I say you have been cheating the master, for I saw you change the dice several times."

"Oh, you—you wicked wretch!" cried Quartley, apparently appalled with the enormity of the fellow's wickedness. "May I go to the bottom of the sea before I reach the shore if I've more than the one set of honest dice about me!"

"If you have not, perhaps one of your friends has," said the gentleman, a little cooler, and evidently somewhat shaken by the tone and attitude of injured virtue, so well acted by the farmer.

"Well, if you are all so innocent, you and your friends won't object to be searched," put in the steward.

"Searched!" almost screamed the farmer. "Who are you to talk of searching gentlemen?"

"Well, if you are innocent, you wouldn't object to being searched," said the yachtsman; "and all I can say is, that you'll be searched either with your consent or without it, and if loaded dice are not found upon you, you shall be taken ashore at once; but if they are, why, as I'm captain of this ship, you shall all three have something to remember her by as long as you live."

"I would fight till I died," replied the old man, "before I

GAMBLERS AND GAMBLING 181

would submit to such a thing at the dictation of a man like that," dramatically pointing to the steward; " but if *you* desire such a thing I am perfectly willing to submit, and if you find on me or on either of my friends anything which warrants this brutal conduct, do what you like with us."

This ingenuous and well-acted little speech a little took the wind out of the enemies' sails, but it didn't prevent the search; and what a search it was! The three friends were required to strip to the skin. This indignity they stoutly protested against, and only submitted to when they saw preparations for using force.

It was very comical to see the three friends standing there, each guarded by a couple of stalwart fellows, and wrapped in blankets, while the whole of their clothing was being carefully examined. My readers are, of course, prepared for the result of the search—nothing to incriminate them was found; so their clothing being restored to its proper uses, the farmer, again assuming the air of injured innocence, said:

"Now, sir, I hope you are satisfied you have been playing with gentlemen?"

"Well, I can't say I am satisfied, sir," replied the yachtman, "but I've given you my word, and you may go; my man still swears he saw foul play, and I believe him, but in some way you have been too many for me. Get off, and thank your lucky stars."

The dingey was brought round by a couple of the sailors, and the three friends stowed in her. A fresh breeze had sprung up while they had been in the yacht; above their heads was a darkness dreadful in its density, and beneath them the now turbulent sea yawned black and awful. Beyond all reality the situation seemed terrible to their excited minds; the voice of the malicious steward coming out of the darkness increased their fear.

"You know what to do with the —— scamps, my lads," said the voice, with sinister suggestiveness.

Of course, the farmer and his pals put the most awful construction on the steward's words, but fear didn't quite depose the old man's reason nor rob him of all his natural cunning.

"Look here, my men," said he, addressing himself to the sailors, "it's a nasty, dangerous job to be fetched out of your warm bunks for, but you land us safely on yonder beach and there's a fiver a-piece for you."

"All right, gentlemen, we'll put you ashore in a jiffey," answered one of the men.

In ten minutes more the sailors had earned and received their money, and Quartley never in his life disbursed a tenner with more pleasure.

"Never no more, my boys, never no more will you find William Quartley taking on this sort of job on the briny," said he.

Mr. Quartley was not only clever as a gamester. He followed at different times many occupations, and, at a pinch, could turn his hand to many methods of getting a living. He had been an owner of horses and a trainer, a professional backer and a bookmaker; and, as occasion required, he adopted either of these callings. Among the horses which he owned, or partly owned, was an extremely useful old slave, called Delamotte—useful not only because he could win a race when required, but equally useful at times when he didn't win. They had him in a couple of races down in the west country, both of which looked absolutely a gift for him, so the farmer and his gang took the old horse down, with the purpose of winning two races and landing a considerable sum in bets; and it was really important they should do so, for the firm had experienced a rough time—was, indeed, in pecuniary difficulties; hence it was once more a case of Delamotte to the rescue.

There was a respectable entry for the race on the first day, and the confederacy expected and desired there would be a fair field, so as to enable them to invest the little bank they had at a reasonable price. One can imagine their dismay, then, when, on the numbers going up, they found the old horse was opposed by a very small field of the poorest quality, and instead of getting 3 or 4 to 1 to their money, they would have to lay big odds on; but as it was now too late to make *other* arrangements, they were obliged to let the horse win. The small stake they wouldn't be able to handle at present, and the trifle they could win at these long odds on was little more than would pay expenses.

Quartley and his friends were very much upset at this disappointment; but the farmer, with his usual resourcefulness, hit upon a plan for helping the exchequer.

"I tell you what it is, my lads," said he; "it looks like being a bad field again to-morrow, although it's the principal race. The public is sure to rush on our horse, at any price, as soon as the lists are marked up, so I'm going in for a 'joint' outside to-morrow. I can make a cert of getting a bit there." So on the morrow Quartley was betting ready money at a judy on the course.

In those days a good deal of the betting, especially on the principal race of the day, was done before the numbers went up. All the fielders had marked up their lists for Delamotte's race as soon as the business of the day commenced, and as this was the fourth race on the card, most of the public money had been invested before the numbers went up. Of course, everybody believed the horse would run. He had been put about most industriously by someone, not only as a certain starter, but as a "snip" for the race; and to give his backers assurance on these points, he was kept marching up and down the paddock an hour before the time for it.

The farmer cunningly contrived to have his list marked always just a little under the odds which the other bookies were offering to accept about Delamotte, so that he took most of the money, which amounted to something like a hundred and fifty pounds.

When the numbers were hoisted for the race, and there was

no Delamotte among them, there was a general howl among the farmers and yokels outside who had "done in" their sovereigns and half-crowns.

"Why, Delamotte beant running, Master Quartley," said one of them.

"I see he beant," replied the farmer; "but, of course, I can't help that."

"Yes; but you'll gie I my money bock, won't 'ee? You know I for many years, Master Quartley."

"Of course I do, friend; but that would be more than my life would be worth. You see, I be a member of a society of bookmakers in London, and it be against the rules to give money bock."

At this the countryman, sidling up to the farmer, whispered:

"That's arl right, Master Quartley; but you can gie I mine bock on the quiet."

Like Mrs. Malaprop, Quartley had a habit of making the most ludicrous blunders in the names of persons and things. I remember meeting him one day coming out of Bushey Park, when I was going for a stroll through the beautiful Avenue of Chestnuts. "I have just met your friends, the *Gracey* brothers, going through the *revenue*," said he. And he always spoke of Sir John Astley as the "Jolly Barrow Night."

He was a fair old flat-catcher, and there was no subject too simple for the exercise of this gift, and few occasions where he did not see opportunities of catching a flat, and when no opportunity offered itself, he very often manufactured one. He was staying at Brighton for the Sussex fortnight, and while walking along the Marine Parade he had observed a number of ladies' hair-pins, which had been shed in the process of the fair ones' promenading. One would scarcely think this simple fact could be turned into grist for Mr. Quartley's mill, but so it was; this gave rise at the time to some trifling betting as to the number of pins met with in a given time, or as to who should find the most in a certain distance.

GAMBLERS AND GAMBLING

The following evening at dinner the subject cropped up again. Betting men, over their wine, will bet about anything. The farmer said he would undertake to find forty hair-pins between the Royal Crescent Hotel and the bottom of the Marine Parade.

"Done!" said a young one who was present, and who had been one of the party the day before, and who, moreover, had been curious enough to count the number he saw during the time, so he thought he had an advantage over the old man, who apparently had not been so cunning; and as the young man had only counted about ten in the distance, he thought he had a real good thing; but, as I shall show, he reckoned without his host.

The bet was for a fiver, and the money being posted, a small portion of the party sallied out to decide it. Quartley said:

"Of course, I have both footpaths and the carriage road, so that I find forty hair-pins between here and the bottom of the Parade." The young man tried to wriggle out of this, and confine him to one footpath only; but clearly that would have been unfair to Quartley, and was therefore not allowed.

"I shall take the horse-road first," said he, and away he trudged down the broad roadway; but he met with very little success there; indeed, after doing the whole distance he discovered but two pins. The young man got quite jubilant now, and began to make the running, which was exactly what the farmer wanted.

"I'll lay you another fiver," says the young one.

"Not for me," said the old man; "you can lay me ten pounds to five if you like."

"No, no, I'll not do that; but I'll lay you twelve pounds to eight."

This offer suited Quartley even better, so after a little haggling this bet was made, and he proceeded with his search again. This time up the pavement nearest the houses, and now, as was natural, with considerably more success, for, of course, ladies did not walk much in the horse-road. Still, the success was not of a character to give him much hope of winning his wager, as he found ten only on this journey. He had now to find twenty-eight on the pavement next the sea; so the young man was still further elated, and he wanted to double his last bet, which, of course, was not good enough for the crafty one, who declared he now wanted very long odds.

"Well, what odds will you take?" inquired the young man.

"Twenty-five to five," replied Quartley.

"I'll lay you thirty to ten," was the answer, and before the search was recommenced this bet also was made.

Matters soon began to assume a more promising aspect for the accepter of the odds, for within a foot of each other he found three pins almost as soon as he started, and before he had gone fifty yards he found a dozen more.

"Ah! ah! I thought I should drop on them down this side," laughed Quartley; "there's ten ladies walk down here for one going down the other side, especially after dark, which is the time hair-pins mostly get disturbed. Here, I win for an even tenner more."

The young man, now looking rather as though he had himself swallowed one of the hair-pins, declined any further bets; but another member of the party offered to take ten pounds to five, and was at once accommodated.

Of course, before he had reached the limit of his search, the forty pins were safely stowed away in Mr. Quartley's pocket, and all the money that astute gentleman had won, amounting to fifty-two pounds, was very soon there also. And it never occurred to any of the party to notice the newness and untarnished condition of those hair-pins.

During one Goodwood Meeting many years ago, Quartley made one of a party of five who had taken a cottage at the pretty village of Singleton for the week, and among the party was a man in many respects very like the farmer himself. He was a wideawake fellow, cute and clever, but very unscrupulous, and was frequently taking down even his own pals with "put-up" jobs. He was a tall, thin, one-eyed man, with a rather eccentric get-up—a parsonic suit of black, with a white top-hat, very low in the crown and broad in the brim, which he must have had specially made, for no one ever saw a head-gear the like of it, and he was known among his friends as Bos. The little incident I am about to relate concerning this man and the farmer shows how very possible it is for the sharpest biter to be bitten—is, indeed, a neat case of diamond cut diamond.

The first morning after the party's arrival at Singleton the farmer awoke about six o'clock, and turned out with the intention of walking up to the course before breakfast, a distance of about three miles. He knew the walk would prepare him for the substantial meal provided, and he thought it possible that, among the horses and jockeys who would be doing their morning's work there, he might pick up something which would be useful later in the day; but he was fortunate enough to fall across this something useful long before he reached the course. It is a stiffish hill for a fat man with a corporation and habits such as our farmer's; so when about half-way up he sat on a stile and dropped into profound thought. I don't suppose the marvellous landscape, stretching out before his eyes like a beautiful panorama of wooded hills and fertile vales, bathed in all the golden glory of the early morn, charmed him as did the sight of a huge flock of sheep browsing on the slopes of that lovely hill, for in this flock of sheep he saw what was more to him than gorgeous scenery—a possibility of making a bit.

As he sat turning this possibility over in his mind, he saw the owner of the sheep, a rosy-faced, good-tempered farmer, come striding across the field toward him.

"Good morning, farmer!" said Quartley. "These be a nice lot of sheep you have here; they be yours, I guess?"

"Yes, they are mine, and they are a flock of nice sheep," replied the farmer.

"Can you tell me the exact number in this flock, farmer?" asked Quartley.

"Yes; there are three hundred and seventy-five in this flock; but it's a very funny thing, I was asked the same question half an hour ago by a gentleman who sat on that very seat. And he was very particular to have the exact number."

"Indeed! that is remarkable; but what sort of a man was he, sir?"

"Well, he was a sort of man once seen never forgotten; he was a one-eyed chap, dressed in a suit of black, a bit like a parson, but with a funny white hat on."

As the farmer made this reply, Quartley's eyes fairly scintillated with the fun of the situation, and the possibilities hidden behind it.

"Now, look here, farmer," he said, "I know that young gentleman, and I know what his little game is; and what's more, I mean to spoil it, and I want you to help me."

And then he painted his friend Bos in such colours as easily induced the simple countryman to lend himself to Quartley's wily purposes. Instead of finishing his journey up the hill, he descended to the village, not wishing at present to run against Bos, who, he now knew, had gone up to the course before him.

A couple of hours before the time of the first race the party of five was in the waggonette, which had been ordered, and the poor horse was struggling up the hill toward the course. When they reached the stile, Bos ordered the driver to pull up and give the poor animal a rest.

"Fine flock of sheep," naturally enough remarked one of the party.

"It is a nice flock," said Bos. "I wonder how many there are in it?"

And then some of them began guessing, but Quartley appeared but little interested in the discussion; but when Bos proposed they should each one have a guess for a sweepstake

GAMBLERS AND GAMBLING

of a sovereign each, he readily joined them in it. Each one wrote the number he guessed against his own initials on a sheet of paper. Some of the party were very wide of the mark. Quartley and his friend Bos were, as my readers feel assured, much the nearest the mark. Bos guessed 370, Quartley 360.

"Me over anybody for a fiver," said Bos.

"Done!" replied Quartley; "make it a tenner."

This, of course, Bos was only too delighted to accommodate him with; and so hot did both get over the matter that the betting only ended when Quartley had staked his last sovereign in the hands of one of the gentlemen who were present, for he had wisely insisted on having no owings in a bet of this kind. And so the stakeholder held eighty pounds between them.

"How shall the bet be decided?" asked Quartley; "it will be a big job to count them."

"Perhaps this is the farmer coming across the field," said Bos; "if it is, we will let him decide it. But let no one be allowed to speak to him but Mr. Smith."

This reasonable condition being assented to by both sides, Mr. Smith addressed the gentleman as he approached: "Will you be good enough to tell us if this is your flock of sheep, sir?"

"Yes, it is, sir," answered the farmer.

"If you know the exact number, will you be kind enough to tell us that also, just to decide a little wager?" said Smith.

"Certainly; with pleasure! There's exactly three hundred and fifty sheep in that flock," replied the farmer.

"Three hundred and fifty!" almost screamed Bos. "Are you sure you haven't made a mistake, farmer?"

"No, *I've* made no mistake, sir," replied the farmer; "there were three hundred and seventy-five *when you asked me* at six o'clock this morning, but I've drawn out twenty-five of the fattest for market."

And the company, finding how the crafty Bos had fallen into his own trap, didn't spare him, nor was he for a long time allowed to forget the circumstance.

CHAPTER XXI

OLD-FASHIONED WELSHERS

My early Experience—Joe Manning—Johnny Quin—"The Captain."

I HAVE often wondered what could be the derivation of the word "welsher" as applied among betting men. I have heard many, but none which has seemed to me perfectly satisfactory. A friend whom I have just consulted on the subject says there is no doubt it was suggested by the old rhyme commencing

"Taffy was a Welshman, Taffy was a thief."

But I am not prepared to accept this derivation either, and am afraid my friend has allowed his judgment to be warped by prejudice, after a prolonged residence in private apartments at a fashionable Welsh watering-place, where they kept a cat, or, I should say, a great many cats. However awkward my readers may find the derivation of the word, a good many of them will experience no difficulty in supplying its definition, for they have had, in the course of their racing experiences, practical illustrations of it. I don't suppose the word welshing has any great antiquity, but the practice is as old as gambling of any sort, and it has not been confined to the turf alone.

A form of welshing was very common 150 years ago, during the insane rage for lotteries. Of course, a good many of these gambling schemes were genuine enough, and among the millions of blanks some were fortunate enough to draw prizes of immense value. But those systems had their blacklegs and welshers. It was no uncommon thing for lottery offices to be

OLD-FASHIONED WELSHERS

opened, and after receiving from great numbers of poor dupes, the managers, as they were called, would do "a guy," just as we have seen the same class act on race-courses in the present day. Sometimes, however, instead of levanting and closing the office in this sudden manner, they would conduct a bogus draw, in which the prizes would be so ridiculously out of proportion to the blanks that they frequently led to riots and sometimes loss of life.

My very earliest personal experience of betting on horse-racing has doubtless been the lot of many of my readers. My first acquaintance with a welsher was when a youth—I needn't say how long it is ago. I found myself at a race-meeting. I knew nothing of the horses or jockeys or anything, but I had half-a-crown in my pocket, so made up my mind to invest it, and as the jockeys paraded their horses in front of the Grand Stand, for lack of better judgment I selected the one I considered wore the prettiest jacket, and planked down my half-dollar on him. Of course, it was a most silly thing to do, but, as luck would have it, this very horse won at 5 to 1. According to my hazy method of calculation, I made out there was twelve and sixpence coming from the bookie to whom I had confided my half-crown. Don't laugh, gentle reader; I have seen the same mistake made many times since those days by much older and cleverer people. However, I went back gleefully to the spot where I left my bookie and my half-crown; but the bland-looking, elderly person, with the black surtout coat and shiny top-hat, was nowhere to be seen. He'd been shouting a good deal, and I thought that probably he was dry and had gone to get a drink, so, unsuspecting guile in such a gentlemanly-looking elderly person, I waited with composure his return; but when I found the numbers up for the next race and the betting in full swing again, I began to think I must have come to the wrong shop, so I moved away in search of my bookie. During my ramble round the outside of the enclosure—on the opposite side to where I had made my bet—I came across a man with a remarkable family likeness to the gentleman, only he was wearing a light jacket with blue stripes and a white hat. Still feeling confident he was my man, I made for him and demanded my twelve and sixpence. He simply said, in an indignant tone:

"Go away, sir! What do you mean?"

But before I could explain my meaning, I was hustled away by a couple of roughish-looking men.

"Yo've bin welshed, ain't you?" asked one of these gentlemen.

"Well, I don't know what you mean by welshed," I replied; "but I backed the last winner with that gentleman for half-a-crown, and I want my money."

"Look 'ere," the man said, "did the joker wot bet wi' yo wear a black coort like a parson, and a shiny black top-hat?" This I was obliged to confess was so. "Theer yer are agen," he said, turning appealingly to his companion; "dain't I tell yer the d—d old thief was at his games agen!" Then turning to me, he continued: "The feller wot did yo is that other gent's brother; yo cum to-morrer an we'll find 'im for yer. Ye mustn't 'inder that gent in 'is busniss, or yo'll get locked up."

I didn't find it convenient to "cum to-morrer"; indeed, it was a good many years before I was able to attend Wolverhampton—or, for the matter of that, any other—race-meeting.

Welshing during my time has had three distinct periods, each marked with characteristics peculiar to itself. From earliest recollections of the turf up to about 1872, welshing was a very mild sort of thing, and its professors were, for the most part, rather elderly men, with a dejected, decidedly seedy and out-of-elbows sort of look about them. I don't believe it was generally so flourishing a sort of business. There was no organised ruffianism, such as we hereafter became so familiar with; indeed, there was no union of any sort among them, consequently little strength. When one of these mean sneaks secured a few pounds he was only too anxious to be off with it, thinking himself lucky if he escaped a cruel pummelling at the hands of an enraged crowd or a ducking in the nearest water.

They were mostly a quiet, inoffensive set of men, and but for their thieving propensities, quite harmless.

I think my next experience of racing will illustrate pretty correctly the character of these old-fashioned welshers. And for this purpose I must revert to a story told in an earlier chapter, where my reader will remember my friend Collins supplied me with an infallible method of backing horses which was to produce untold wealth, and a ring full of broken bookmakers.

I will not repeat how this marvellous system terminated, but looking round about Upper Norwood, East Molesey, Edgbaston, and, indeed, many of the genteel suburbs of London, and most of our great cities, it is easy to gather evidence that the portion of my dreams relating to the bookies is still some little distance off fulfilment. As my readers are aware, it was at glorious Goodwood I made my *début* as a backer. For the first three or four races no favourite won, so my system now called upon me to take 40 to 20 a horse whose name I have forgotten. The bookie I had done my business with so far was rather a meek-looking little fellow, very quiet—I liked him for that. He wasn't much of a swell to look at. I didn't object to that either, knowing so many substantial people affected a seediness in attire; he was dressed in a well-worn suit of black, giving him rather more the appearance of an underpaid curate, minus the white choker, than a common betting man. This also pleased me, so I handed him four nice new fivers, and when, a few minutes afterwards, my horse had won, I ran off the stand with my friend, eager to touch my first winnings. On my way I said to my friend:

"What a nice little fellow that is we've been betting with—so very civil and obliging!"

"Yes, he is very civil," answered my friend; "but you must remember we have done nothing but lose to him so far, and it's easy for anyone to be civil when they are winning your money."

"Ah! You—you'll find him quite as agreeable now he has to pay," I replied. "But where is the gentleman? That's his place against that pillar. Another gentleman seems to have taken up his position." Then, thinking of my Wolverhampton experience, I felt a sinking sensation come over me. I didn't for a moment imagine my quiet little friend was a vulgar welsher; but began to think, after previous experience, I was a bit of a fool not to have taken steps to assure myself of the stability of my bookie before I began betting with him. However, we waited, and he didn't turn up; we searched for him, and couldn't find him; so we began to make inquiries, and found that he was a notorious old welsher named Manning, then, in all probability, on his way back to town to enjoy himself with the unusually large and easily got plunder of a couple of young fools.

This last experience sufficed for the remainder of my life. It is true I have been welshed many times, and for very large amounts, since those days, but not by the common welsher.

Some two months after this incident I went with my friend, the theory inventor, and some other acquaintances, to Warwick Races, and on alighting on the platform at the Great Western Station, the first person I set eyes on was the meek-looking Mr. Manning, with the same seedy suit of black and melancholy visage. I and my friends surrounded him, demanding the sixty pounds. The little gentleman looked somewhat alarmed, but he affected immense surprise.

"What do you want sixty pounds of me for, gentlemen?" he meekly inquired.

"What you welshed me of at Goodwood," I replied. "Come, no nonsense; pull it out!"

"Goodwood! young man, you are quite mistaken. I'll take my solemn oath I never was at Goodwood in all my life."

And then he called upon the Almighty, in the most choice and powerful language, to bear witness to his truth; also to afflict him with all sorts of horrors if he had ever been near Goodwood, or knew where it was. He was a cowardly little villain, and trembled with fear, doubtless possessed with a lively recollection of some previous rough handlings by other victims. Well, what could we do with him? It was clear he was the man, but it was equally clear he had scarcely sixty pence, much less sixty pounds, about him. And no amount of punishment we could inflict would get any of my money back. So I was weak enough to believe I was proposing something clever when I said:

"Now look here, Manning, old fellow, I know all about you, and if you don't make a clean breast of it, confessing you're the man, and also promising to pay me a bit at a time, as you may be able to, we'll take you down to yonder pool of stagnant water and duck you within an inch of your life."

Of course, he confessed instantly, and promised all I asked, and much more. What would he not have done to get clear of us at that moment? And he snivelled in most abject fashion over my weakness, which he was cunning enough to call kindness. I saw a good deal of the poor old wretch in after years, but need scarcely say didn't get a penny of the sixty pounds. I rather think he whispered me occasionally for bits of silver to help him home after some of his unsuccessful excursions, presuming, no doubt, on his very early connection with my racing career. I haven't seen poor old Joe now for many years, but suppose he has gone the way of so many better men with whom I became acquainted in my early racing days, and who still hold a place in my memory.

As far as observation goes, I don't think many of the

"chosen people" have gone astray in this direction—for these wary gentlemen the game was never good enough—but I am sorry to record the fact that I remember one sheenie welsher, and I daresay there are some old racing men who will remember him better than I do. He was a big dark man, with a most pronounced Semitic cast of face, and a stoop in his shoulders; the appearance of having in some part of his life lost something he was for ever seeking to find. Like his friend and contemporary, Manning, he wore a quiet, almost sad expression, perhaps not the most desirable, yet one of the endurable parasites of racing. He was called "big Nathan."

An equally well-known old traveller in the same line was poor old Johnny Quin. I have frequently heard him called "the honest welsher," I suppose the adjective being used here in the comparative sense. It was not that he refrained from plunder where he had the opportunity, or that he was ever known, willingly, to repay the victims he had robbed; but I have known highly respectable members of the ring lend him half-a-sovereign to go to a race-meeting or to help him home again after an unsuccessful meeting, and these amounts he never failed to repay. One good-hearted—albeit, perhaps indiscreet—bookie, who was frequently Johnny's banker, was soundly abused for this practice.

"Ah well, we've all to live," he would say, "so has this poor old devil; he lives on the involuntary contributions of the new 'mugs.' How many of us are doing the same in a different way? Good luck to him!"

I have said that these old-fashioned welshers were almost a harmless set of men. Compared with the class which succeeded them, they were honest gentlemen. They were mostly very poor, and I have often thought they were welshers less from choice than necessity.

The most notable example of the class I have hitherto written of was a man known for many years as "the Captain," and by this name only shall he be known here, not only

OLD-FASHIONED WELSHERS

because he lived to occupy a far different position on the turf and in commercial life, but because he has left behind him some who inherit only the better traits of his character and the worthiest traditions of his life. Of this singular type of his class I shall now have to speak.

The Captain was known wherever there was racing all over England, and, taking him altogether, his was the most interesting personality which has ever appeared on the turf in the shape of a welsher. In personal appearance he was a remarkable man; he was thick-set and rather above the average height; his face, although badly pock-marked, indicated considerable shrewdness and natural intelligence; his eyes, small, keen, and restless like those of a bird of prey, were always on the lookout for victims; he wore his iron-grey hair cropped short as with a clipping machine; he made up for this, however, by cultivating a splendid moustache of the same colour. In his bearing he affected the high military style of which he was uncommonly proud, and which, doubtless, had secured him his nick-name. In his manners he was suave and gentle, and polite almost to excess, and he exercised, in the practice of his despicable calling, a patient perseverance, industry, and ability which—applied in a more legitimate course—might have secured him a big position in life. As it was, they got for him several rows of houses, and with them a certain sort of consideration and respect, which the world always concedes to wealth, or reputed wealth, and to success—however achieved.

The Captain was, indeed, the only one of the welshers belonging to his school who got money and saved it; to begin with, he had more ability than his fellows, and what, even more than this, accounted for it, was the fact of his being a steady, sober sort of fellow, with the one fixed idea, never to " part "—for any purpose, or to any person—when he had once secured a bit. I have heard him confess that, in his early days, he seldom went through the formality of taking a railway ticket to the towns he was intending to honour with his presence, and as he was never burdened with superfluous personal luggage, he frequently managed to dispense with the necessity for unpleasant leave-takings with indulgent hosts and hostesses; and as for admittance to the various race-course enclosures, I am not aware that the clerks of courses supplied him with complimentary tickets, but I am quite certain he never paid for admission.

He was in the habit of leaving his home, bound for a race-meeting, with no money at all, or next to none, and every night without fail, whatever sums he had been able to put his "thieving irons" on, much or little, and by whatever means obtained, it was turned into Post-office Orders and despatched home, so that if it should happen that he got caught and "turned up," there was but small chance of recovering anything from this astute practitioner.

"They might tear the clothes off my back," I have heard him say, "there was always some benevolent farmer or sympathetic village tradesman ready to rig me out with a better suit. They might duck me in the pond and cudgel me till I was half dead, but I had always the consolation of knowing that the money was safely at home."

It was very amusing to hear him tell, in after years, of the toil and hardships he endured, the cruelties he occasionally suffered at the hands of enraged mobs, and the ingenious tricks he practised to elude the enemy. It was, as a rule, hazardous business to take on Yorkshiremen, and the Captain had a wholesome fear of the Tykes. They were not only keen on the welsher, but when they caught one they were apt to be inconsiderate and brutally vindictive; indeed, they have been known, on more than one or two occasions, to handle them in such a way as to leave them of little service as welshers—or in any other capacity thereafter—and I believe, from what he said, the worthy Captain had himself suffered at the hands of these stubborn and unforgiving Yorkshiremen. However, he ventured to Doncaster on a certain Leger week when so many favourites were beaten every day that he found himself able to remain in the ring all four days, and so successful had be been in finding "flats," he had been able to despatch quite a nice little parcel each night to his excellent wife at the metropolis of the Midlands where she resided. Towards the end of the business, on the Friday he managed to lay a gentleman twenty pound to five against 2 to 1 chance, which was decidedly indiscreet, because it had the effect of making the punter suspicious, so, without the Captain knowing it, he kept his eye on him, and he made up his mind to resist the temptation to see the race, in order to be able to do this till the race was over. But before it was over—in fact, before the horses were at the post—the Captain left his place and leisurely made for the exit gate, having cast a furtive glance on all sides, to be sure none of his clients were within sight. None of them were in sight, so he was considerably surprised when in an instant after the Yorkshireman was at his side, as though he had sprung out of the earth ready armed, like a certain example in mythology.

"What bist t'after!" inquired the Tyke, glaring savagely at him.

"All right, my boy, I'm not going to run away," cheerfully answered the Captain; "come with me if you're frightened."

So the Tyke followed him to a part of the ring which was pretty clear of the crowd. When there, he turned his back on the Yorkshireman, and appeared to be counting his bank. In the meantime, the horses had started, and very soon, unluckily for the welsher, the Tyke's horse won. Whatever sensations of fear or anxiety may have possessed the heart of the gallant Captain at that moment he didn't permit his face to betray, but turning lightly to his companion, he said:

"Look here, my friend, I've had a very bad day, and I find I haven't enough with me to settle with you; but it will be all right, I assure you. Just jump into a cab with me. I've got plenty down at my lodging, and I'll pay you honourably; I'm no welsher, I assure you," and his high military bearing, combined with his gentlemanly and persuasive language, was too much for the poor Tyke. Scarcely daring to doubt, yet feeling slightly uncomfortable, he went off with the Captain, who chartered a hansom, and was soon on the way to his lodgings, He pulled up at a respectable-looking little house near the Turf Tavern. The Tyke was about to pay the cabby and discharge him.

"I'll see to him," says the Captain; "he can wait a few minutes while I have a cup of tea, and you must have one with me while you're here, and then he can drive me with my luggage down to the station." This all looked so straightforward that the Tyke was made much easier in his mind.

"Here, missus," cried the Captain to the good woman of the house, who was in the little back kitchen by herself, "I'm back a bit earlier than I expected, and I've brought a friend with me; get a cup of tea for us, sharp, while I go upstairs and put my things together."

This he proceeded to do, while the good woman busied about the sitting-room, laying the table for her lodger and his friend. Now the cunning Yorkshireman, as he came in, had noticed an entry at the side of the house, and while now relieved of much of the doubt which had before possessed him, he thought he wouldn't throw a chance away, so, as the Captain went upstairs, he slipped out to the cabman.

"Look here, cabby," says he, "an tha sees yon chap come doon t'entry just call me oot of t'house, and I'll pay th' well for it." Then he slipped as quickly into the house again and waited for the Captain to join him at tea, and pay him the twenty-five pounds. The table was laid, the tea was "mashed," the bread and butter ready, a bit of cold meat, the remnant of the Captain's dinner, on the table; but the Captain tarried so long the Tyke became anxious, and the old woman rather alarmed. At last she impatiently hammered the stairs with the haft of her bread-knife, screaming out at the top of her voice:

OLD-FASHIONED WELSHERS

"Th' tay be ready, sir; thou'lt have it cold!"

There was no response, and no sound of movement in the room above. The Yorkshireman could bear the suspense no longer, so he joined the old lady in the kitchen.

"Hadn't you better go up to his rooms and see what he's after?" said he, a dreadful suspicion coming over him.

The old woman at once acted upon his suggestion, knocking violently at the door; still there was no response. She tried to open the door; it was locked. Then she began to scream. She knew, she said, the gent had been and made away with himself because he'd lost his money at the races. The Tyke had been already more than half disposed to that opinion, and when the cabman assured him he had neither come down the entry or through the window that way, he felt horrified with the certainty of it. What was to be done? They were dumb with the horror and fear of it. A little knot of neighbours had now collected, and someone proposed they should either break open the bedroom door or fetch a policeman who would do it. So cabby was sent in search of an officer, and after a time, having succeeded, the door was burst open, and the Yorkshireman and two or three of the bolder spirits among them followed the policeman into the room, prepared to be still further horrified. They found, however, no indication of a dreadful suicide; no man was in the room—dead or alive. There was a dilapidated old papier-mâché portmanteau not worth carrying away, and that was all that remained of the Captain. The active and intelligent officer, after looking up the chimney and under the bed, turned quite savagely upon those about him, demanding to know why he had been fooled in his manner. The door had been locked on the outside, and the key carried away. This was evidently a manœuvre to gain time while he secured his retreat, worthy the military reputation of my hero. After the officer had made a careful examination of the premises, inside and outside, he began to cross-question the cabby, more than insinuating that he had either allowed himself to go for a little nap or over to the Turf Tavern for a little drink, and so allowed the man to escape. The poor cabby, exasperated at this imputation upon his honour and truthfulness, swore, as only cabbies can swear, declaring he had neither closed an eye nor moved from the spot, so that he couldn't have escaped down the entry. It remained for a sharp lad, instead of an active and intelligent officer, to discover an altogether different and easy means of escape, which was, after all, ridiculously obvious. This was a low wall which formed the boundary of the little yard, over which a person might almost step into a similar little yard, and thence down another entry leading to a street running parallel to ours.

By this means, then, and while the busy housewife had been laying the table for two, had the Captain escaped, and he was on the way to Birmingham hugging himself complacently after another brilliant victory; amusing himself as to what the old woman would say when she found he had taken his departure without the usual formality, and what cabby would charge the Yorkshireman for his exciting job.

The remarkable strategy and resourcefulness of the gallant Captain in this episode clearly qualifies him as a General among welshers; his grasp of the situation, determination, and courage, were characteristic of the man, and worthy a better cause.

On another occasion he was plying his nefarious occupation at the aristocratic little Hunt Meeting, Stratford-on-Avon, but with only indifferent success, and it was on the last race but one when he secured a bite of any value. A couple of formidable-looking countrymen came up while he was offering 3 to 1 on the field for this race; as the straight men were limiting their offers to 6 to 4, the countrymen took the bait, and invested three sovereigns, and then went on the stand to see the race. But they returned before the race was run, and before the Captain had thought it necessary to make tracks. Some unkind acquaintance had put him away by darkly hint-

OLD-FASHIONED WELSHERS

ing something derogatory to the character of the layer of long odds, so they forsook the pleasure of seeing the race for that of keeping an eye on the man with their money. The Captain saw them and appreciated their motive, and resolved, if possible, to outwit them. The horses had started, and were indeed half-way home, when he walked quietly into the urinal, which was a flimsy, temporary erection—a few boards against the hedge dividing the betting ring from the adjoining field.

The young men kept their eyes fixed on the entrance, which was also the only means—apparently—of exit. While they are watching, the race was over, and their horse had won, and beginning to think their bookmaker a rather unnecessarily long time behind the boards, they entered the place themselves, but the bird had flown. Instead of their bookmaker, they saw the big gap he had made in the hedge as he had torn his way through it. Instantly they resolved to go in pursuit of their money, or revenge. Naturally, they were about to rush across the field towards the highway, supposing the welsher, as green as themselves, would take the nearest way back to Stratford. It was therefore unlucky for the fugitive that at the moment he broke through the hedge an unsympathetic wretch, on the very top of the stand, happened to glance into the field below, so he was able to instruct them in what direction the Captain had gone, which was exactly opposite to that which they were taking. Away they went, having this good scent, as fast as they could run, and when they arrived at the top of the field they were rewarded with a view of their cunning bookie walking leisurely at the side of the hedge in the next field. Almost before the Captain was aware he was pursued they came up with him. The welsher once more grasped the awkward situation; he knew that to run was out of the question, and forcible resistance mere madness; he must needs try once again his oldest and most useful defender, his ever plausible tongue. The enemy came towards him, cudgels in hand and murder in the eye. Under these circumstances, it was difficult for him to secure an opening for his powerful tongue before they opened fire with the cudgels; however, he made the effort.

"Look here, young men," he cried out before they were within striking distance, "if you want to get your money, just hear what I've got to say." They lowered their cudgels for a moment to hear what he'd got to say, and he went on with his speech, with assurance of another victory. "I'm an honest old man" (a good deal of emphasis on the "old man") "and I've met with great misfortunes. I've been betting every day I've had a chance for three weeks, and I've lost every blessed day. I'd only twenty pounds when I came here to-day, and all that went on the first three races. What could I do? A starving wife and family at home. I took your three quid because a fellow told me the favourite couldn't possibly win, and Mr. Wilson himself had told me it was a cert for his; so I put your three nickers on Mr. Wilson's; and now I'm broken-hearted, and haven't a shilling to get home with."

"Oh, that won't do for us," said one of the countrymen, the murder, however, being no longer in his eye; "you must have money about you," and with that they proceeded to run him over. Every pocket was searched, but no coin was found. It didn't occur to them to take his boots off; he had a watch and chain on, and judging they would, most likely, confiscate these, he made a virtue, and something else, of necessity.

"Now I'll tell you what I'll do to show you I mean going straight by you young men. I've got a gold watch here which I wouldn't sell for fifty pounds—not that it's worth more than fourteen or fifteen, but it was a present from my poor old mother who's now in heaven; then the chain is worth six or seven pounds. Now I owe you nine pounds; lend me thirty shillings and make it ten guineas, and I'll hand you over the watch and chain for security—that is, if you'll promise me not to part with it for a week; but let me have it back on sending you the ten guineas."

After more of the Captain's eloquence they were subdued,

OLD-FASHIONED WELSHERS

and advanced him the thirty shillings, and he entrusted them with this precious heirloom of his family on their solemnly reiterating the promise to let him have it back on repayment of the ten guineas. And so they parted, the Captain to the bosom of his virtuous family in Birmingham, and the two countrymen to Stratford, where they lived, and where they soon made the distressing discovery that the watch and chain were excellent samples of *Brummagem* ware, but not gold; really fairly good imitations of it, and worth altogether perhaps fifteen shillings.

There can be but little doubt that had the daring spirit, clear-sightedness, indomitable energy, and other noble qualities which went to make the bold welsher what he was been exercised in any legitimate business, he would have been a notably successful man. This would appear to have been the opinion of a number of people beside myself, and it was not an uncommon thing to hear the expression of this opinion. One gentleman held it so firmly, he decided to back it by risking a considerable sum of money. This was Mr. William Taylor, who, with his brother George, were well-known bookmakers, hailing from the Emerald Isle. These gentlemen were devout Catholics, and were both of them among the most straightforward and benevolent men I ever met with. Will Taylor, being impressed, as I said, with the evident ability of the Captain, determined upon the Quixotic task of his reclamation. The Captain's plausible tongue had almost convinced him that it was only want of means which had prevented him shining in some straight way long before—indeed, it would appear it had been by the merest chance he hadn't been a saint instead of a welsher.

"Supposing I start you with a small bank to begin with," said Mr. Taylor, "will you promise me to bet fair and go straight?"

"I should think I would, Mr. Taylor," the Captain replied.

"Why, it's the opportunity I've been waiting and longing for all my life."

"Then you shall start to-morrow at Warwick," said the philanthropist. "I'll provide the necessary tools, and be behind you to the extent of a hundred pounds to begin with, and I'll make people acquainted with the fact as far as possible, so you may be able to get a little betting."

With the tears of gratitude welling up in his eyes, and loud in praise of his benefactor, the Captain took his departure; and on the following day behold him in the ring at Warwick, equipped and eager to commence his new career as a legitimate layer, declaring on *his honour* to Mr. Taylor, and to all whom it might concern, that nothing on earth should make him go crooked again if Mr. Taylor would only stand by him. Well, the first race is over, and the philanthropist, full of excitement, rushes off to see how the new bookie has fared.

"Well, Captain, what have you done?" asked he. But he need scarcely have asked; the Captain's beaming countenance proclaimed the good news, "a skinner" to begin with, which was set down as an augury of good. A clear book for £27 gave him heart to bet even more vigorously on the second race, and he was rewarded by even better results; he had yet another clear book for nearly £40. Again Taylor hurried up to the "joint," and the Captain almost embraced him in his effusive gratitude.

"Oh, what have I been doing all these years?" he exclaimed. "I've been at the wrong game, I can see. Why, if I'd only gone straight long ago, I should have been a rich man now."

Taylor, seeing things going so well, and feeling sincerely anxious to help on the good work as much as possible, now recommended some of his friends who punted in small amounts to do business with him, vouching for his honesty, and even going as far as to have himself a few bets with him. So on the

OLD-FASHIONED WELSHERS

third race his betting had so much increased that another "skinner" resulted in a win of upwards of £60. This made him about a hundred and thirty to the good, and gave rise to visions of rows of nice-looking houses to be called "Straight Villas," with an industrious penciller collecting the rents.

The result of the fourth race, alas! demonstrated the futility of human hopes, and knocked the "baseless fabric" of the Captain's dreams all of a heap, for it produced a low, selfish sort of punter, with no desire, like friend Taylor, for the reclamation of an erring Captain; and this man had the ill-grace to put a tenner on the winner, and as it was a large field, although favourite, it started at 3 to 1, so that this inconsiderate punter was entitled to £40. Mr. Taylor, of course, expected there would be a loss on this race, so promptly made for the spot which the Captain had selected as his "pitch." He was rather surprised to find, instead of his gallant friend, one of the punters whom he had guaranteed waiting to draw £40. You may perhaps better imagine than I can describe his feelings when he found the numbers up for the next race, and no Captain. Indeed, the pitch was "to let" for the remainder of the meeting. He had intended returning to Ireland after Warwick, but the conduct of his protégé so vexed his philanthropic soul, he remained in England, travelling about from meeting to meeting, for several weeks, in the hope of meeting with the ungrateful welsher. After about a month, he suddenly came across him at another Midland meeting; and so far from trying to avoid him, the gallant Captain put on his high military style, saluting his friend and would-be regenerator with the boldest effrontery.

"You're a nice sort of fellow," began Taylor; "nice sense of honour or gratitude you must have to treat a man as you have treated me. You rascal! You ought to be whipped off the face of the earth."

"Come, come, Mr. Taylor; draw it mild," the Captain replied. "I was really obliged to bolt at Warwick."

"Obliged to bolt! How so?" asked Mr. Taylor.

"They backed the winner," answered the inveterate welsher, looking astonished that any human being should be weak enough to expect him to remain at his post under such circumstances.

"How much had you to pay the winner?" asked the philanthropist.

"About sixty pounds," was the reply; "and if I'd paid, I should have had to part with all I'd had the trouble of collecting on that race, and about fifteen pounds of my previous winnings. I couldn't do it—I really couldn't, Mr. Taylor."

"Yes; but didn't I tell you I would be by your side," said that gentleman, "and if you required it, find the money?"

The irredeemable old scamp sighed deeply, and in quite pathetic tones replied:

"It's no use talking, Mr. Taylor; I tell you I *couldn't* pull it out again. I didn't think it possible I could get sixty pounds back again that afternoon, as there were only two more races; and as the punters had begun finding winners, I thought they might perhaps go on doing it."

The high-principled and generous Irishman, recognising the incorrigible character of the creature upon whom he had wasted his humane efforts, and feeling that nothing he might say or do would have the slightest effect upon him, let him go his way, only registering, mentally, a solemn vow that he would be guilty of no more Quixotic feats of knight-errantry on behalf of fallen humanity in the shape of confirmed old welshers.

For several years after this the Captain continued his welshing career; but he was becoming an old man, and he had lost much of his old dash and daring. And his soul revolted at the brutal methods of the new school of welshers which was just springing into existence. He had invested some money in a commercial undertaking, and that looked like meeting with considerable success; but it didn't go well with his old occupation. But after all, I do believe the factor which most strongly influenced him in his decision to relinquish his nefarious profession was an intense yearning to mingle in good society; to meet on equal footing men of position and respectability, who had been in the habit of looking upon him and his occupation with contempt. To attain this purpose, there was nothing he would not do; he would grovel in the dust, or spend and lose his dearly-loved and hardly-earned money like the veriest "mug." He succeeded in this object, as he did in most of the matters he set his mind upon; but the price he paid for the distinction he coveted was out of all proportion to its value, and will scarcely be believed by those unacquainted with the latter part of his history, and who only remember him as the hard-headed and shrewd old welsher.

Two or three years after the relinquishment of his profession of welsher he reappeared on the field of former glories in the character of a gentleman backer, and so adroitly did he manage matters, he was soon "taken on" by most of the leading pencillers of the ring, and was found betting to a considerable amount of money, with an account every week at the clubs and at Tattersall's. He became possessed of an intense desire to become a member of one of the best and most respectable sporting clubs in the country. At first he failed in this attempt; but with astute management, and after what he called "indomitable *per-sev-ver-ance*," his numerous efforts were crowned with success. At most of the clubs, just at this time, there was a rage for high play at cards, and the game of baccarat was the one most in vogue. The club I have referred to was no exception to the rule, and no sooner had the Captain become a member than he was seized with a mania for baccarat; and night after night, when he was not away racing, he might be found, eager-eyed and earnest, doing battle with the fates at the baize-covered table.

Fate was not kind to him—perhaps it resented his desertion of a profession wherein it had secured for him so much profit and renown—and now, like a very butcher, it had the knife in him. In his own line he never had an equal; at this green-baized table he was a child contending with men. Anyway, he lost heavily, and nearly constantly. He couldn't give it up—it had become a mania with him; he almost lived at the club, and the play had got to be a necessary part of his existence. It was known that monkeys had settled on the roofs of all his rows of houses. Trying to recover what he was losing at cards, he began to bet heavier and recklessly at racing, with the inevitable result that there came a Monday when the Captain's racing account was missing, and he found himself obliged to retire from his beloved club in an absolutely stonified condition. Poor old Captain! I saw him many times after that, walking about in complete poverty, reduced to lying in wait for the pals of his better days in order to beg the means for a dinner. He was now too old and broken in spirit to make fresh attempts to raise himself from his dreadful condition. To return to the only mode of life in which he had been successful was out of the question; and if he had attempted it, he would certainly have failed. Welshing had undergone a complete change; its methods would have disgusted the Captain's suave and gentlemanly spirit, and it would have been impossible for him to have mixed with its then turbulent professors; clearly welshing had become an impossibility for him. The friends and acquaintances of his prosperous days, naturally enough, gave him the cold shoulder; indeed, treated him with the contempt which he deserved—deserved for being a fool and not a rogue; not because of a wasted and dishonourable life, full of low lying and thieving; not because of splendid abilities perverted to vilest uses; not even because he owed them anything, or had done them personally any wrong, did they despise him, but simply because he was poor.

It was clear there were no possibilities, no place for him even, in this life, and nothing for him to do but to die. This the poor old wretch did some five years ago. Of course, I am not going to excuse or extenuate the execrable profession of welshing of any kind; but I am bold to reiterate an opinion I have elsewhere pronounced, which is that the Captain, with all his faults, was a gentleman, compared with the vile wretches who succeeded him in the welshing profession, about whom I shall have something to say in my next chapter.

CHAPTER XXII

THE BRUTAL SCHOOL OF WELSHERS

How I came by a Limping Gait—The Battle of Ewell—" Punch" and his History.

THE old-fashioned welshers of whom I have written so far are an extinct race. They were not a credit to the turf, but, as I have said, they were endurable parasites. They fleeced the unwary, and made the young beginner pay his "footing," content to rob their victims and sneak off with the plunder. The *modus operandi* was highly interesting, and, as I have shown, their trickiness and skill in evading the enemy testified to rare natural abilities, and often afforded amusement to those interested as lookers-on. These comparatively innocent old welshers, with their simple methods, were succeeded by what I may style the dark ages of the turf, when welshers "came not in single file" but in whole battalions, terrorising the ring, and setting all lawful authorities at defiance. It would seem as though the good news had been conveyed to the purlieus of thievery in all our great cities that here was a field of labour for the thief, where to ply his occupation in broad daylight, and in sight of the very guardians of the law, without fear of interference; nay, more than this, where they might be guaranteed the protection of their old enemy, "the copper," if they should have the misfortune to be caught and overpowered by those they were robbing.

Some of my readers, whose experience of the turf does not go back as far as these dark days, will discredit this description of matters, and be inclined to charge me with exaggeration, and worse, though strictly true, and any old racing man who lived through those days with his eyes open will endorse what I say. Many times I have seen these vagabonds caught in the act, and when their victims, seeing legal protectors refuse to help them, rose in their indignation, taking the law into their own hands, and were about to inflict well-merited punishment, the policeman would step in to guard the thief, taking him into custody, only to release him the moment he was perfectly safe. More than this, I have seen the welsher, when pursued, run into the arms of a policeman, demanding his protection, and getting it, too, with the same result.

No wonder, then, that these people greatly increased in numbers, and as they went about in gangs, became powerful, and were indeed a terror not only to backers but to layers also. If a man had been plundered in the most cruel and barefaced manner, the advice generally offered by his experienced friends in the ring was, " You had better put up with it. It's more than one's life is worth to interfere with them."

Welshers were not only thieves, they were composed of the very residuum of thievery. No such blackguards and irredeemable ruffians would ever have been permitted to follow their nefarious occupation, for such a length of time, in any other civilised country under the sun. The brigandage of Italy in its worst times was nothing to it, and if it had been allowed to continue and grow to the present day, it would have put a stop to racing. Indeed, it was only when it menaced the very existence of a noble sport that steps were taken to check it, and all honour is due to the magistrates at Ascot who so construed an Act of Parliament as to warrant them in sending welshers to prison, which aforetime had never been done, thus creating a precedent which many magistrates have since followed, to the purification of the turf in a remarkable degree.

Some of my readers may incline to the opinion that I have

overdrawn the picture and am unduly severe on welshers of the period under notice. I answer that exaggeration were almost impossible, and personal experience warrants me—if excuse were necessary—in the use of the strongest language at command. I owe it to the unspeakable brutality and ruffianism of these thieves that I have gone maimed and limping through nearly thirty years of my life, and which I shall do through all that remains of it, knowing no day in all the years, and but few hours, without more or less of pain. It is therefore natural that I should feel bitterly, and say what I feel. At the same time, I know that there are thousands of racing men who would bear witness that I have not spoken a bit too strongly against these cowardy pests of the turf.

I cannot better illustrate their character, and the condition to which the ring was reduced in the early seventies, than by giving "a round, unvarnished tale" of my sufferings at the hands of welshers.

I was betting in the ring at Brighton, in partnership with W. Knee, who is at the present day one of the most widely-known starting price merchants in the provinces. I was betting, and my young friend was booking. Up came a man who will be remembered as Big Fisher, one of the most notable scoundrels of the gang then travelling; he took ten pounds to five the favourite, posting with me his fiver. After he had turned away, my partner remarked:

"If this favourite wins, I shall want you to stop a tenner he welshed me of at Worcester."

"That was before you joined me," I answered; "and, of course, has nothing to do with me. But if he wins, and you intend stopping it, you had better take the money, and settle with him when he comes."

As the favourite won, I awaited with some anxiety the return of Fisher, knowing him for one of the most violent and dangerous of all the thieving fraternity. It was not long before he put in an appearance, and my partner handed him his fiver back, which was all he considered due.

"What the —— does this mean?" inquired the ruffian.

"It means that I've stopped the tenner you owe me for Worcester," replied my friend.

The welsher, foaming with rage, dashed the money on the ground with a volley of the most fearful oaths, and at once went for my partner, who was then a well-built, powerful young fellow, nearly as heavy as Big Fisher. In an instant a crowd was around them, composed very largely of "the boys," and all was confusion. The combatants were on the ground together, and it was clear that Fisher, unaided, would fare badly; but the thief was not to go unaided, for I distinctly saw one of his pals, a fellow named, or nicknamed, "Butcher," deliberately kick at my friend while they were on the ground. This was a bit more than I could stand, so I rushed in and pulled Butcher away. The fight was, of course, soon over, as the police were near at hand; but I have painful reasons for remembering the diabolical expression of Mr. Butcher's face as he turned away from me, saying:

"Look after yourself, you —— ——. We'll do you next. We know you're a —— policeman."

The latter remark, I afterwards learned, referred to my acquaintance with the celebrated Scotland Yard detective, Tanner, with whom they had seen me talk occasionally, although, on no occasion, had they or their doings been the subject of conversation.

Well, I thought the matter had blown over, at any rate for the present, and was just beginning to bet on the following race when a little fellow came hurriedly past me, and, without looking at me, earnestly whispered, "Keep your eyes open, the boys are on you," or words to that effect. I turned to look after this would-be friend, and as I did so I received a fearful blow on the side of the head; in a second I was on the ground, being kicked all over. I was literally surrounded by the ruffians; but I well remember seeing among my assailants Big Fisher, Butcher, and a dreadful thief from Birmingham named Sam Unwin. In two minutes, and before assistance could reach me, I was served fearfully. Among other injuries, my leg was broken in the ankle, and the joint dreadfully dislocated, the muscles being so badly lacerated as to preclude the possibility of ever becoming sound again.

I was carried to my lodgings in the King's Road, suffering excruciating pains, and there I lay for many weeks. In the meantime, articles had appeared anent the subject in various newspapers; a sort of committee, composed of a few well-known members of the ring, took the question up, and warrants were issued for the arrest of such of the miscreants as I was able to identify. They, however, left the country or kept out of the way for a long time, and the following year the matter was allowed to drop. I had all along made up my mind that neither I nor any one individual ought to be singled out for the purpose of prosecuting these villains, not only because I knew the danger to the individual, but I felt it ought to be undertaken by a body representing the whole ring, in the interests of the ring, and of the public. Butcher, from what I afterwards saw of him, no doubt relinquished his disreputable calling; anyway, I never remember to have seen him following it from that time. The other two, after my affair had blown over, continued their thieving career as boldly as ever, and I have known them more than once assisting at scenes as shameful as that described. They were both drunkards as well as thieves. Big Fisher dropped out of sight many years ago, and I should say he had either drunk himself to death or died doing time in one of His Majesty's prisons. The last time I saw Unwin was a few years ago; he was too old and emaciated to get about the country racing; so he was employed on Saturday nights outside a "cag-mag" meat shop in one of the low parts of Birmingham, touting for customers. Soon after this I heard of his dying in abject poverty in one of the slums of that city.

These men were not exceptions, they were fair samples of what welshers had now become, and the treatment I received was not more brutal than scores of respectable men underwent at the hands of these or other members of the fraternity.

At Lichfield, a year or two after my case, I witnessed a scene more horrible than that wherein I was concerned, because the victim was an elderly man, and apparently in a feeble condition. A firm of welshers had established themselves in the ring; the ruffian who acted the part of bookmaker was perched on the top of a high stool. He had hung round his neck, by means of a broad yellow strap, a large satchel, on the front of which was emblazoned, in gold letters, the name of one of the best-known bookmakers. This, by-the-by, was a very common practice, and, in more than one case I have known respectable bookmakers permit their names to be forged in this way, and the public thereby gulled, because they were afraid of the consequences to themselves if they interfered.

Well, the respectable old gentleman I have referred to, it appeared, had deposited two sovereigns with the welsher, taking him twelve pounds to that amount a certain horse which won, and, of course, he demanded of the thief, who had borrowed the straight man's name, the fourteen pounds he was entitled to. In the days of the old-fashioned welsher he would have found the "pitch" to let; not so with the modern type of welsher, he maintained his position with an effrontery bred of constant success; so the old man handed up his ticket.

"How much do you want?" asked the welsher in the business-like manner of the straight man.

"Fourteen pounds, sir," replied the old gentleman.

"Number 725, fourteen pounds," shouted the thief to his fellow-thief, who acted as his clerk, and who, after pretending to look at the book, looked innocently up at his master, remarking:

"The gentleman's put the wrong horse down; he backed a loser," and the welsher tears up the ticket into little bits, and throws them into the old man's face.

"Go away, you damned old scamp," says he; "what are you trying on?"

Some old gentlemen would have gone away terrified at the savage demeanour of this bookmaker, supplemented as it was by the rude and uncomplimentary remarks of a little band of square-headed ruffians by whom he was immediately surrounded. But this old gentleman, with more valour than discretion, was not of that metal. He was an excitable and passionate little man, and he commenced a violent argument, and when he found himself being hustled about by those surrounding him he made a snatch at the satchel, which was the signal for "the boys" to begin their work. In about one minute the poor old man was kicked into unconsciousness, his pockets rifled of watch and money, and I have no doubt that, although no bones were broken, he had received injuries which would trouble him as long as he lived, and probably shorten his life. The welsher and his confederates got clear away to continue the like business elsewhere.

Occasionally these ruffians met with their due; and once they did so, I remember, under amusing circumstances.

A few of my elderly readers will remember the famous Battle of Ewell, which was much talked about at the time.

A gang of welshers, hailing chiefly from Manchester, Nottingham, and Sheffield, and known as "The Forty," were very much in evidence in those days. A party of them, during the Epsom Summer Meeting, had quartered themselves at the pretty little village of Ewell, at whose capital old hostelry some of us have rested many a time for a drink on the way. It is a few miles from the course, and on one of the highways to

London, and as in those times vast numbers of those attending the races went by road, it is easy to imagine, if you don't remember, what a busy place the little village was on "the Derby Day." A couple of the pleasant party I have named lodged at a cottage down one of the lanes, and after the labours of the day on the downs, hither they repaired for a good feed and unlimited booze. On the Derby Day in question, after these two young men had so regaled themselves, they strolled into the main road and joined the crowds who were watching the carriage-loads of jovial folk returning from the races. Some will recognise the two men when I tell them they were known as Punch and Iron Mask. Punch was a cobby-built fellow, with a big head on broad shoulders, and a flat nose on a face as big, and about the colour of an old-fashioned copper warming-pan. His pal was a much taller man, with a slight stoop, very long arms, and a cadaverous-looking face, with huge jaws and prominent cheek-bones, which almost obscured his wolfish little eyes. And they were both supposed to be able to scrape a bit; indeed, they were quite a terror to quiet folk, but, as is generally found to be the case with such, they were both at bottom arrant cowards.

They had no sooner taken their stand on the high ground forming the footpath on one side of the road than they proceeded to pelt the carriage people passing by with rotten eggs, sods of turf, and sundry other objectionable missiles, while other of the onlookers contented themselves with blowing peas through a tube, and less objectionable annoyances. Most of the passengers took it all as a matter of course, and bore it as became the day and the occasion. A carriage, drawn by a pair of high-stepping horses, was coming by, and a couple of young swells with two ladies, evidently of the blue blood, were seated in the carriage. Punch and his friend, in an unlucky moment, thinking this was an excellent opportunity for a little extra display, shied a huge sod, which caught one of the ladies on the head, sadly frightening her, and what was worse, utterly spoiled her headgear. This resulted in a surprising deviation from the usual state of things, and instead of the coachman having orders to drive faster, the horses were stopped suddenly, and out jumped the two young swells, and in an instant they were face to face with their ruffianly assailants, and the most remarkable part of the business was that the welshers immediately recognised in the two swells a couple of their victims on the course.

"You two blackguards will have to fight," began the shorter of the swells, "or else you will have to be locked up; now, which is it to be?"

"Hear, hear! bravo, little 'un!" shouted some of the bystanders, and it was clear there were enough honest Englishmen present to see fair play, and who, English like, dearly love to see a fight. The welshers blustered a bit to begin with, but seeing no way out of it, threw off their jackets, and prepared for the fray. "You take Mr. Flatnose," said the gentleman who had spoken before, "and I'll have a go at this big thief who welshed me to-day."

The taller of the gentlemen protested against this arrangement, and wanted to slip into the big one, but the little one wouldn't hear of it, and so began the famous battle of Ewell.

As the two fights began at the same moment, it is rather difficult to describe the early stages of them. Punch was a Lancashire man, and believing if he could succeed in getting a grip of his opponent he would be able to trip him up and fall on him, according to the custom of the boys in his country, and surmising at once that he should have no chance in ordinary fighting, immediately he stood before his opponent he made a dash to get hold, but instead of the gentleman he got hold of a blow straight from the shoulder, and delivered on Punch's poor flat nose with a force and precision which not only scored first blood for the gentleman, but made the bully's thick body spin, and his eyes strike fire, ere he flopped on the earth like a lump of lead. When they picked him up he would have run if there had been any use doing so; as it was, he had evidently very soon had enough, and the men who had volunteered to second him had almost to throw him at his terrible enemy. This time his attempt to rush the gentleman was of the feeblest description; he was instantly seized by the scruff of the neck, and the swell held him there till he had sufficiently pummelled him, and then sent him reeling to mother earth. The gentleman was satisfied, and Punch was more than satisfied, and was glad to sneak away without inquiring after the fate of his pal.

Meanwhile, Iron Mask, having an immense advantage in size and the length of his reach, was not doing quite so badly as Punch, and that is all that can be said for him, for, despite the length of his reach, he had never been able to touch his little opponent, who, in point of science and condition, was as far in front of him as was Tom Sayers to an untutored yokel; so he got peppered on nose, and eyes, and high cheek-bones to such a purpose that his wife would never have known him.

It took something longer to bring this result about than Punch's punishment had taken, but it was just as effective, and before they had been at it many minutes Iron Mask knew he had no chance whatever, so instead of coming up to time, after a stinging thump in the ribs, which had nearly knocked the life out of him, he quietly turned his back and was for slinking away after his friend Punch.

"No, you don't go like that," said the gentleman, following him up and taking hold of him. Iron Mask, seeing him at such close quarters, suddenly turned round, a very devil gleaming in his eyes, and letting fly at the gentleman, caught him a nasty blow on the side of the head. This naturally exasperated the swell, so he set about him in earnest. Ding! dong! like little sledge hammers, on ribs, mouth, and nose went the iron fists of the gentleman, till the big welsher was out of puff and utterly cowed, and again would have sought safety in flight. "You don't move from here," said the plucky little swell, dodging round him, but keeping a safe distance, "till you apologise, and say you have had enough; and if you don't do so, I'll set about you again."

Anything was preferable to this, and he proceeded to apologise in the most abject fashion, and declared, I am sure with more truthfulness than he was accustomed to use, that he *had* had enough, and only then was he allowed to follow his friend to the little cottage down the lane.

The two swells, who had not troubled to remove their coats, and as cool as though nothing had happened, proceeded down the road to where their carriage awaited them, and drove off amid the cheers of the crowd, and so ended the Battle of Ewell. Iron Mask has been dead these many years; but it was only the other day that I came across Punch, within a few yards of one of the principal sporting clubs of London; a poor, shrivelled-up old wretch, ragged and bootless, and hungry, lying in wait for sporting men, whom, he had reason to know, have tender hearts, and stand the "whispering" of the most worthless objects, whose sole claim to charity is their poverty and bitter distress.

Before I have done with Punch, it may be worth while giving a short account of his history, and how he became a welsher, gleaned from material supplied by the redoubtable old welsher himself, the truthfulness of which I have no reason to doubt.

I was walking thoughtfully through the classic precincts of Old Drury. The names of several of the streets I passed had given my thought a certain drift—I was living in the past—the offices of the *L.V.G.*—whither my feet were tending—the wicked autocrat who holds in the hollow of his hand the destinies of all connected with those offices, as well as the wretched myrmidons of his tyranny—editors, printers, and such-like—were all dead and buried, or yet to be born, as far as I was concerned. The pale-faced hungry urchins that fight for the end of my cigar, as they wallow in the mud—the wretched, ragged creature, pressing to her dirty bosom the putty-like face of a tiny child, as she flits past me into the darkness of one of these courts—the blear-eyed *thing* that was once, perhaps, a man, who reels out of the gin-shop, and rushes after her—all, all, are shadows merely. The only realities are the beautiful women, with spotted cheeks and powdered hair and flowing robes of silk ; and the gallant gentlemen to match, all associated in my mind with the names of these streets, and who are thronging the chambers of my imagination.

I was dashed down from this high society, and awoke from these pleasant reveries by a rather determined tug at my coat-sleeve. Perhaps it was a second or third sort of knock of the door, as it were—I cannot say, I had been so busy with my thoughts.

"Beg yer pard'n, Mister Old Guv'nor," said a gruff voice. "Yer don't remember me, I reckon—I'm one o' th' old boys." But I did remember him; who that had ever seen that face could forget it? Poor old Punch, whom I had not seen for many years, and whom I thought dead long ago. For a moment I felt inclined to slip a few coppers into his hand and hurry on. I don't want to say anything that would hurt his feelings, as he will probably be reading this account of himself; but in his palmiest days you would never have mistaken him for a member of the aristocracy, a Church of England clergyman, or a Bank of England clerk even. On the contrary, in those days he very much resembled a—no, I won't say what he resembled. I'll only say he looks very much worse now, because, after all, to a bird it does make a world of difference the kind of plumage nature gives him ; and I hold with Carlyle that clothes play a much more important part in the world than simple folk believe.

Recognising in him a living type of the real old-fashioned welsher, and perhaps of another sort, too—on second thoughts —I believed it might be advisable to give him silver instead of coppers, and that it might even be worth while to cultivate his acquaintance. I may say that I was never in the secret of his proper name; consequently, I was obliged to address him as "Punch," the name by which he was known on all the race-courses of England for many years, and by means of which hundreds of my readers will readily identify him.

"Why, surely you are old Punch?" I began. "I thought you were dead long ago."

"Well, Guv'nor," he answered, "I've bin welly nigh dead many times lately, an' I've bin awful hard up, times is so different; th' old game's played out, and I'm too old for graft; but I know you won't mind givin' a lift to one of the old 'uns for the sake of old times?"

I gave the poor old broken-down welsher what appeared to please him, and on leaving him, I said:

"And now I'll tell you how you can earn a bit more. Go home and jot down, if ever so roughly, a few particulars of your own life; how you became one of 'the boys,' with some of the tricks you have played."

"I can do that fust-rate," he responded, quite earnestly. "I'll go home and write it down, and let you have it."

Several weeks passed, and I saw nothing more of him, and I had ceased to expect the fulfilment of his promise. Two months after, however, I found a dirty envelope addressed to me in quite an unfamiliar hand. On turning out the contents, I found a large sheet of a whitey-brown sort of paper, not too clean, covered with writing, done, I should think, with a stumpy blacklead pencil, and in hieroglyphics which taxed all my powers to decipher.

Poor old Punch had done his best to tell me something of his life.

When a young man, it appears he was a mechanic earning good wages in the town of Leeds. He began his racing experiences by having his half-dollar on a gee-gee occasionally at the lists in that town. He was—perhaps unfortunately for him—rather successful, consequently he began to bet in larger amounts, winning at one time as much as a hundred pounds, and so he was induced to give up his job at the works and follow racing as a profession. The first place he visited with this purpose was Nottingham race-course, and there, no longer relying on his own judgment, but listening instead to tipsters and touts, he began to go wrong. Going on to Stamford, he continued to lose his money, when one of his pals suggested that instead of backing horses he should commence business as a bookmaker. And doubtless he started with the intention of being an honest bookie; but losing all his bank, it is equally certain he very soon became a notorious welsher, as unscrupulous as he was audacious and clever.

The first day he began in this line of business he considered he was very lucky, for he "got thirty pounds and went with it" to London, henceforth to become a denizen of that great city of refuge, which sheltered, and still shelters, many no better than he, who dwell in the gorgeous splendour of the West End, instead of up a filthy court in Drury Lane.

Being now able to come out as a "toff," he must needs try his hand at Goodwood, where he discovered a gold-mine, and worked it to some purpose. There were crowds of simple young swells, like fat geese, waiting to be plucked, and he plucked a good many of them, earning in the four days a very considerable sum of money. He travelled from thence to the gay town of Brighton, where he got introduced to all the old hands at the game, and where he himself in turn got plucked, for they taught him a new game, played with a little box and two square bits of ivory, and known as "hazard." And so he "did in" all his ill-gotten Goodwood earnings, and had to start afresh at Brighton, where he was again very successful at his flat-catching business; getting in his net, among others, the late Lord Stamford for fifty pounds. But, like better men, a mad infatuation drove him to "the box," and again his pals, as he put it, "skind" him.

He then made tracks for his own "North Countrie," and at Richmond and elsewhere made money. At York he met with his first serious check. In attempting to get away, he was collared by his suspicious clients, and had his good intentions frustrated. I have spoken elsewhere of the hard-heartedness of these Tykes, where welshers are concerned, and they seem to have handled poor Punch rather roughly, but it appears there were valiant pals to the rescue. The famous "Stalybridge Infant" was there, and, not liking to see the brutality of the mob, or for some other sufficiently good reason, he was induced to join in the fray, and with such effect that the enemy was scattered, one man receiving a blow which stunned him, the lookers-on believing him dead. This resulted in Punch getting away, but it also resulted in the "Infant" being "run in," and having to appear before the magistrates. Being unable to produce a prosecutor, the police trumped up a charge of attempting to pick pockets. The charge was as untrue as it was clumsy, and fortunately the Infant was able to offer amusing ocular demonstration of the absurdity of the charge.

"Look here, your worships," said he, stretching towards the bench his huge arms, with hands at the end of them as large as legs of mutton, "your worships can't believe it would be possible for me to pick pockets with these!"

There was roars of laughter. The magistrates evidently did not believe it, for they straightway discharged him, only stipulating that he should remove his leg-o'-mutton hands from the locality.

Punch then went to Doncaster, where he had to be particularly wary, but by the aid of a good "make-up" and a constant change of clothes, he was able to do a good stroke of business, taking down some of what he calls "the tip-top mob."

His next adventures were among the cannie Scots. At Musselburgh he found in the ring a real beautiful "J" in the shape of a half-drunken colonel, to whom he laid an even "pony" against the favourite which won. He immediately slipped out of the ring and changed his clothes, with a white hat instead of a black one, and was back in a few minutes. The Colonel looked at him very hard, and with an evident want of confidence, asked him for a "pony." Punch was, of course, indignant, and easily persuaded the Colonel he had made a mistake, but he finished up by generously forgiving him, and then laid him a tenner against another horse which, unfortunately for the welsher, also won. He was now, therefore, unable to go into the ring again.

In the evening he saw the Colonel go into his hotel very drunk, and catching sight at the same time of the notorious old welsher, Johnny Quin, he pointed the Colonel out to him.

"Now, Johnny," says he, "you ready your book with a tenner, losing bet, against that swell, and follow him into the hotel and claim it." Johnny being supplied with the Colonel's name and other particulars, he boldly faced the soldier, and demanded ten pounds, which he declared he had won of him.

"I have not got it down," said the Colonel, "and I forget all about it, but I suppose it's all right; but it's rather funny I keep on paying, and never receive any bets I win."

However, Quin got the tenner off him, and promised to look after the people who were indebted to him.

"You go on to Perth, sir," said Johnny; "I can put you on some good things, and most likely get the money which is owing to you." So to Perth the gallant Colonel went; Punch, keeping in the background, followed him there, as did also the cunning little Quin, and sundry others of the gang, and they didn't lose sight of him until they had plucked him for a large amount.

With varying fortune, for many years Punch continued his disreputable occupation. At times the buffets of the fickle goddess drove him into deep waters, and he met with rough usage at her hands. At other times he made heaps of money, lived on the fat of the land, and dressed like a swell; and there is no doubt what he tells me is perfectly true—if he had saved his earnings like "the Captain," he would now have been a man of fortune, with a charming villa in the suburbs of his native town, a respected member, perhaps a committeeman, of several important clubs, and an honoured pillar of various political associations. Who can tell? I have seen these honourable positions held by men made of no better material than poor old Punch, men who lived for years by his methods—or worse. Punch, like many a better man, has missed his golden opportunities, and they will come to him no more. For him there remains no honourable offices, no charming country villa, but a painful pilgrimage to something quite different.

CHAPTER XXIII

WELSHERS AND WELSHING

How Brown became a Welsher—Welshers Abroad—Punch and the Pigs.

WELSHING is a phase of turf life which has occupied my thoughts a good deal, as it has been a constant subject of my observation. I have elsewhere shown that I have ample reason for disliking the followers of this particular form of thieving; but I have met among them men who are so evidently the victims of adverse circumstances that one finds it impossible to withhold from them some little pity and commiseration. Here and there among them you find smart, well-educated fellows who have forfeited good positions and gone wrong through inherent wickedness. On the other hand, many of them were born and reared in an atmosphere of thievery, and so handicapped from the beginning by conditions which made it almost impossible for them to be other than they are. One of the saddest cases of this kind was that of a man I knew almost as soon as I began racing. He possessed, I believe, great natural ability, was quick, clever, and thoughtful, and not having, I should say, a bad heart. Doubless he was as unscrupulous in his methods of getting money as others of his class, and what he got he spent so recklessly, when years and illness came, and he was no longer able to get about the country, he became, like so many of them, a common beggar. When I met him last, which is some years ago, I had a long and interesting conversation with him, and in reply to my question as to what first induced him to take up welshing profession, this is what he told me, and I will give it, as well as I possibly can, in his own words:

You have known me a great many years, Old Guv'nor, and must remember when I was a smart young fellow; but didn't know me before I took on the welshing lay. Ah! that's a long time ago, and yet it don't seem so very long looking back. I'm an old man now, and my life has been a wasted one. I'm nearing the end of a long race—you may call it the Beacon Course. I've passed the distance-post, one of the beaten lot. It's true I had a bad start, and have never been able to make up the lost ground, and it's too late now.

You want to tell how I became a welsher, do you? Well, I don't mind, for it can make no difference to me now. So I'll tell you all about it, fair and square, not trying to make myself look a bit better than I am; and when I've done I'm afraid you'll be saying I ought to be ashamed of myself for an old scamp. Well, perhaps I had; I know I've been very bad—I don't know of anybody quite as bad. But before you begin flinging stones, just you look right into your own heart, because you are better acquainted with that article than anybody else is, and really know, if you would only be candid, how very little you have to boast about. Besides, bad as I am, and as I always have been, don't you go to imagine that I am every bit bad all the way through. If I choose I might call to mind a few things which, maybe, will be put in the other scale; although I fear it will make but a sorry show when the balance comes to be struck.

Well, then, to begin at the beginning, I must tell you I was born, as the saying goes, of poor but dishonest parents. My earliest recollection of life was a dirty marine-store dealer's shop in a great manufacturing town in the North of England, kept by my parents. I could never understand why our shop was called a marine-store. I never saw any sailors there, or, as far as I remembered, anything to do with the sea. It was a dreadfully dirty establishment, this shop of ours, which faced the dirty street. The stock-in-trade consisted of sundry pieces of household furniture, household utensils, which nobody seemed to buy, dilapidated cutlery, worn-out spoons, and broken cruet frames, which here and there showed signs of having once been electro-plated, a few worthless carpenter's tools, boxes containing tarnished brass hooks, rusty nails, old screws, and other familiar objects in brass, wood, and iron, which had been there as long as I could remember. You passed through "the shop," as we called it, into our living room, which was almost as dirty as the shop. Beyond this living room was the mysterious chamber of the establishment; this was what once had been a little scullery. The door which had led into the yard had been bricked up before I could remember, and the shutter of the small window was kept nearly always closed. This was father's sanctum, into which I was forbidden to enter. I nevertheless managed more than once to get a good look over it; I know there was a strong wooden bench with a large vice screwed to it, with files, shears, hammers, and all sorts of tools lying about. There was also a blacksmith's hearth and a pair of large bellows which were worked by a leather strap and a long rod of wood. The fire was kept always burning, and very often my respected parent was locked in the place, working by himself. At such times I could hear him hammering away at metal things or blowing up the fire.

In those early days, being of an inquiring turn of mind, I often got a whacking as a reward for asking inconvenient questions, and for prying into matters which my father said didn't concern me.

As much to get me out of the way as for any other reason, my father sent me to a day-school in connection with the Church of England, and I really got very fond of it, learning to read and write with a rapidity which not only amazed my worthy parents, but surprised my master also, and, I suppose, pleased him too, for he went so far as to have me at his own house two or three nights in the week, along with several other promising boys, where he gave us instruction in higher matters than we were allowed to learn at the school. I was now about fourteen, and it was the happiest part of my whole life; in fact, I may say it was the only part of it where I knew anything at all of happiness. But this good time came to a sudden and very tragic ending, and even at this distance of time, all grimy and black with sin as I am, I cannot look back to those only few happy years of my life without a strange lump rising in my throat, and I can't help thinking that they who brought about my expulsion from that school may have something to answer for.

It came about in this way. There was a great lanky lad among my schoolfellows, about my own age but much taller. He was the son of the grocer in our street, and he and I didn't get on well together. At first I wanted to be friendly with him, so took the liberty of calling at the grocer's shop for Sam Bland to bear me company to school; but the grocer, who was one of the churchwardens, and considered a very religious man, wouldn't allow it, and bundled me off the premises in what I thought a rather cruel manner. The boy, I suppose taking the cue from his father, after that missed no opportunity of annoying me, and he finished up with giving me a nickname which stuck to me as long as I remained in the neighbourhood. He called me "Young Hot Pot." I didn't know the meaning of the expression, so didn't care for it very much, as I called him names in return, which, I daresay, I thought quite as cutting. "Young Sand the Sugar," I remember, was one of them.

At last the quarrel came to a head. We were in the playground, and, as usual, got to high words.

"What do you mean by calling me 'Hot Pot,' you lanky devil?" I asked, and he immediately retorted:

"Because your father's a thief, as everybody knows, and buys stolen property, and keeps a hot pot always ready to melt it up, and—"

But before he could get any farther with his speech I had landed him one fairly on his mouth, and then, before he could recover himself, another and another on nose, eyes, and all over his face. In fact, I was all over him, and I think he was too much astonished to retaliate till I had knocked all power of retaliation out of him. The boys screamed out, and very soon the master put in an appearance. Poor Bland was picked up bleeding and badly bruised, and taken home, while I was taken by the collar through the schoolroom and locked in a dark cupboard under the stairs, where I lay trembling for more than an hour. I was dragged out by a couple of the strongest of the pupil teachers.

"Stand forward, Brown," said a severe-looking old gentleman in a white choker and gold-rimmed spectacles, whom I knew for one of the managers of the school and clergyman of the adjoining church. "We have been inquiring into your brutal conduct to young Bland; we have heard all that has to be said about it, and have decided to have you thrashed and expelled the school in disgrace."

I was beginning to say a word in my own defence, for I felt how unfair it was to try a lad in his absence, hearing only what was to be said against him; but they wouldn't hear me. Bland's father stood there, looking as though he would have liked to execute one part of the sentence himself; but this pleasure was denied him. I was seized by two of the teachers, while another belaboured me with a stout cane.

When I got away from them I made for home, and told my mother all that had happened. She consoled me with the assurance that when my father returned I would get some more.

In the evening my father came home, and my mother repeated to him the whole story, and when she came to the "hot pot" part of it there gathered on the face of my father a look I shall never forget. He glared on me like a savage.

"You go upstairs and undress," he hissed out. "I'll give you something to remember."

I knew what this meant, but was obliged to obey. He followed me in a few minutes, and making me undress, he thrashed me with the strap off the big bellows till I was covered with wales and bruises. It was not the first time by many that this sort of thing had happened, for whenever things went wrong he vented his temper upon me. I was a big lad for my age, and, I suppose, tolerably sharp too; and at these times I couldn't help reasoning with myself about the cruelty and unfairness of my parents. But I never dared to reason with them, so I made up my mind I would stand it no longer, but would run away from home and try to get my own living, and I felt sure, if I could only get to London, I should be able to do this. I began to make preparations at once by stealing from the shop odds and ends of metal, and anything else which I thought wouldn't be missed, and which I could readily turn into coin. Mind you, I didn't look upon myself as a thief for this pilfering from my own father, and at that time I didn't think of being a thief. Indeed, I can remember how I lay a-bed for hours at this very time, wide awake, and dreaming of becoming all sorts of good and great things.

However, before I could carry out my plans, something occurred which upset them all, and perhaps changed the whole course of my life. My father and mother and myself had just sat down to supper, when a ringing of the bell, attached to the shop door, told us someone had come in, and almost at the same moment a fellow, whom I knew as Hookey White, came hurriedly into the room.

"I want you, Ned," he said to my father, and the two passed into the workshop, my father bolting the door after them.

They had been there but a few minutes when Hookey was let out again, and without exchanging a word with my mother, he passed quickly through the shop again and into the street.

My father was back in the workshop, with the door bolted again, and I could hear him busy blowing up the fire on the hearth.

I didn't think much of this, because something like it was a common occurrence, but I was alarmed immediately after Hookey had gone, for the bell again rang, and two powerful-looking men marched straight through the shop into the sitting-room. Before they could prevent her, my mother rushed to the door of the scullery and shouted through the keyhole:

"The D.'s are here, Ned, and want you!"

"Don't you disturb him, Mrs. Brown," said one of the men, "we will see him in there." This, however, was easier said than done, for it was a stout door, and well secured.

They demanded admittance, and my father shouted that he was busy, but would be with them in a few minutes; and we could hear him blowing at the bellows, vigorously, all the time.

Seeing that my father didn't mean to open the door, they threw themselves with all their force against it, trying to burst it open, and they seemed to shake the very house to its foundations; but the door didn't give way. I stood there trembling with fear, while my mother, in a fearful rage, swore at the policemen, and threatened them with the poker.

They managed eventually to burst open the door, when my father asked them quietly what they were making such a fuss about.

"There's been a robbery, and you are suspected of receiving the swag," said one of them, "and we have a warrant to search your house."

"Well, search away," sneered my father, as cool as possible, "and if you find any of the swag here you can run me in."

"You may say that," replied the D., "for I see you have got the pot on, Mr. Brown, and you know we shall not be able to recognise spoons and forks in that."

"There's no spoons or forks there," answered my father, "but only a few old silver watch-cases that I got in the way of business."

While this was going on, a couple more officers in uniform had come in, and kept watch over us while the detective began the search; hardly had they commenced it when one of them picked up a small brown paper parcel from underneath the bench.

"What's this?" asked the officer.

"You know better than I do," was the reply; "it don't belong to me." And as they unwrapped the parcel, disclosing two or three silver forks and spoons, he continued passionately: "Oh, this is a plant, I see; I swear you have brought these things with you!" cursing them fearfully all the time. But suddenly fixing his eyes on the articles, he seemed to recognise them, and screamed out: "It's that thief Hookey who has put me away, and you have bribed him to do it!"

And then he sank quietly on a chair and suffered them to put the "darbies" on his wrists. I saw them take him and my mother out of the house, watched them going down the street, amid a gaping and jeering crowd, and then I went back into the room and cried until I fell asleep.

Well, I needn't give you the particulars of all that happened to me at that time, or of my father's trial. My mother came home the following day, but I never saw my father again. He was found guilty, and as he had several convictions against him, he got a "stretch" of fifteen years. But he did not do much of it, for he "pegged out" in eighteen months.

My father and mother all along had been in the habit of taking on a lot of booze, especially my mother, and after my father had gone she seemed to do nothing else. She kept the shop closed, and rarely left the house, or received a visitor; she provided me with plenty to eat and drink, but wouldn't pull out for clothes or pocket-money; but as she allowed me to go where I liked, and do pretty much whatever I wished, I thought it no harm to appropriate the saleable remains of the shop; and this kept me going for nearly twelve months, and was the means of getting me into some middling company.

My mother didn't seem to care for anything, if I was only at hand when she wanted a fresh supply of gin, and she always

WELSHERS AND WELSHING 237

appeared to have plenty of money for this purpose. One night, when I was nearly sixteen, I went to bed about eleven o'clock, leaving my mother, more than usually drunk, sitting by the fire. When I came down next morning I found her lying on the hearth dead. In trying to get up she had evidently fallen on the fire and been burnt to death. I rushed from the house and alarmed the neighbours, and, of course, it was not long before the house was full of them, with a doctor and a couple of policemen. Well, they could make nothing more of it than I have told you.

During the day my mother's brother, James Shrimpton—Uncle Jim, as we used to call him—put in an appearance, and seemed to take possession of me and of all my mother's belongings. After the funeral there was a sale, and I went with Uncle Jim to his home, a dirty little hovel up a court in one of the worst slums of the town. I wasn't quite such a kid as he took me for, so I rather put him one on when I asked him, after a day or two, how much money he had found in our house, and what he had received from the sale. I was the more curious about this, perhaps, as I couldn't help seeing that he was now flush of coin, and living very differently to anything I had seen before; besides which, he had never done a day's work since my mother's death. He assured me he had found but little in the house, but this and the proceeds of the sale, after paying all expenses, left fifty pounds in hand.

My uncle had been in the employ of a man who attended races with a stock of stools, betting boxes—or "judies," as we called them, because they were very like the Punch and Judy shows—printed cardboard lists, and all the other things used by the poorer sort of outside betting men. These things the man hired to the bookie, making a pretty good thing of it. During his visits to the races, Uncle Jim had occasionally supplemented his work as an assistant judy-keeper by acting as clerk for some of the bookies, and so had become acquainted with the business. He told me all about this, and proposed that the fifty pounds should be used as a bank to start bookmaking in a small way, and that he should bet and I should clerk for him, sharing the profits, and he painted it in such glowing colours that I readily consented. I liked the idea of travelling about from place to place. All the fun and excitement of such a life—as he painted it—had a great attraction for me.

So it was not long before we had knocked together a little judy of our own, resplendent in bright red baize, and all the paraphernalia of a betting man's "joint." I remember how proud I felt when I saw it put together for the first time on Worcester race-course, and I watched my uncle, with tin tacks, affix our pasteboard sign to the front of it with a swelling breast, for it bore this legend:

"Shrimpton and Brown:
To Win, and 1, 2, 3.
All In, Run or Not."

I certainly believed I was then on the way to fortune; and, mind you, it was our purpose at the beginning to bet on the square, and pay up. Welshing had never entered into my head; in fact, at that time I did not know the meaning of it.

Well, I and Uncle Jim bet together at that judy on the race-courses all over the country for more than three years, with good and bad fortune. When we won we spent our money freely, so that we never got together much of a bank. We had a good many ups and downs. At first, like new beginners at every game, we had to pay for experience. I remember, nearly the first time we opened the joint, a respectable-looking cove taking odds to a sovereign—which was a big bet for us—and giving a country fiver in payment, and Jim gave him four beautiful good quids in change. The man had backed a wrong 'un, so he didn't turn up after the race; but I don't think he would even if he'd been on the winner, as we discovered afterwards that the note was on a country bank which had been closed for more than twenty years. At another time a fellow came up with a ticket for a winner, and drew a couple of sovereigns. He had scarcely turned away with the money when another came up, claiming the same amount with a ticket bearing that identical number. Of course, we demurred to the payment, but it was useless, for on finding the ticket which we had just torn up, we found that the numbers had been cleverly tampered with, and altered from a losing number to that of a winner. There was no doubt these fellows were working together, but it was equally certain the last comer had the genuine ticket; so we had to pay him £2 also. These and similar experiences sharpened me up a good deal, and perhaps prepared me for the life I was to lead.

As I have said, we never made much progress, and at last we had a very severe run against us. The bank was weak when we arrived on the course at Liverpool for the Grand National week, and there the bad luck continued the first day; favourite after favourite won, and at night the bank was one; we hadn't a quid left between us. I remember we held a council of war in my bedroom. The question was: Should we retire from the field defeated, or raise the sinews of war by "popping" our watches, rings, and other matters of jewellery?

The latter course was decided on, and we also agreed that we would make this capital spin out till we came to the Grand National, betting little on the smaller races, but taking every shilling we could on the big one, so we should be able to stand our ground; keeping well before the public, gaining its confidence more after every race, and then have a dash against Huntsman, and "go for the gloves"—that is, lay as much as we could against the favourite, which was a very hot one. If we could get him beaten, the bank would again be flourishing; but if he won! Well, we should have to do "a guy," which means get away, and henceforth be known as welshers. Ah, my friend, you are shocked! but if you will allow me to break in here with a bit of moralising, I would like to ask if anybody knows how many there are among the well-to-do bookies, and backers also, of the present day who have just once in their lives gone for the gloves; I venture to say, if the truth could possibly be known, the world would be considerably shocked as well as surprised. But it has "come off" for these people, and they are for ever more worthy members of society.

So we began to bet on the big race in earnest, pinning our list to the front of the judy, marked with the prices we were prepared to lay against each of the thirteen runners; but as we contrived to have the list showing liberal odds against the favourite, and a little under the odds the other twelve, our betting was naturally almost confined to laying against the favourite, and we did a roaring trade against him. The result was that before the flag fell we had laid the odds to more than a hundred pounds, and had that amount in hand. Nobody seemed to suspect us, consequently we found no difficulty in slipping behind the judy while everybody was intently watching the start for the race. We made for a temporary wooden stand a hundred yards away, where we might watch the race and at the same time keep an eye on our judy.

"The moment we see the favourite beaten," whispered Jim, when we had paid our shilling and climbed toward the top of the stand, "we must rush back to the joint."

"And what if he wins?" I asked, rather dolefully.

"Oh, he won't win," Jim replied; "we have twelve chances against him. Surely one of them will beat him!"

"But suppose he should happen to win?" I persisted.

"Well, then, we must guy with the swag over to the station, or jump into a cab."

The horses were on the way, and there was no more talk. I shall never forget my sensations as the horses came tearing

WELSHERS AND WELSHING

past us. The first time round one or two came a cropper; how devoutly I prayed that the favourite might be among them. I was fairly shivering with fear and excitement, a cold sweat broke over me; I was actually obliged to hang on to the arm of my pal, for I felt I couldn't stand for the few minutes which was to decide so much for me. In my heart I didn't want to be a welsher, and all the misery and horror of the years which were to follow seemed crowded into those few minutes.

The favourite, as I said, was a horse called Huntsman, and I quickly found he was not among the fallen, for Lamplough, his jockey, had him well in hand; he jumped beautifully, and appeared to be going better than anything, and when the jumping was over and they came into the course, my heart sank, for I could see the favourite still there, and bang in front. As they came to the straight run in the field of horses presented a long straggling tail, with only two of them prominent. For a moment there were excited cries, which revived my hopes and brought the colour to my face.

"Bridegroom wins!" and "Bridegroom! Bridegroom!" was re-echoed on every side; for it was evident young Ben Land was making a tremendous effort, and for a moment it looked like him beating the favourite; but only for a moment. Lamplough called on Huntsman for a final effort, and he answered gamely. As they passed the post—the favourite four lengths in front of Bridegroom, and nothing else within hail of the two—Jim whispered hoarsely: "It's all over; we must guy."

We took a last look at the judy, where already the people were beginning to assemble with the expectation of receiving their winnings; slipping off the stand, we crossed the course and got on to the main road, and jumping into a cab, ordered the driver to take us back to Liverpool as fast as he could go. When there it didn't take us long to pack our traps and get to Lime Street Station, where we got the next train home.

And now you know how I became a welsher. You would

like me to tell you some of the strange dodges and adventures of a welsher's life, would you? Well, well, perhaps I may one of these days, if I can only get rid of this plaguey cough.

It is certainly more than thirty years ago since the true story I am now to relate had its origin. That every particular of my story is true is well known to plenty of people living at the present time, for they knew the circumstances better than myself, and were more intimately acquainted with my principal characters. Four pals belonging to the old welshing school were at "glorious Goodwood" in pursuit of their usual occupation of flat-catching. There were a good many flats about that year, and the merry little band had a rare old time of it, netting among them several hundreds of pounds, living like fighting cocks every day, and getting gloriously drunk every night.

At the end of the Sussex fortnight it became a question what they should do with themselves and the nice bit of "swag" which an unusual amount of luck, and considerable industry, had brought them. Toby Pearson, who was in a chronic condition of drunkenness, although he took nothing stronger than ale, said he knew a nice little pub for sale in Whitechapel, where they did their own brewing, and a good business in ale and porter; and he proposed they should club together and buy it, and so have a home over their heads, and a bit of something certain, when things went a little crooked, as too often they did.

"Pub be d—d!" snarled old Jack Roach; "if we kept a pub we should want only one customer beside ourselves, and that would be a bloke to buy the grains. Let us cut up what we've got, and do what we like with our own. I mean to buy a mangle and things, and start the old woman with a laundry."

"I fancy I see you turning the mangle," sneered Harry Jones. "One thing's certain, the old woman would have to do all the work while you collected the accounts and spent them."

WELSHERS AND WELSHING

This led to high words, which might, perhaps, have culminated in a fight if it hadn't been for Tom Buckley, who was quite the superior man of the party, and its tacitly acknowledged chief. Those who remember Tom when he was a well-known figure in the betting ring and among the outside judy men on the race-courses, especially at the London Suburban Meetings, where at one time he bet as straight as any of them, will not need to be told that he was a fellow with really good parts—with a head on his shoulders which ought to have landed him in a good position. Tom had been sitting quietly listening to his pals' proposals, and thinking all the time of a scheme of his own, and just as Jack Roach was doubling up his leg-o'-mutton fist, getting ready to have the first knock on his pal, Tom stepped in between them.

"Don't you be a pair of —— fools!" said he. "What are you going to get by fighting? Have a drink, and hear what I've got to propose."

There was an instant clamouring all round to hear what Tom's scheme was; but not until they had had a drink all round, and something like good humour was restored, would he consent to tell them what it was.

"Well, look here, lads," he said at last, "I believe I can put you on a job where we can double the bank, at least, without much trouble or risk; and where we can have a jolly good time of it, too."

"Bravo! bravo! Go it, Tom!" screamed out Toby, in whom the last glass had just produced the noisy state of drunk. "That's the joint for me, my lads, and Tom's the boy to work it."

"You stow your —— trap, Toby," interposed Jones, "and let Tom pitch the lay."

"Well, this is what it is, lads," began Tom, who saw that unless he got them quickly interested in his scheme they would be for scrapping again, "there's some racing over in France, at a place called Dieppe, next week; let us work the joint there, and I'll bet we put together a nice parcel. They think over there that all English betting men are clergymen's sons and bankers, and they've never had any crooked betting men there at present; anyway, not any from England."

"But we don't know the country," interposed Toby Pearson, "and wouldn't that be rather awkward when we had to 'guy'?"

"I've thought of that, and all the rest of it," Tom replied. "You leave all that to me. Harry knows a bit of French, just enough to shout the odds; Jack can stand by him and wear the satchel, and you, Toby, can do the clerking."

"And what will your 'graft' be?" asked Toby suspiciously.

"Oh, I'll be the 'blue in,'" was the reply.

And as he was the best dressed, most gentlemanly, and cleverest member of the party, they all agreed that he would be the man for that business.

"It will cost something to get us all over there," proceeded Tom, "and perhaps we may 'blue' a bit the first day, because we must go 'straight,' and perhaps that won't cost us anything. The big race is on the second day. We can put up a list on that, and get all the stuff we can. The second day we'll have a carriage and pair posted as handy as possible, and while *mounseers* are watching the big race, we'll just slip quietly off and drive like blazes back to the town and take the first boat back to old England."

The plan was well thought out, and looked feasible enough, and apparently was not very risky. So their few things were soon packed, and the promising quartette were on their way, and brimful of hope respecting the wealth which would accrue from the plunder of the Frenchmen, and each one busy also with schemes for disposing of it when they returned to England.

When they arrived at Dieppe they quartered themselves at a comfortable hotel in a quiet locality. On the night of their arrival they commenced the good time Buckley had promised them, enjoying themselves in a right jovial manner, and with such quietude and modesty as usually characterise Englishmen of this class. The worthy host endured with meekness much that he would have objected to from his own countrymen—but then, were they not English *milords*, and running up a pretty bill?

They drove a showy carriage on to the course the first day, and set up the "joint." And when the racing commenced, Harry Jones, in a horrible jargon he called French, proceeded to bawl out the odds, but somehow the natives didn't bite quite so freely as expected, consequently they did not do as much business as they had fondly hoped; and when they returned to the hotel at night they were somewhat the poorer for their day's work, which was a state of things they were unaccustomed to, and didn't relish.

"Never mind," said Tom consolingly, after a good dinner, "they'll come at us better to-morrow, and we shall make it all right on the big race."

Jack Roach growled and wished himself safely back with the old woman. And Toby, who, not being able to get good English ale, had drunk an inordinate quantity of the wine of the country, which he, nevertheless, styled "*wash*," was more sour and cantankerous than ever, and it took Tom all his time to preserve the peace. And he daren't get drunk himself, because he knew if he did there would be the dickens to pay, and probably they would all get locked up, and so miss the opportunity he was looking forward to.

The following day, Tom having completed all his arrangements, they went down to the course as before, and as Tom had predicted, the natives took to them more kindly, with the result that before the numbers went up for the principal event they had taken something like a couple of thousand francs on that race; mine host of their hotel having contributed a portion of that amount, as well as introducing a number of his compatriots, who had done likewise. After the numbers were hoisted they did even much better, owing partly, no doubt, to this useful introduction, but even more largely to the fact that they were able to lay better prices than their neighbours.

Well, the big race is being run, and our friends have laid every horse at some price, so it is impossible for them to have "*a skinner*" if they stand their ground, and "a skinner" being what they intend to have on this occasion, they didn't trouble to wait for the result, but while their numerous clients were busy with that purpose, they quietly slipped to where Buckley waited with a carriage and fleet horses, and were very soon back at the hotel. The luggage was brought hurriedly downstairs, packed on the carriage, and when the agitated hostess—who was in charge while her husband was enjoying himself on the race-course—presented the bill, Jones was put up to try to make her understand that it had been all arranged with her husband. She looked perplexed and doubtful; but what could she do with four burly Englishmen whom she had heard her husband address as "*milords*"? She let them go, and in good time they and their luggage were on board the steamer, bound for Merrie England. They strutted about the deck smoking big cigars with an air of consequence becoming their nationality, and successful exploits.

Tom Buckley, who was not so bold as his friends, but much cleverer, keeping in the background, is presently alarmed to see a number of gendarmes step upon the deck, looking keenly about them, evidently in search of somebody. He takes in the situation at a glance, and knows who is wanted.

He was alarmed, as I said, but does not "lose his head." The gangway is guarded, and escape thitherward clearly impossible; but with that resourcefulness for which he was remarkable, he instantly hit upon a means of escape, which seemed promising, and which actually turned out even better than it seemed.

A poor young mother sat on deck in the midst of her three crying children; with a tiny one at her breast, she could do nothing to pacify the others. Tom, good-hearted fellow, saw in this little domestic scene a possibility of killing two birds with one stone—swiftly seats himself in their midst and begins hugging one of the squalling brats to his fatherly bosom, and thus so effectually blinds the inquisitive eyes of the gendarmes that they overlooked him altogether, while they haul his three friends to the nearest prison, and he goes gaily on to his native land with a fair share of the plunder; and I remember seeing him the following spring going strong and well in Barnard's ring at Epsom, and betting like a leviathan on the Derby.

Meanwhile, the other poor devils had been tried and found guilty, and were then expiating their offence with twelve months' "hard." And this was not all their punishment. They not only had to do the time and the labour, but they were charged a very heavy price for a most scanty prison fare; and, after this, all their money which remained was confiscated, in payment of the fine which was a part of their sentence.

After a time they all got safely back to their own land, and met again on their own happy hunting grounds. Harry Jones never went bookmaking to France again; I never heard whether Tom Pearson saved enough to buy a pub, and I don't believe Jack Roach's "old woman" ever got that mangle; but I do know that Tom Buckley, for years after, was knocking about London and the surburban meetings betting to a good deal of money. But I have neither seen nor heard of either of the quartette for many years, and I presume they have either gone over to the majority, joined the Salvation Army, or become respected members of society, like so many I have known who were, once on a time, no better than they.

I will conclude this chapter with a short story of our old acquaintance, Punch, and then I shall have done with the welshers.

Many years ago Punch had set up his "joint" in the shape of an old-fashioned, humble judy on the race-course at Chester. He weathered the storms of the opening day without finding any necessity to do a shunt, nursing himself rather carefully for the second, which was the Cup day, which, as I have shown, was a very common practice. He made up his mind to go easy through the first two races which preceded that famous race, so he might be the better able to land a *coup* thereon. But, alas! Punch was but mortal, and a mortal not blessed with much power in resisting temptation. And when he found in the second race a moderately good field, with one pronounced blazing hot favourite in it, he could not resist the temptation to take the money. It was a case of 6 to 4 on; but by dint of hard work, and accepting a little less than the market price, he found himself with an unusual number of clients, and, when the betting was over, a satchel full of silver, with a liability, if the favourite won, as far above his possibility of meeting as it was beyond his intentions.

The favourite was on the card as running in a bright scarlet jacket, which Punch looked upon as fortunate, that being so easily discernible in the distance. Immediately the flag fell the eager eyes of the welsher were looking out for the scarlet jacket, making ready to move off the moment he had reason to apprehend the slightest danger of it being found in front. No sign of it, however, being there, he boldly held his place, especially as something in yellow was leading by twenty lengths.

The cry of "The favourite wins!" as they passed the post, and a hasty glance assuring him there was no scarlet jacket among the runners, struck him with dismay, the whole truth of the situation flashing through his mind in an instant. He had left it rather late, but he made a determined bolt. Unfortunately for him, some of his clients saw him, and rushed after him with the dreadful cry, " A welsher—a welsher!" Punch was fleet of foot, and he dodged with amazing rapidity through the mass of human beings, and getting safely through the crowd, reached the street leading up to the city. His enemies, in full cry, were after him. He bolted up a side street, but the pursuit continued, and it was evident some of the pursuers were gaining on him, and worse still, his wind was giving out. As he ran, casting his eyes in every direction for a haven of refuge, he espied a large pair of gates with the small door in them open. Being now almost exhausted, he leaped through this door, slammed it to, and turned the key, which fortunately was in the lock. In a few seconds eight or ten of the leaders of the hunt arrived at the gates, only to find their entrance barred. While some of them held a hurried consultation, others thundered at the gates, and after a little time it was decided to storm the citadel. With this purpose they began to climb on one another's shoulders, when suddenly the doors were thrown wide open by a lad, and a countrymen stood there in a "float" loaded with fat pigs ready to drive away.

"What the devil's all this row about?" inquired the driver.

"A welsher ran in here a few minutes ago," answered one of the leaders, "and we mean to find him."

"Well, find him, then," was the surly reply; "he canna' get away from this yard without coming through these gates." Then turning to his lad as he drove quietly out of the yard, he said: "And you, Jack, shut the gates and lock 'em when the gentlemen have gone."

Of course, as my readers will surmise, with the driver and his load of fat pigs the welsher had gone also, neatly covered with straw, and the worthy driver bribed with a promise of a couple of sovereigns if he got him safely out of the city.

The better part of the story, however, remains in the sequel. It didn't take long for a part of the company to search every nook and corner of the premises, while the remainder kept guard at the gates. Of course, the search was unsuccessful, and as there was no possibility of escape otherwise, it occurred to them that the surly driver had done them, and got the welsher away with the pigs; whereupon they seized the boy and swore they would hang him if he didn't tell them all about it, and where the float and pigs were bound for, and they so worked upon the fears of the lad that he made a clean breast of it, and a very few minutes more found as many as possible packed in and on the top of a "fly," tearing through the city in pursuit of that float. Some distance before you reach the confines of Chester at its northern boundary they came up with the object of their pursuit. To jump off the fly and "hold up" the driver of fat pigs was the work of an instant.

"I'll tell you all about it," cried the trembling wretch; "he's under the straw among the pigs."

In another instant the grunters were bundled into the road, also the straw, but there was no sign of Punch.

"Why, dom him," cried the driver, between rage and fear, as white as a ghost, "he's bin an' welshed I as well!"

The fact being that while the man had gone leisurely along with his float and fat pigs, whistling with glee to think what an excellent day's work he had done, Punch had quietly slipped out, behind, and made the best of his way to the railway station; and the baffled backers, appreciating the comical side of the situation, burst into a roar of laughter, the principal subject of regret among them apparently being that they had missed seeing the race for the Cup while they had been chasing a welsher.

CHAPTER XXIV

NOBBLING

In at a good Thing—"Going for the Gloves"—How the Favourite was got at.

My readers may take my word for it the account of nobbling a favourite, which I am about to give them, is in all particulars substantially true; but as some of the actors in the affair are still living, I am not using the real names of either horses or men. Nevertheless, as the race referred to is an historical one, and the facts which follow were known to a good many people, there are still alive those who will have no difficulty in supplying themselves with the date and names.

On the first day of good old Warwick Races, at a time when it was among the best of all provincial meetings, I was there—now a full-fledged member of that highly industrious fraternity known as "the bookies." I was not what was known as a leviathan; but I bet to a considerable amount, and, like my fellows, when I knew, or thought I knew, anything, I was not very particular how much I betted. I was, moreover, well off in the matter of friends who "were in the know," and, as I have already shown, I was frequently "in the cart," suffering from too much knowledge, although it did occasionally happen that my information was reliable, and turned to good account.

I had just begun to bet on a Hunters' Flat Race; there were three runners only, and it looked, on public form, a certainty for a horse I will call Soldier, who had won no end of these races, and although he was carrying top weight, the public speedily made him a hot odds-on favourite against Musty, an old hunter whom he had met and beaten many a time before, and a "dark horse" whom nobody knew anything about, and whom, for the purposes of this veracious history, shall be named Senator. I was not laboriously at work on this race, believing that in such a field 6 to 4 was not a reasonable price to accept, and that probably much longer odds would be forthcoming when the betting had settled. One of my most intimate friends, in passing me, quietly slipped a bit of paper into my hand which, unseen by anybody, I managed to get a look at; and this simple circumstance so altered the case that I became at once the most industrious of fielders, readily accepting all the odds which were offered, and to any amount.

Now, unless it may be inferred by a too suspicious reader that this bit of paper contained what is known as a "laying order" against a "dead 'un," I will let him into the secret of what information the paper really did contain—which is more than I did for anyone at the time, not excepting my own partner, who was booking for me. Well, this is what the paper said:

"Bet away, *Soldier won't be favourite.*"

I knew what this meant, and so had soon taken odds to lose a couple of hundred pounds in bets of all sorts and sizes, from fifteen shillings to ten, to thirty pounds to twenty on; and when my partner, who had filled two pages of his book against this horse alone, found time to look up from the volume where I had kept him so busy, he remarked:

"Do you know what you're after, Dyke; or are you going mad? We're standing to lose more than two hundred pounds Soldier, and haven't got a penny out of either of the others."

"Write away!" was all I could spare time to whisper.

And away we went till another page or two was filled, and all, so far, against the favourite.

NOBBLING

But now some "squarheads" began asking after the dark horse, Senator. Five to two, bar one, had been freely on offer, and was freely laid against this stranger; but not by me or my particular friends. Soon two's was the best offer, and he was eagerly backed at that, and quickly shortening prices, till they laid good odds on him, and only then did I lay a shilling against him, and even then no more than would ensure me against being a loser in case he should get beaten. In the race, Senator, who had all the allowances, simply made hacks of his opponents, as he would had he been giving them a couple of stone each, instead of receiving about that weight from them, for he was a great horse, and many times in after days proved himself a wonderful chaser—one of the best, indeed, the century had produced.

In the early part of the following year I found Senator entered in the Grand National, and so little had the handicapper valued his previous performances that he had let him in at a trifle over 10 st. I was acquainted with his owner, and trainer, and all connected with him, and had reasons for believing that he had been tried a real good horse, and one another stone would not have stopped—with health and fair play—from winning the blue ribbon of steeple-chasing. In due course I had my orders, and proceeded to back him at long prices to win a good stake. The owner and some of my friends backed him very heavily, to win among them something like £50,000. Unfortunately, the sportsmen of our town were divided into hostile parties on this occasion, for another townsman owned a very good chaser, named Sandy, and had him in the Grand National, and, as he thought, with an excellent chance of capturing it. And so it came about that there was not only a sharp division but a bitterly hostile feeling between the owners and principal supporters of Senator and Sandy. As was natural, this feeling led to some high words and heavy betting.

Mr. Robert Sharp, or, as he was commonly called, Bob

Sharper, was not the nominal owner of Sandy, but people have been heard to declare that there wasn't a hair of his tail belonging to anybody else; anyway, Sharper was the chief backer and manager of the horse, and the undoubted leader of the Sandyites. He was at the time a professional bookmaker, and was reputed well off. Before he became a bookmaker his employments and method of living had been of a questionable sort; and, indeed, he had been for many years, and was even now, looked upon as rather a shady character. He was an unscrupulous and determined fellow, who would permit no obstacles to block his way that might be removed, with safety to himself, either with force or guile.

The leader of our faction was, in many respects, too much like Mr. Sharper, although possessing clearer antecedents and a better character. Everybody called him Big Dick, and his bets were booked and his account settled in that name, and I doubt if many doing business with him knew that his real name was Richard Coalmere.

Well, these two estimable gentlemen were obliged to come into frequent contact in the ring when they were abroad racing, and at the chief resort of sportsmen in our good town when they were at home; and they seldom met without canvassing the merits of their rival horses, and rarely parted without supporting their fancies with bets, some of which were for very large amounts—so large that it might have been an inconvenient matter for either to settle on losing, unless a good deal of squaring was done before the race.

Sharper concluded that all the large bets which he laid Big Dick and others would cost him nothing to get back, because he looked upon Senator as a local fancy, and when he got to London and met the leviathans there, if he wished to do so, he would be able to effect a profit on all these transactions, so he continued to lay against the horse to all comers the quoted odds.

"You'll see," he would say, "what price Senator will be

when these people have put all their bit of money on; instead of being twenty-five to one, I shall be able to cover at forties."

In this case, doubtless, " the wish was father to the thought," but it was destined never to be realised, and instead of going back to forties, Sharper was horrified and alarmed to find him steadily growing in public favour, the price, day by day, being reduced.

This meant utter ruin to Bob Sharper if Senator should win, and it had now become impossible to cover the bets he had laid against him, as that would mean ruin in case he got beaten. So this dilemma drove him into desperate courses, and he decided to brave it out, trusting to fate in some way to help him out of the difficulty before the eventful day; and if fate didn't help him, he would call in the assistance of his own indomitable will and resourceful ingenuity, and with them mould fate to his own vile purposes. The friends of Senator, having got all their money on at the long odds, made no secret of the merits of their wonderful horse, nor of the trial he had won, which made the race look a good thing for him, so that before the day he had become the actual favourite. This fact, instead of arresting the pencil and nimble fingers of Sharper, only served to increase his zeal in laying against him; and not satisfied with this, he indulged in some very heavy bets with Big Dick, Sandy over Senator, " one to win."

To those who had watched him, and were pretty well acquainted with what he had done, it was evidently a case of "going for the gloves," but this was a matter which was just whispered of here and there, but which the public never for a moment suspected.

One of Sharper's most intimate friends was an ex-steeple-chase jockey, who was at the time training a few jumpers, and who had much in common with him, and it was rumoured that the two had been associated in some questionable dealings and doings on the turf. It was to this ex-jockey, Shem Helas, that

Sharper turned in his trouble for help, and an urgent summons had brought Shem on a visit to his old friend.

"What on earth is the matter, Bob, that you have sent for me in such hot haste?" asked Shem, when the two worthies were quietly closeted in Mr. Sharper's snug private room.

"Well, I've sent for you, Shem, because I can't do without you," began Bob, very deliberately. "I've got myself into a hole over the Grand National, and you will have to get me out of it. I've done a thing or two for you in my time, and I think you will admit you owe me a good turn."

"Well, and I'll do it for you, Bob, if I can. What do you want?"

"Well, I want the favourite for the Grand National stopped," replied Bob bluntly.

"I am sorry for that, old man," answered the other. "In the first place, I've backed Senator myself to win me a couple of hundred, and—"

"Oh, never mind your two hundred! I'll give you that and a monkey on the top of it if you can stop him," interrupted the bookmaker. "And it must and shall be done."

"But you speak as though I were going to steer him in the race," replied Shem; "and you know his trainer and the son who will ride him are standing to win a very large stake. They do him and feed him themselves, and watch him so carefully that there's no chance of getting near him."

"I know all that, and what's more, I know they are pretty sure to do the trick if we can't stop them; and then I'm a broker. You know where they stable their horses for Aintree; go down there and get as close as possible to them, and don't spare any money or trouble; and if we can bring it off, you are a made man."

After long and anxious consultation the friends parted, and Shem, with a heavy purse, was on his way to Liverpool.

The next time they met was the day before the big race,

very early in the morning, in Bob's bedroom at the Adelphi Hotel.

"Well, what luck?" asked Sharper eagerly.

"I wouldn't trust anything to writing," replied the other, "but I think you'll say I've done a good stroke of business. They have only one horse here except Senator, and I've rented the very next box to them, and what's better, I've got the loft which runs over all the five boxes. I told the landlord I wanted it for my lads to sleep in."

"Ah, that's good, very good, Shem!" said Sharper, shaking his friend warmly by the hand. "It won't do for me to be seen near the place, but you tell me exactly what tools you want for the job, and I'll have a parcel here for you to-night."

Two days before that fixed for the race the trainer of Senator and his two sons had arrived at their quarters, within an easy distance of the course at Aintree. The favourite's box was a large and lofty loose one, which they had used many times before, and knew well. There was a small box in connection with it, where they stowed the hay and corn, and everything necessary for their horse, all of which they had brought with them. From early morning till midnight, during the two days preceding the race, one or other of them never lost sight of the animal on which so much depended; and when they did leave for the night, they supplemented the ordinary lock on the stable door with a huge padlock they carried with them.

Senator, on the morning before the day of the race, had done his work on the course in grand style, not only inspiring his backers with increased confidence, but making heaps of new friends, with the result that he was backed during the afternoon in the ring, and in Liverpool at night for immense sums, and was now a very hot favourite.

When the trainer left his horse and double-locked the door upon him, it was with a feeling of intense satisfaction that the noble animal had come so far safely through the dangers which always beset the favourite for a big race, and I have no doubt

R

he went to bed and dreamed—as some of the rest of us did—of the glorious victory which awaited him on the morrow. And none of us dreamt what a sorry morrow it would be for our party. It came to us a keen, crisp, bright March morning, and I turned out earlier than usual. I was too anxious and excited to lay a-bed. I was stepping out of the hotel when I saw approaching me one of the most important members of our party—the one, indeed, who had been chiefly responsible for working the large commission for the owner and others. The first glimpse of his face convinced me some calamity had happened; his eyes were wild and restless; his face, haggard and drawn, appeared to have aged ten years since I left him a few hours before.

"What on earth is the matter?" I gasped. "Nothing amiss with the horse, I hope!"

"It's all up with us," he replied, and he almost had to hold on to me to save himself from falling. "The horse was as well as possible when the old man locked him up last night at eleven o'clock, and when he went at five this morning he was coughing his heart out, and was so dull and stupid they could scarcely get him up. We shall run him, because we don't know what may happen, but the old man says he couldn't possibly get the course. So you had better get as much of your money back as you can, and don't breathe a word to anyone."

"But how has it happened?" I asked. "Surely he has been got at, and you must suspect someone!"

"No, we don't; the locks have not been tampered with, and everything was found exactly as left last night."

I went up to the course with a heavy heart, intending to get out the best way I could before the secret of the horse's condition transpired, but Bob Sharper was one of the earliest in the ring; it was evident the secret was known to him, for he commenced knocking the favourite out, and never left him till the flag was down.

NOBBLING

The first time round, the noble horse, handicapped as he was, jumped faultlessly, and for three miles led the field in gallant style, and the guilty villain who had caused him to be nobbled trembled with fear, and doubtless had for a short time some dreadful sensations. But it was soon all over, and the good horse had to succumb. It was some time before the mystery of the nobbling of Senator could be cleared up, but I think it was made tolerably clear how it was done when a light jemmy was found in the loft, and right over Senator's manger there was abundant evidence that the boards had been prised up and replaced.

CHAPTER XXV

ON TRAINERS AND JOCKEYS

The Reward of Civility—A Horse in the Bog—Jockeys and Owners—George Fordham—Tom Cannon—A Jockey caught Napping.

I HAVE had considerable intercourse with English trainers of the race-horse, and ample opportunity for becoming acquainted with their peculiarities. As in all other professions, of course, there is to be found among them a few who may not be all we could desire. Speaking generally, I believe they are thoroughly straightforward and honourable; able and hard-working in their patrons' service, and absolutely loyal. There is perhaps no class of men which comes in for as much undeserved abuse from the ignorant and unthinking followers of racing. The nature of their occupation tends to make them cute, and loyalty to their employers compels them to be "close." These are among their most notable characteristics, and as in nearly every case they were jockeys before becoming trainers, these most necessary qualities for their occupation were implanted and fostered in their early days, and have become a part of themselves. The following short anecdote will, however, show that one of the closest of them was amenable to the opening pressure of a little act of kindness.

The truth of the old adage, "Civility costs nothing," was demonstrated to me in a remarkable way at the Manchester Autumn Meeting in 1870. It not only cost me nothing—it got me a bit. I was staying at the Merchants' Hotel, Oldham

Street, which was kept in those days by my friend, old Stephen Pettitt. The evening before the Cup was run for I was enjoying a little "snack" in the comfortable dining-room upstairs, having for my next neighbour at the meal a well-known Northern trainer. I was able to show him a few of the customary courtesies of the table, and we became on chatty terms. When he arose from the table I noticed him take out a small pocket-book, and then run over all his pockets in the evidently futile attempt to find a pencil. "Here you are, Mr Blank," I observed, handing him one, "just what you want. I've another in my pocket; you are quite welcome to this." It was a small matter, scarcely worth naming, but I could see that he was pleased with the attention. Later in the evening I met him in the smoke-room, and he insisted on my having a drink with him. He did not know me, but I knew him well by reputation, which gave him the character of a particularly "close" man, able to keep his own counsel, and some of his acquaintances used to say he was harder to draw than a hedgehog, and that if you wanted to know any of his good things you would be quite as likely to get at them by reading his remarks about them backwards as any other way. I was not likely, therefore, to believe he was going to make a confidant of me. And yet, as the sequel will show, so deeply had a trifling kindness touched his rugged nature, he actually did so.

"What's gooing to back for t' Cup to-morrow, young mon?" he asked, just before we parted for the night.

"Well, I think of going a little on Star and Garter," was my reply.

"They'll likely lay odds on that chap," said he, and then was going on his slow way; "but Fearnowt, my lad—"

"Oh, you may depend upon that!" I broke in. "I shall fear nothing, for it looks, according to the book; a snip for Star and Garter."

"Oh, d—n the book!" he answered; "thou'll not take much notice of the book when thou know'st as much as I do.

Fearnowt, my lad, Fearnowt will win t' Cup; and what's more, he'll win again on Saturday."

I saw at once the ludicrous mistake I had made by interrupting him, thanked him, and wished him good-night, making up my mind to have a go on his tip the following day. During the racing I saw my friend several times without having an opportunity of speaking to him. When the numbers went up for the Cup, I was vexed to find that it was a very small field; in fact, the presence of Star and Garter had frightened away all but Fearnought and Discretion. As soon as the betting commenced the public rushed on Star and Garter, with the result that those who were, like myself, "in the know," got some respectable prices about Fearnought, who at the finish was well backed by some of the cleverest men in the ring down to 2 to 1, while others laid 7 to 4 on the good thing. As the betting indicated, the race was entirely between the two. Wood was riding the favourite, and once I thought it was all over and my money gone; but Gray, on Fearnought, put in some very pretty work when nearing the winning-post, and, to my great joy, got home by a neck, and I had a very substantial reason for feeling thankful for Mr. Blank's "straight tip," which was entirely due to a little well-timed civility.

The next day was Saturday, and I had some reasons for wanting to get home, but the hint I had received about Fearnought winning a second race induced me to stay with the determination of playing up my winnings on him for the second race. I found his number hoisted with three others in the Heaton Park Cup, and there Prince, with old Job Toon up, was a warm favourite. Johnny Osborne had this time the mount on Fearnought., and I felt glad it was so, as he was one of my favourite jockeys. I was just preparing for the intended dash on him, when I caught sight of my friend Blank a few yards away, looking very hard at me. Fancying he wanted to speak to me, I made for him.

"Have backed t' hoss this time?" were his first words.

"No; but I was just going to do so," I replied.

"Well, maybe he'll win, but he'll have a stiff job. He'll likely run in the Trafford Handicap later on, and that looks easier for him," was his answer, as he walked hurriedly away. He was meeting the four-year-old Prince at 2 lb. for the year, and giving considerable weight to old Winyard, so I looked on. After all, the race was a very pretty one, but he was beaten about half a length by Prince. After missing one race, Fearnought and Prince were both pulled out again for the De Trafford Handicap; but this time Prince had to put up a penalty, and was giving Fearnought 13 lb. on the previous running. This made it look like "a moral" for my champion to beat Prince, and, with nothing else to fear, I felt capable of playing up my winnings, and staking my shirt as well on him, but there was another among the runners who inspired fear within me; this was the five-year-old Pretty John, ridden by my old friend, Johnny Osborne, and backed by every square-head in the ring as though there was nothing else in the race. Everything conspired to shake my confidence, but I bethought myself of my rugged friend's remark, and went manfully to work, backing Fearnought at about 4 to 1 to win a very good stake. This was one of the prettiest races of the meeting between three—Gradwell now was up on Fearnought, Gray on Ralph Lambton, and old Johnny on his namesake. It was close and exciting, and at the finish you could have covered the three with a sheet; but Fearnought secured the verdict by a neck, and Ralph Lambton beat the favourite by but a shade farther, Prince this time being nowhere.

It is not within the scope of my present purpose to write of the celebrities among trainers, such as the Scotts, Days, and Dawsons of my time, but to give just two or three sketches of a very different class, who confined their operations, for the most part, to the small leather-flapping meetings.

As I have remarked, they are proverbially a cute race, and

in nothing do they prove this more than in cases where they have the misfortune to be invited, by suspicious stewards, to explain the reason of a horse running perhaps a couple of stone better to-day than he did yesterday. The horse's "well-known bad temper" does frequent and efficacious service, as we have seen more than once recently; and that is doubtless in some cases a very valid reason. But then, how about the market? I am afraid it is not the horse's temper which affects that.

I remember a notorious west-country owner and trainer many years ago whose horse opened a hot favourite for a certain race, and then, for no reason which was apparent, went right out of the betting; and need I say he was nowhere in the race? The following day he was in a similar race, and the owner backed him for pounds, shillings, and pence, and of course he won. This was too glaring even for Worcester, so this worthy was cited before the stewards.

"Now, Mr. Blank," said the senior steward, "will you kindly explain to the gentlemen how it happens that your horse has run so much better to-day than yesterday?"

"I will do that with pleasure," replied the owner. "It's in this way, your honours. My jockey got the horse in a bog yesterday, which lost him the race; to-day I showed him how to steer clear of it."

This explanation was confirmed by the jockey, and being adjudged entirely satisfactory, both left the dock—room, I should say—without a stain on their characters, and it never occurred to the wise stewards to seek for an explanation about the betting.

Thirty years ago old Ben Land was a well-known owner and trainer, and in the western counties he cut and dried many nice little jobs. In his time he had a few useful horses, but he didn't despise the "leather-flappers" and the small plums which were to be picked up at some of the little country hunt meetings. He had a flapper called Skyrocket running at one of these meetings in Wales, where the management was entirely in the hands of amateurs. The judge was a fox-hunting old squire, nevertheless a mere country bumpkin, and old Ben was not slow to see some possibilities in this fact, so he planted himself quite close to the judge to watch the race, and when he saw that at the finish it was going to be reduced to a match between his own horse and one of the others as they came towards the winning-post, he began crying out lustily:

"Skyrocket wins! Skyrocket wins!" and as they passed the post, he shouted: "Skyrocket's won, sir!" so the judge put up Skyrocket,'s number. He afterwards admitted that he thought the other had won, but the gentleman at his side was so confident, he concluded he was, perhaps, mistaken. Everybody else was quite positive he had been so in hoisting Skyrocket's number, who was a pretty good second.

The relation of jockeys and owners has undergone considerable change during my acquaintance with the turf. I remember when jockeys were in the habit of looking up to the gentlemen who employed them with no little measure of respect. And a jockey who dared to give a saucy answer to such men as General Peel, Sir Joseph Hawley, or Lord Glasgow would have stood in imminent peril of losing their license. Alfred Day, old Tom Alcroft, or Tiny Wells would never have dreamt of behaving towards their employers as I have seen little chits of lads behave in recent years. It must not, however, be supposed that the lads are solely to blame; owners have, in a large measure, themselves to thank for this state of things; the lads are pampered and puffed up, and made so much of. And they are in a position to earn so much money that it is almost a wonder we find any of them with the slightest remnant of modesty about them. As far as I am able to judge, the new order of things set in with little Jimmy Grimshaw, and it has been growing steadily worse ever since.

The fact is, the system is to blame, and requires a radical

change. At present owners are too dependent upon a few popular light weights, and there are not half enough jockeys. Among the many hundreds of lads in our training stables, I have no doubt there may be found the material for scores of riders as capable as those before the public, and it is a pity some means cannot be devised for giving these lads fairer opportunities. In this direction, I am persuaded, there may be found a means of diminishing an evil which is well understood and very generally deplored, but which those in authority appear to lack the nerve to tackle.

Time was when owners of any note kept their own jockeys, who rarely rode for anybody else. Their names never appeared in the few newspapers or calenders which chronicled the races they were engaged in. They not only rode, but they had to groom their horses and take them about from meeting to meeting, and if a generous master gave them a guinea when they rode a winner, they considered themselves lucky. And the hardships many of them underwent it would be impossible for a modern jockey to realise, a bare recital of which would now make a fifth-rate member of the profession bristle with indignation. Jockeys nowadays scarcely groom themselves, much less their horses, and have highly-paid valets to fetch and carry for them; when at home live in mansions, smoke shilling cigars, and drink wines which a bishop could not afford.

Instead of walking or ambling weary distances on a wretched nag to the scenes of their labour, some of them travel with quite a retinue of followers and servants, and lounge away the time in luxurious first-class carriages; while their earnings during the eight months of the year they are at work make the salary of the Archbishop of Canterbury or the Prime Minister look simply ridiculous.

I have been frequently asked to say whom I consider the greatest jockey of my time; and looking through the long list, I find many who were almost faultless masters of the art, and

TRAINERS AND JOCKEYS

it may seem invidious to award the palm to any particular one, and in doing so I am aware that my opinion will not be endorsed by some racing men of long experience and great judgment. It is, after all, a matter of opinion; and while I hold to my own with some tenacity, I am bound to respect that of the friends who differ with me. I give it, then, as my own humble opinion, that looking at the subject from every point of view, and "taking him for all in all," George Fordham was the greatest jockey we have seen for forty years. Kitchener, Tiny Wells, Tom Alcroft, the elder Grimshaw, French, Harry Custance, Fred Archer, Tom Cannon, John Osborne, and probably two or three others, may be named as the great horsemen of my time. I have known no more determined finisher than poor Harry Grimshaw—witness that grand race between him and Fordham on Fille de l'Air and General Peel in the Claret Stakes at Newmarket, in 1865. Who that saw it will ever forget it? I certainly will not

"While memory holds her seat in this distracted globe."

Wells, Custance, and Archer were equally great at a finish. Tom Cannon had beautiful hands, and could handle a youngster with anybody. Osborne had that marvellous judgment of pace which got him home many a time, where any other jockey would have been beaten. They were all great in a way; but I fail to find in either of them, in an equal degree, that combination of qualities which go to make the great horseman as, in my opinion, distinguished Fordham. At a finish he had no superior; his terrible rushes were the dread of his opponents; and while he never took an unfair advantage, by the occasional use of what was known as "*kidment*"—an accomplishment almost peculiar to himself—he succeeded in throwing the oldest hands off their guard. The most wonderful thing about him, perhaps, and where he surpassed all other riders, was his gentle treatment of rogues; what others failed to do with whip and spur, he did without them, coaxing them, as it were, to do their best. Once at Newmarket I remember him riding quite a close finish on a notorious rogue; and winning while patting a horse's neck and talking to him, when there was not the slightest doubt that the mere sound of a whip, or the suggestion of a spur, would have stopped him. In fact, I never knew any jockey who could get so much out of any sort of horse without the employment of these overrated implements of torture, and I question very much if they are of anything like the value some riders set upon them, and I believe more races are lost by their excessive use than are won by them. His generous helpfulness to young jockeys, his amiable disposition, and his many personal good qualities, have, of course, nothing to do with this question; but I hope some day to have an opportunity of doing justice to them also.

A few seasons ago I often heard it remarked how wonderful it was to find Charley Wood, after being away from his profession so long, riding so well, and it speaks volumes for his steady, regular habits; for it must be remembered it was not a case of being suspended for a season—he was off for more than nine years.

Poor old Fordham retired at the second October Meeting at Newmarket in 1875, and we never expected to see him resume his profession; and at the time of his retirement, I believe he had no intention of doing so. Circumstances, however, happened which induced him to alter his purpose, and to the delight of his hosts of friends, he reappeared at his favourite battle-ground, the scene of so many brilliant exploits—Newmarket Heath—at the Craven Meeting in 1878, and I shall never forget the reception he met with. His first mount was on Pardon in the Bushes Handicap; his old opponent, Archer, just managed to do him on Advance. Then standing down for one race, he was found up again on Pardon in the Bretby Plate; and this time he was victorious, beating Dunkenny (who was on odds-on chance) and four others. And who that witnessed his return to scale will ever forget the enthusiasm which greeted the popular and unparalleled horseman? Hats were thrown in the air; hundreds struggled to shake hands with him. These and other signs of excitement and delight testified to the fact that he was still the best beloved of all jockeys.

After this, the great jockey went on riding as brilliantly as of old; but it lasted for only a few seasons. It then became evident that his health and strength were gone, and at Windsor, in 1884, he had his last mount on Aladdin. He lasted, however, for a few years longer, and died at Slough, which he had made for years his home, October 12, 1887.

I was on board one of the Bournemouth boats, bound for a sail round the Isle of Wight, in company with an ancient friend of mine, who is also a well-known and genial turfite of the punter species. But even at that hazardous profession he has managed to hold his own—and a bit of the bookies'—for many years; and, in fact, as my friend Richard Henry Fry has more than once declared (I suppose with sufficient reason), he is "no catch." We were slowly steaming past the glorious East Cliffs, when I drew his attention to the beautiful marine residence occupied by Tom Cannon, and just discernible among the pines. Now, it so happens that the great horseman is almost a demi-god with my old friend, and this incident was quite enough to set him going in a glorification of his idol, which lasted till we were well past the Needles.

"I have seen all your great jockeys for the last fifty years," he said, "and not one, taking him all round, could give him a start; and in handling a tender two-year-old, none that could come near him."

"I know you have won a pile of money following him," I said. "Just tell me what you think was his greatest achievement."

"Well, it's difficult to choose where there is so much to pick from," he replied; "but it has always seemed to me that his getting home on Enthusiast for the Two Thousand Guineas was one of the most wonderful races I ever saw. Of course, I backed him, as I generally did, no matter what he rode; but it went a bit against the grain that day, I can tell you. I knew Donovan was a great horse, and didn't well see how he could be beaten. The 'heads' were laying four or five to one on him. Besides, among the runners were Gold, and Pioneer, with Jack Watts up, and several other useful animals; and to tell you the truth, although I was obliged to back Cannon, according to a little theory of my own, which I was trying at the time, I felt something like throwing the money away. The bookies didn't think much of my chance either, for I was able to get about thirty to one. And what a race it was!—I shall never forget it—Tom Cannon, to my surprise, sticking close to Fred Barrett on the favourite, and Watts lying at their girths. Of course, I expected at every stride to see Donovan leave them, but he couldn't do it; and just on the post Tom seemed fairly to lift his horse, and get home by a head. It was not Enthusiast that won me the money that day; it was Tom Cannon, my lad, and no other jockey in the world could have done it."

On this subject the old man would endure no contradiction, and perhaps he was right.

There are few jockeys who have not some time been "caught napping." One of the most amusing and glaring cases I can call to mind occurred at Worcester.

The late venerable Colonel Forester was rather an irritable old gentleman at times, and not the most philosophical loser in the world, as I am from personal experience able to aver. He was not a heavy bettor as a rule, but when he had an unusual amount on one of his brother-in-law's (the Earl of Bradford) or on anything coming from Stanton, you might bet your boots they were very hot goods. Therefore, should you find him laying long odds, and to a good deal of money, on one of his own, hot wouldn't be the word for it. I remember, however, his doing this on one occasion when he did not win—that was not his fault, or the horse's either, for the matter of that. It was simply a case of the jockey caught napping.

The Colonel had a useful old hunter named Professor, running in a race at Worcester. The opposition was very small, and also very bad. The Colonel laid me thirty-five pounds to twenty on his old horse, aud I very soon discovered that I had made a bad bet; this was the experience of several other layers also, for nothing else was backed for a shilling. The only one which had the remotest chance with the favourite was a stable companion ridden by a lad out of Wadlow's stable. George Lowe, at that time a very capable gentleman rider well known all over the west country, was up on Professor. I can see them now as they came up the straight for the finish, Lowe's horse cantering home a hundred yards in front of his stable companion, and the other two, or three, a long way in the rear. George had a look behind him, and seeing the state of affairs, deliberately pulled his horse up, and determined to actually "win in a walk," never for a moment dreaming that the stable companion would beat him, even if he could, and the others, he knew, were hopelessly out of it. But nothing had been said to Wadlow's lad, and when he saw what had happened, instead of easing his horse, he set him going with all his might. The gallant Colonel and the other layers of the odds began screaming at George to go on. He never realised what it all meant, till twenty yards from the post he saw the outsider upon him. Then he tried to set the old horse going again; but it was too late—the outsider had won. I rode from Worcester to Birmingham that night in company with Colonel Forester, and I shall never forget it, and I don't think poor George would either had he been there. The old man had, I believe, at some time been unfortunate enough to have some of his bones badly broken, but I feel certain his sufferings then were mild by comparison.

CHAPTER XXVI

A TRAINER'S STORY

How he was broken—How mended.

It was Christmas Day—I won't say how many years ago. As far as the weather went, it was anything but an ideal Christmas Day. Instead of the hard earth being wrapped in a mantle of pure white snow, there was mud, and slush, and water everywhere under foot; and in place of the bright, crisp air one loves to associate with that blessed day, it was moist and misty, and clung on to one like impecunious relations. It was impossible to wipe it off. It produced a sense of dreariness and chill which was harder to bear than the coldest frost, and penetrated to the very temper of a man. It was such a day when one closes the shutters with a bang and lights up early—a day one longs to shut out. On such a Christmas Day, of course, the best place for a man is the bosom of his family, in his own home. But supposing a man has no family or home, or that the exigencies of his circumstances forbid him those blessings on that particular day—well, all I can say is, that he could scarcely be in a better place than the cosy bar-parlour of the old Woolpack. Everybody knows the old Woolpack Hotel, with its huge gateway in the centre of it, through which the famous old coachman, Peedle, fifty years ago, used to drive his team of reeking horses, and the celebrated London stage-coach, "Tally-Ho." Everybody knows the great yard, where the coach used to load and unload, and change horses, and all are familiar with the time-worn front of the hotel itself, with its

A TRAINER'S STORY 273

great bay windows, and balcony running the whole length of it, which was used as a hustings, from which the Tory candidate for the county, and his friends were in the habit of holding forth to our enlightened fathers.

But everybody didn't know that cosy bar-parlour where we were assembled on this particular Christmas Day; on ordinary occasions that was an experience reserved for the select among the residents in the good old county town, and the neighbourhood. At race time, however, it was reserved almost entirely for the use of a few racing men—trainers, jockeys and others—who had made the Woolpack their home, during the races for many years past.

After dinner on the Christmas Day in question, old Timothy Westland, the trainer, Shute Holmes, and several other celebrated professional cross-country riders, several notable bookmakers, and at least one well-known owner of race-horses, were the occupants of the bar-parlour. After a dinner which can be no better described than by simply saying it was worthy the house, the handsome hostess, and the day, this jovial company, as befitted the occasion, felt on very good terms with themselves and all mankind; and if they didn't indulge in a "feast of reason and a flow of soul," there was an abundant flow of good-fellowship, and of something beside, accompanied with cigars of the choicest brands, and conversation became animated and interesting.

"Look here, gentlemen," said old Tim, "we are unfortunate in being obliged to be away from home this day, but as the races are to-morrow, and we live so far away, it was unavoidable, so we must make the best of it, and enjoy ourselves as well as we can. In the first place, I'll ask you to drink a toast, which all will do most heartily. Here's to our absent friends—God bless them, and may they have a happy Christmas!"

This short and homely speech was received with acclamation, and the toast honoured with enthusiasm.

"And now," continued old Tim, "as the weather isn't the

sort to be out of doors in, and as the billiard-room is locked up, and we can't very well sing songs, I'm going to propose that we amuse ourselves telling tales."

"Hear, hear, hear!" shouted the company as with one voice.

"And I propose," cried out Shute Holmes, "that Mr. Westland tells the first story."

This proposal also, was cordially received; whereupon old Tim laid down his cigar, gave a cough or two by way of preparation, and with a swig at his grog by way of clearing his throat, began:

"Well, gentlemen, I don't mind telling a story, only, as I don't know any romantic fairy tales, you will have to put up with something that's true; and as I have heard say that truth is often stranger than fiction, perhaps a chapter out of my own early life would amuse you. And when I've done, perhaps my friend, Shute Holmes, will give us a short jockey's story, and I know we have an owner in the company who tells a good story; and then Will Froste as an old bookmaker, is sure to cap the lot.

"I'm going to tell you a little story of how I got broken by a man, and mended again by a horse. You all know that in my early days I was a rather famous light-weight jockey. I made a good deal of money in those days, because I was very successful, and rode a great many winners; but I made the money for somebody else—that was the trainer I was apprenticed to. I did the work, and he nailed the stuff. But, Lord bless you, in those days neither owners nor the punters who followed you were a hundredth part as generous as they are in these times. Nowadays a jockey turns up his nose at a tip of a pony or fifty pounds; we used to be thankful for half a quid, so that I wasn't able to save a lot of money during my apprenticeship, and as I put on a good deal of weight towards the end of it, when I was my own master I found myself too heavy to get many mounts. That brought me to cross-country riding, and I daresay you will have heard, if you don't remember, that I was able to take my own part at that.

"It was while I was at this work that I got married. I married the girl I'd been sweet on from a nipper, and we were very happy. In the course of three or four years, finding a little family springing up about me, I began to think it was time to make some sort of provision for my lass and the youngsters, in case of anything happening to me. I was doing pretty well, earning plenty of money to keep us all well. But I couldn't help asking myself what would happen when I got too heavy for cross-country riding, or if some accident should befal me.

"This led me to think of my present business, and having the offer of four or five horses belonging to a very good fellow, I made up my mind to start. It happened at the same time that there was a lovely little place to let called Rose Cottage, within half a mile of Winton Downs, which is, as you know, one of the best training grounds in England. Rose Cottage had attached to it a compact little farm of about two hundred acres, which had been used before for the purpose of training jumpers, so I had everything nicely ready to my hand.

"I had never tried to save much money so far, but I'd managed to get a good home together, and perhaps I'd got £800 or £900 in the bank when I took Rose Cottage. Well, I began business there as a trainer, and I did very well with our small stud; I think we won in our turn. I and the missus were very happy—we never knew the want of money, although we weren't rich; we kept a good house, which was open to all our friends, so perhaps you will be able to guess that, although we lived well, we didn't save much.

"I now became acquainted with the man who was to break me—an Irish owner and trainer and horse-jobber, named Jack Hawke. I met him first at Manchester, where I was running a horse, and where he was running several. In a fatal moment I invited him to Rose Cottage. He came almost at once, and we became great friends; he had a glib, plausible tongue, and a manner that would cheat the devil. He told me how much he liked the place, what a quiet spot it would be to ready a Grand National winner, and then he entrusted me with the secret that he and his brother had got a Grand National winner at their place in Ireland, the best lepper in the world; and he finished up by proposing that they should send all their horses to me to train, and that he or his brother Joe—who was a topping cross-country jockey—should ride them. So certain did he make it appear that we should all win a fortune, and that quickly, I agreed to take their horses only, although it obliged me to break with my first and best patron.

"Well, as you already know, I daresay, I trained the winner of the Grand National for them, and Joe Hawke rode him, and I won a nice bit of money. But somehow I didn't get rich; I am afraid I spent too much, for I was really anxious to make everybody belonging to me, and about me, happy, and I always felt I couldn't do enough for the Hawkes.

"They now imposed a condition upon me that I should not only keep all the secrets of their horses, and their own intentions in respect to them, but that I should do all my own backing through them. This I looked upon as only a natural precaution. I did very little through the summer, as I had laid myself out for the jumping business, and as my style of living had now become a trifle extravagant, towards the opening of our next season I had run out of all my ready money, and I told Jack Hawke as much, for I may tell you that both he and his brother now lived, almost entirely, at Rose Cottage.

"'Never mind that,' said he, 'when the jumping begins we'll be getting you a lot of stuff, and meanwhile you can have whatever money you want of me, just giving me merely the security of your name, on a bit of paper, then you can pay me back again out of your winnings.'

"This I thought was very noble treatment, so I signed what he brought me almost without looking at the paper, I felt such an unbounded confidence in him. Then I began drawing whatever money I required, for I may tell you that what they paid me for their small stud of horses was not half enough to keep Rose Cottage going, now the Hawkes were with us.

"Well, the season commenced, and I believed we should win races with all our horses; and when they ran with Joe Hawke up, I asked his brother to back them for me, which he did, or professed to do; but we were beaten time after time, and Joe had always some plausible excuse for it. I was now owing them so much money, I began to get nervous. The only race we had won for the first two months was a selling hurdle race, and the horse that won was so very much inferior to all the others that when they proposed he should run and take his chance, unbacked, I quite agreed with them; but you can imagine my feelings when he won in a canter. I didn't then imagine foul play, but I couldn't understand him starting a red-hot favourite, and Hawke buying him in for two hundred and fifty guineas. However, when I spoke to them about it, they assured me they hadn't a penny on, and I was bound to believe them.

"Other matters besides racing began to go badly with me. My first-born, a beautiful little boy who was the pet of everybody about the place, his mother's very life, and the light of my eyes, was taken with the fever and died. It was a sad blow for me, but I thought my poor girl would never get over it. She was heart-broken, and lay for more than a fortnight between life and death, and I thought I was going to lose her also.

"I was obliged to leave her. We had a beautiful young chaser in a race at the Manchester New Year's Meeting; he was bottom-weight in a handicap steeple-chase, and had nothing to beat, and as I had tried him very good, it looked a cert for him. I told my patrons so, and they agreed with me; and it was arranged that Joe should ride him, and I should have a couple of hundred pounds on. This was a big plunge for me; but I was anxious to get out of debt, and it did look such a moral. When I had weighed out for the horse and saddled him, I went into the betting ring to see what price was laid. There were eight runners, and the fielders were laying three to one on the field. The favourite was quite a commoner, that I felt confident we could beat with a good deal more to carry than we had. My horse was evidently liked by the good judges, and was being backed at fives. I went on to the stand to see the preliminary; mine was the gentleman of the lot, and pleased everyone so well that he became first favourite. I was in a fever of excitement while they cantered slowly down to the starting-post. After they had started, a very old friend came running up the stand to me.

"'What have you backed?' I asked him.

"'I've backed yours,' was the reply; 'but I needn't tell *you*, I suppose, I'm in the cart.'

"'What on earth do you mean?' I inquired.

"'I mean what I say,' said he. 'I'm on a wrong 'un, if ever I saw one. When there was a rush to be on yours, I, like a fool, without knowing anything, followed the heads, and dashed my pony on; but it was no sooner on than I tumbled it was all wrong. Tom Restill, who laid me, never left him, or missed a shilling, and I'm not such a fool as not to understand what that means; he's a safe 'un, I tell you, whether you are in it or not.'

"I tried to laugh at him, but I'm afraid it was only a sickly attempt. 'You are mistaken,' I said, 'for I am standing two hundred pounds with the owner. Still, you might run down and see how Restill bets now; I see they're coming up the straight, and my horse is bang in front.'

"While he ran down for this purpose, my eyes were riveted on my horse, who jumped faultlessly, and came past the stand, the first time, leading four lengths. I lost sight of them on the far side, and didn't get a clear view of them till they came into the straight again, and then I was thunderstruck to find my horse wasn't with them. I saw him walking through the crowd down the course after the others had passed the post.

"'Are you satisfied now?' inquired my frined, when he rejoined me. 'When your horse was leading lengths and jumping beautifully, old Restill went on quietly laying all he could, and never missed a bob at any price, and he's the man that's had the job.'

"I felt too ill to argue the matter with my friend, so I got rid of him and went into the paddock to meet Joe and the horse.

"'What does this mean?' was my first question to the jockey.

"'It means that he refused a fence on the far side of the course,' was his reply.

"'That's very strange,' I said; 'he never knew how to refuse a fence since the first one he jumped.'

"'You speak as though you thought there was something wrong about it,' said Jack Hawke, who, I found, was standing at my elbow.

"'There's a lot I don't understand; but perhaps you wouldn't mind telling me with whom you put my two hundred pounds on?' I said.

"'Old Restill—' he began, but stopped suddenly, as though he realised that it might not be policy to mention names. 'No, be damned to you, I'll tell you nothing!' he hissed, while I could see the Irish blood rush into his face.

"He turned from me abruptly, and I stood for a minute or two like one in a dream. I knew something dreadful was going to happen; but I didn't realise how dreadful it would be. My head lad, who was a countryman of the Hawkes', and their creature, went home with the horse, and I saw no more of them that day. Ours was the last race, and the rings and paddock were nearly deserted before I could make up my mind what to do.

"I was anxious to get home to my poor wife, but I felt I

must have it out with them before I went, and also that I would see Restill and demand to see his book, so I determined I would remain in Manchester that night and attend the races the next day. This I did; but when I made inquiry for the Hawkes I was told that they had left Manchester the previous evening; nor could I find Restill. It appeared he had found it convenient to be taken suddenly ill, and had gone home.

"I wouldn't stay for the racing, but hurried off to catch the first train. As I passed the weighing-room one of the officials ran out and handed me a telegram, which I found was from my wife. 'For God's sake, come at once!' was all the message said.

"I had nearly two hundred miles to go to reach my home; so, wiring that I was on my way, I took the first train, my head and heart all on fire with terror and excitement, and my brain utterly bewildered. What could this short strange message portend? If it had not been sent by my wife, I should have concluded she was worse, if not dead. Perhaps something had happened to another of my little ones? Fearful thoughts of accidents, fire, and even murder haunted me all the way; and although going express rate, the train seemed all too slow for my anxious heart.

"It was ten o'clock at night when I reached Rose Cottage. I found the door locked, which was unusual when I was expected. I gave a sharp rap, and the door was at once opened by a strange man; you know the sort—a thick-necked, bull-dog-looking ruffian, and I saw another standing in the hall.

"'Who are you, and what brings you here?' I asked him in dismay.

"'We are in possession for Mr. John Hawke,' he replied. 'That's all we know, and if you want to know more you must see him.'

"Without wasting more words on them, I rushed upstairs, where my wife was still confined to her bed. I found her very ill, and almost broken-hearted. Well, I needn't tell you what

I felt that night, or how I got through it. For the sake of my poor lass I undressed and pretended to sleep, but sleep was out of the question. Long before daylight I was up and at the stables, but I found them also in possession of strange men, who, to all my inquiries, could do nothing but refer me to Mr. John Hawke. After comforting my wife as well as I could, I made my way to the town, five miles away, for the purpose of consulting my lawyer. He wanted to know what I had signed when Hawke lent me the money. I couldn't tell him anything about it. Of course, he pitched into me for signing anything without solicitor's advice, and told me in plain English I was a fool for signing anything I didn't understand. However, he promised he would go in and see Hawke's solicitor, and get at the nature of the deed I had foolishly put my name to. I sat in the office waiting for him perhaps an hour, but it seemed a day, and at last he came back, looking very serious.

"'You have done a nice thing for yourself,' he began. 'It's a lot worse than I thought. Why, you have assigned everything you have in the world to that blackguard by an absolute bill of sale, and it's no use kicking against it; all the lawyers in the country, with the Lord Chancellor at the head of them, couldn't get you out of the hole.'

"Of course, I raved and fumed, and threatened to do all sorts of things to the thieving Irishmen, who had no doubt deliberately robbed me, and, like the filthy blackguards they are, had abused the confidence I had placed in them. But it was all to no purpose; in a few days I and my sick wife and little children were turned adrift from my pretty home at Rose Cottage. I soon saw the trap I had fallen into, and I knew enough to satisfy myself how I had been done; and during those days I do believe I should have killed those villains or made away with myself, if it hadn't been for the thought of what would become of my poor lass and the little ones; and often and often, when she began to get better, she cheered me up.

"'It will be all for the best in the end, my lad,' she would say. 'It will teach you a lesson for the future; and as for those dreadful men, don't think about them; they'll be punished without your troubling.' It was very hard to think so at the time, but I believe the little woman was wiser than I was.

"One day, about a month after being turned out of Rose Cottage, I was surprised to find my first patron, Mr. Lones, finding his way to our humble lodgings. I was the more surprised because, to tell the truth, I considered he had every right to charge me with bad treatment in pitching over the man who had first started me, for the sake of strangers. I looked at it in this way, but, bless your heart, such thoughts never entered into his head—leastways if they did, he never showed it. He had a heart of gold, had that old Lones. He was that kind and affable like that my poor lass fairly broke down, and had to go upstairs to have her cry out, and it took me all my time to prevent myself blubbering in the old man's face, especially when he said I could have his horses back if I could find a decent place for them, and he would let me have what money I wanted to make a start. And as an earnest of his intentions, he insisted on me taking £50 on account. I shall never forget his kindness; and if the dear old fellow was alive, and here now, I think he would tell you that I did my best to repay it.

"Well, I went on very quietly for two or three years. I hadn't any very grand tools to work with, so wasn't able to save a lot of money. Still, I saved what I could, and I managed to buy a little horse out of a two-year-old selling race, because he appeared to me very unfit, and capable of a lot of improvement. I gave him plenty of work, and did him well, and in about a month you wouldn't have known him; so I entered him in another selling race, and I hadn't the slightest doubt I could win, so I persuaded my friend Lones to have a hundred pounds on. I had fifty on myself, which was all I could afford; if I had been better off I should have had a monkey on, so good did it appear. It was at Lichfield; there were only five runners. A horse that had won the previous day, and had been bought in for seventy guineas, was made an even money favourite. Mine and two of the others were pretty nearly equally backed at about five to one. The one without a friend at all was a wretched-looking three-year-old filly named Rails, owned and trained by a local man. And as she stood in the paddock to be saddled, I am sure nobody would have given a fiver for her; but I was struck with her beautiful action the moment she moved. I drew Lones' attention to it, and remarked: 'If anything beats us, it will be that ragged-looking mare.' It was a good start, but before they had travelled a couple of hundred yards my little horse and the ragged mare were out by themselves lengths in front of the others; and the gap was increased as they came within a distance of the winning-post. Neck and neck they came along, locked together, and I saw at a glance my horse couldn't get away from Rails; and when my jockey began to ride, I knew it was all over. The outsider won by a length. I rushed down to meet them coming in, resolving that I would make Lones buy that wretched-looking mare, whatever she might cost. She hadn't turned a hair, and wouldn't have blown a match out, so little was she distressed as they walked her towards the sale ring. I rushed to find Mr. Lones, but he was not to be found, so fearing to lose her I went to the sale. The auctioneer had asked several times if there was any advance on £50, and there was no response. The meanness of her looks frightened everybody. 'Make it fifty guineas,' I said, and was astounded when I found her knocked down to me at that price. 'Put her down to Mr. Lones,' I said to the auctioneer, and then I went in search of my patron and told him what I had done. I told him I had bought him a horse that I thought was possibly worth ten times what I had given for it. 'Well, then, you keep it for yourself, my lad,' said he. I told him I had had the mare charged to him, and that I really hadn't the money after paying the fifty I had lost over my own horse.

"'Then let them charge it to me,' he replied; 'you and I will settle that by-and-by,' and I could not persuade him to become the owner of that wonderful mare at such an absurd price, and yet I am sure he held my opinion that she was worth a lot more. The fact was he thought that as she had caused me to lose on my own horse, I ought to have whatever profit there might be in her. I took them both home, and the following week I entered my little horse in another selling race, and there was a field twice as large as at Lichfield, and much the same class.

"'I don't like asking you to back the little horse again, after your bad luck at Lichfield,' I said to Mr. Lones, 'but I believe he'll win.'

"'Yes, I think he will,' he replied, 'because he may not meet a Rails this time; but what are *you* going to have on?'

"'Nothing at all,' I answered; 'I shall have to be contented with the stake.'

"'Oh, that be blowed!' answered the generous old man; 'I shall put your bit on with mine.'

"There was a kind of lump in my throat which prevented my answering, so I hurried off to weigh out and saddle my horse, expecting that he would most likely put me a tenner on. I didn't see him again until after the race was over, which my little horse won by a couple of lengths. My first inquiry, when I returned to the ring after weighing in, was for the price of the winner, and you may imagine my surprise when I found mine had finished a good favourite at five to two. Running against Lones, I said:

"'I'm sorry you have had such a poor price, sir. I never dreamt of being favourite. Somebody must have had a dash on him. Have you any idea who it is?'

"'Who do you think?' answered the old man, with a merry

A TRAINER'S STORY

twinkle in his eyes, which showed me, at once, who the dasher had been. 'I got a good price to commence with,' he went on, 'and your money will average six to one, and I took the liberty of putting you fifty on.'

"There was no time to tell him then how much I thanked him, for the horse was in the auctioneer's hands. He was a little horse, and although he had won easily, there was not a very strong competition for him, so I was able to get him back for a hundred and fifty guineas. I may tell you the little two-year-old won me several races after that, and a nice bit of money, and then I sold him for a monkey.

"But I must come now to the ragged mare, as I always called her; for it was that wonderful bit of horse-flesh that put me on my legs.

"About this time I was preparing a good-looking three-year-old for a valuable handicap, over two miles, and had got him nearly fit. I hadn't given him a regular trial, but he had done so well in a rough-up with the best we had in the stable, that we seemed to have a real good chance, so Mr. Lones backed him quietly at long prices to win a large stake. A week before the race we arranged to have a regular trial. The principal trial horse was a recent winner over two miles, belonging to a friend of Lones', which he had borrowed for the purpose, and when all was settled, I suggested that Rails should be put in, for the first mile, to make a good pace, as I was under the impression she would be better at a mile than five or six furlongs, which was as far as she had hitherto gone; but from the way she finished, I felt certain she would stay. One of my little lads rode the selling plater; I saddled her myself, and nobody else had the slightest idea what weight she was carrying, everybody, of course, supposing it was a feather-weight, to enable her to make the pace pretty hot for half the journey. I gave my lad orders to make the running with Rails, for the first mile, as sharp as he could go, and then if he found her pumped out to pull her up; but if he found her going well, he was to go on with them, and finish as close up as possible.

"Well, when the flag was dropped my mare rushed to the front, and made the running for half a mile, but she did not seem able to get away from them, and as they neared the mile I fully expected to see the boy pull her up, but he didn't, and she went swinging along in her free-and-easy style, it seemed to me, faster the farther she went, and at the end of the two miles she had won by ten lengths. This was a revelation to me, and I was awfully excited, but didn't shout about it. Lones seemed a bit down-hearted, for although his horse had fairly answered the question put to him, as far as his other trial nags went, he couldn't get over the fact that he had been beaten so far by a common plater, although, as he supposed, at a considerable difference in the weight.

"'I shall scratch my horse,' he said, when we got quietly together, over a nice little lunch at my house. 'He can have no earthly chance if he couldn't beat a selling plater, like your mare, at any weights.'

"'Suppose I told you they were running at even weights, what should you say?' I asked.

"'I should, of course, know I'd no chance, and strike mine out of the handicap at once,' he replied.

"'Well, then, that's how they did run,' I replied, 'and even then you won't be foolish enough not to run for your money, for has not this trial, with my mare out of the question, told you all you want to know? How do you know how good Rails may be over a long course?' and so I talked him out of the idea of scratching his horse for the handicap, which, in fact, he won.

"And after that we knew we had a nailing good mare in the selling plater, so I entered her in several handicaps, and, of course, they could give her nothing but bottom-weight. Some of my friends thought I was mad, but when they saw her simply canter in for the first of them they rather altered their opinion. I won a good stake without much risk, because, although I had made a wonderful improvement in her appearance, she was always a ragged-looking lot, and people did not fancy her. She won the three handicaps right off the reel, for her penalty couldn't stop her; and she won for me and my old friend Lones a lot of money, and I have never looked back from that day to this.

"But for my accidentally, as it were, finding out that we were running her out of her course in short races, Rails might have finished her life as a selling plater, and would never have made the grand name she did as a stayer, and I should have been a much poorer man than I am this day, when I feel able not only to forgive those wretched Hawkes, but almost to pity them."

CHAPTER XXVII

A JOCKEY'S YARN

A queer Judge—Racing in the West Country—George Ingram—The Weymouth Sharp.

Mr. Westland, having finished his story, called upon the company to fill a bumper and drink another toast:

"Here's to the sports of old England, and may they flourish for ever!"

This having been duly honoured, he lit another cigar, settled himself in the corner, and constituting himself chairman, called on Shute Holmes for a story.

"Well, gentlemen, I'll do the best I can, but it can't be expected I can tell a long story like Mr. Westland, or one as interesting; but I've had some funny jobs in my time, and experiences which would read like romance if you found them in a book. But I'm not going to tell any startling tales of my own doings in the pigskin; that may come later on—that is, if I can find a man who will put it together for me. I'm only going to tell you now one or two amusing little things that I have seen, if not taken part in, during my professional career.

"In the early days of my cross-country riding I was employed chiefly in the West of England, and among the small Welsh meetings, and it was my lot to see a good deal of an old character some of you will remember, so I needn't tell you his correct name, especially as he was better known wherever he went as Pudney than as anything else.

"Pudney was a queer old stick, and at the meetings I'm

A JOCKEY'S YARN

referring to he was in those days a sort of little god, filling all sorts of positions. At one place he would be clerk of the course, or clerk of the scales; at another meeting you would find him judge, or starter; and he was generally auctioneer, and, occasionally, you would find him filling several of these important offices at the same time. Pudney had a nasty habit of bending his elbow, and I don't think his pecuniary position was improved by that habit; so, most likely, if he saw an opportunity of earning a pony, and doing a friend a good turn at the same time, it would be rather difficult for him to resist the temptation.

"I remember seeing, at Much Wenlock, either a most gross case of favouring a friend, or the biggest blunder that was ever made by a judge of racing. It was hard to believe it was merely a mistake, because, as everybody knew, the owner of the horse that was favoured—who was a well-known Worcester bookmaker—and the judge were great pals. As far as I can remember, the bookie's horse was called Bravissima, and the owner had backed him for as much money as he could get on in such a market; consequently, he was a very hot favourite. Pudney was judge, and, for want of a proper judge's box, he sat opposite the winning-post in a farmer's muck waggon. There was about half-a-dozen runners for the race I am speaking of, but before they had travelled far there were only three standing up; and I remember well that the favourite came over the last fence three lengths in front of an outsider, which was owned and ridden by a farmer, while the second favourite was a hundred yards in the rear; and as the outsider was blundering through his fences rather than jumping them, it looked any sort of odds on the bookie's horse. However, when the farmer had managed to get his horse over the last fence, he set down to his work and rode like the very devil. We could see he was catching the favourite, and there was naturally great excitement as they neared the winning-post, for the outsider, at the finish, passed the judge first, and certainly

T

won by a good neck, if not half a length. At the moment they were passing the post the bookie rushed up to the side of the waggon, and looking up into the judge's face, significantly said:

"'The favourite's won, Pudney.'

"'All right, *Jarge*,' replied that official, and up went the favourite's number.

"Of course, there was a storm of indignation, and some not over-polite expressions used respecting the judge, and some of those interested in the matter followed Pudney into the weighing-room, trying all they knew to persuade the old man that he had made a mistake; but they didn't know enough. Nothing could induce him to admit a mistake, and he indignantly declared that 'the man in the box' was the only person in a position to judge. And, of course, the owner of the favourite and its backers loudly endorsed this opinion.

"I remember another case which occurred in the same country, and where the two principal actors concerned were Pudney and 'Jarge'; but this time Pudney was starter.

"My friend Jarge was running a mare in a short race, and as he intended backing her, he knew it was of the utmost consequence he should get a good start. And I have reasons for believing he told the starter as much. Anyway, it is certain that Jarge's mare did get a flying start of twenty or thirty yards, and we all thought she was going to get home; but she was beaten on the post by a head, and as Pudney couldn't very well be judge and starter, her opponent's number went up.

"I had it on very good authority that when Jarge and Pudney met that evening, after the races, a short dialogue something like the following took place:

"'Well, you're a nice sort o' fellow, Pudney, to give a pal a fair start,' said Jarge.

"'Oh, you don't think you had a fair start, Mr. Jarge!' answered Pudney.

"'Fair start be d—d!' replied the bookie. 'I call that leaving my mare at the post.'

"'Well, put her in again to-morrow, Mr. Jarge, and I'll see she beant left at the post again.'

"Accordingly, on the morrow she was entered in a similar race, and she had to meet some of the same horses, and the winner among them. The bookie's horse, in spite of being beaten the day before, was again a hot favourite. This time the starter made no mistake. If he had erred the day before, he made amends for it this time, for he wouldn't drop the flag till his friend's horse had quite twice the start she had on the previous occasion, and of course she won. When they returned to the ring there was an awful uproar, and attempts were made to mob, not only the mare and her jockey, but the judge also. Jarge, however, who was a most popular fellow in his own country, and had a large following, gave the office to a few of 'the boys,' and no damage was done. But on this occasion I believe Pudney did have to appear before the stewards, who, after hearing his explanation, acquitted him of all blame. Of course, neither the stewards nor the public were aware of the very intimate friendship existing between this particular owner and old Pudney. But some of us knew of it, and I assure you Jarge had to stand a good deal of chaffing about it in private. Lord bless you, gentlemen! you needn't laugh so unbelievingly. I've seen plenty of things as bad as that in those days, especially at the little country meetings.

"A very amusing incident just occurs to me that took place at Worcester, which in those days was quite a swell meeting; but I won't give you the correct names of either horses or men, because some of them are alive at the present time, and if they were to hear of it, they mightn't like it; but it's as true as it is that I'm sitting here. Harry Slinker was one of the best cross-country riders in England, and he was also a well-known owner and trainer of jumpers; but he was notorious for the strength of his arm, and I think I have seen him do some of the most barefaced pieces of roping that ever was known since that art was introduced. Yet he never seemed to get very rich at it, and some time ago he pitched it up altogether, riding and roping, training, owning, and all the lot of it; and at the present time I am told he is a shining light in one of the noisiest of all religious bodies. So I hope he has pitched up one or two other bad habits which I won't mention; but I don't know.

"Well, the little incident I'm going to tell you occurred in a match. Harry rode a big hurdle-racer called Smelter, and Jack Littleman, of Cheltenham, one of a family of brilliant horsemen, was up on old Ratsmasher. Will Legge, who is now one of the most prominent starting-price bettors in the West of England, was then fielding at the post, was intimately acquainted with Slinker, and had done considerable business with him, of one sort and another. Just before the match was run, these two gentlemen had a few words in private.

"'Well, Harry,' said the bookie, 'must I go for you? It looks good, and you're sure to be favourite.'

"'I don't think it is good for me,' answered Slinker. 'My horse is very unfit, and mightn't jump.'

"'He's a sight better jumper than Ratsmasher. The public won't stand him,' said the worthy fielder; 'but what am I to do?'

"'Can you get me a pony?' asked Slinker.

"'Oh, yes! I'll undertake to do that,' was the ready reply.

"The two horses were weighed out, and started on their journey—a couple of miles over hurdles. Both jumped the first flight, and went on, side by side, towards the second obstacle, which Harry's horse took all right; but that worthy was alarmed to find he had lost his companion. Ratsmasher had refused. However, he made his way to the next hurdles, and finding, on turning his head, that Littleman was still trying to get his horse over the fence, he contrived to make Smelter refuse also, and he went on refusing till Littleman had got his horse over the other hurdle, and had come up with him; and then they both cleared the third fence without any difficulty. Now, it frequently happens that horses which have once refused a particular fence will refuse that fence again, and so it was with Ratsmasher—he wouldn't have that second lot of hurdles; so Harry found himself again making for the third fence by himself, and when he arrived there, he saw that Littleman hadn't yet got his horse over the other. Now it so happened that a kind-hearted country bumpkin, seeing how matters stood, and wanting to do the jockey a service, had removed one of the hurdles to enable him to get past the obstacle without jumping. The countryman, finding Slinker apparently trying in vain to get his horse over the hurdles, cried out:

"'Look 'ee 'ere, gaffer, theer be a hurdle down.' And then, finding the jockey still disregarding his information, and blindly pretending not to see what his kindness had done, he lost his temper and shouted: ''Thee bist a domned nice jockey, thee bist. It's the mon, I see, and not the hoss that weant goo.'

"Jack Littleman got his horse over as before, and, as you will suppose, won at the finish, with a bit in hand.

"Now, gentlemen, I'll tell you a little story showing how easy it is for the biter to be bitten, and then I'll make way for sombody else.

"A good many years ago I was staying at one of the principal hotels in Weymouth, and among our party was a poor old George Ingram, of Worcester, Farmer Quartley, Billy Knee, and several very hot members from Bristol. It was Weymouth Races, and at that time it was the custom to have a day's pigeon shooting in addition to the races. Now, Mr. Gunn, the proprietor of the hotel, was well known to be fond of a bit of betting, especially when he thought he was having the best of it. Indeed, so cute was this Mr. Gunn, he had been more than once suspected of being the author of some got-up jobs, by means of which his good friends at Weymouth had suffered severely. Our worthy host, and all the gang of us, went up to the pigeon shooting at about eleven o'clock in the day. And I must tell you it was the day the Ebor Handicap was being run at York. George Ingram and one of the Bristolians were in the tent, having a quiet drink together, while Mr. Gunn was busy among the shooters, arranging fresh sweepstakes.

"'Look here, George,' whispered the Bristol man, 'I want you to promise me not to have a bet to-day with that old gonuph, Gunn.'

"'Why not?' asked Ingram. 'Surely I can hold my own with him!'

"'Yes, that's all right, old pal, when the business is straight.'

"'Straight or crooked,' persisted Ingram. 'But what's his graft—a plant of some sort, I suppose?'

"'Yes, and got up specially for your benefit,' replied the Bristolian, who straightway disclosed to the Worcester bookie the hole which the wily Gunn had prepared for his guests.

"'Don't you *crack a lay*,' said Ingram mysteriously, when they parted, 'and I'll see him in the hole intended for us, and will make him stand the hotel bill for the lot.'

"Three or four of those present had books on the Ebor Handicap, which was run at three o'clock; and, in between the shooting, a good many bets were made on the race, nor were they particular about laying half an hour after the race had been run, because, considering the distance between York and Weymouth, with the delay of transference, and then the fact that a message would probably have to be delivered first at the hotel and then brought up to the field by foot messenger, it had never been found possible to get a message on the field under an hour, so it was considered perfectly safe to bet for half that time. About half-past three, when Ingram had got the tip that a message had been brought up to the field, by a lad on a fast pony, and secretly conveyed to the worthy host, he shouted out:

"'Now, my boys, I'm still open to bet on the Ebor Handicap for three minutes only, and then the book's closed.'

"'What will you lay me Brown Jade?' asked Gunn.

"'Fifty to five,' was the instant response, while all the other layers crowded round, offering to accommodate him on the same terms. He not only accepted all their offers, but doubled them, so that at the finish he was hugging himself with the blissful reflection that he had done his pals for about four hundred pounds.

"The shooting being over, we all proceeded to make the best of our way down to the hotel. The host and half-a-dozen of his guests were crowded into a large landau, which was not far on its way, when the lad and fast pony were seen tearing along as fast as he could come toward the landau. When he came up with it, he handed his employer another telegram. Gunn tore it open eagerly, and it is certain if he had been perched on the top of the high driving seat he would have fallen into the road. As it was, he went an awful colour, his head fell on the side of the carriage, and Ingram looked terrified, for he thought the man was dying. He was, however, relieved when he saw him lift his head and heard him cry:

"'Oh, you —— thieving villains, you've put the double on me, but I'll never pay a —— shilling!'

"And there is no doubt he would have been as good as his word if he dared have done so; but to begin with, they had most of it in hand in the hotel account. Then he found it wouldn't pay him to holloa very loudly, for not only would the facts come out regarding the false message which one of the confederates had, by wire, squared a pal at York to send ten minutes before the race was run, so as to ensure its being delivered in front of the true one, but the purpose for which his own message was intended would also be discussed. So, after all, poor old Gunn—who long since went over to the majority—had to 'grin and bear it.'"

CHAPTER XXVIII

SHARPERS

The New Firm—A Sheffield Blade—"Cut and Put" Timson and the Trainer—The Swell who fed his Dog on Chicken—Angling for Flats—The Stroud M.P.—A near Thing.

Of the many sharping tricks I have seen or known of, in connection with the turf and turfites, I propose in this chapter dealing briefly with a few which may be amusing as well as illustrative of some of the methods adopted by the sharpers.

I often think "the boys" who follow racing and have to subsist on their wits must, at times, have but a precarious existence, and yet the amount of originality and skill—I had almost said genius—employed in their nefarious occupation, if directed into honest channels, ought surely to provide them with a good living. A couple of newly-fledged bookies from Newcastle-on-Tyne, visiting headquarters for the first time, secured a pitch in the half-crown ring, and prepared to bet on the first race of the meeting. Of course, I needn't tell my readers that "*the boys*" are always on the look-out for young beginners, and they quickly marked the north-countrymen for their prey.

They waited until the numbers were hoisted and betting about to begin, when the most official-looking member of the gang presented himself to the astonished Tynesiders.

"Have you men got your license?" he inquired, in severe tones.

"No, sir; we knowed nowt aboot ony license," replied the bookie.

"Well, you can't bet at Newmarket without one," persisted the bogus official; "but I'll allow you to bet on this one race; but mind, you must not take any ready money before you get the license. Come into my office after the race is over, and I'll give it to you; but if you take any ready money before you get it, you'll not only get no license, but you'll be warned off the Heath."

The bookies were very grateful for the information, and expressed as much.

There were four or five runners for the first race, and immediately our bookies offered 2 to 1 on the field a simple young man came up with a "tenner" in his hand, accepted the odds, but affected surprise when the bookmaker refused to accept ready money, begging to pay or receive after the race for the first event, and on these terms they did quite a roaring trade, laying a good amount against each of the runners. When the race was over they found they had forty pounds to pay the winner, which was immediately claimed and paid; but the punters of whom they expected to draw seemed a long time coming, so one member of the firm made for the office and demanded his license. Of course, there was no license forthcoming, but information instead, which convinced the poor bookie that he had been the victim of a gang of sharpers.

Dodger Luckett had a brother who was a bit of a flat-catcher in his way, and he was likewise a bit of a bookmaker. About thirty years ago a good many racing people from the country put up, when in town, at Johnny Billinghurst's, the George Hotel, just outside Temple Bar, in the Strand. I was staying there on one occasion with this gentleman and other racing men, among whom were poor old Will Frost and Currie Elliott, a respectable firm of fielders, both long since gone, and jolly Bill Knee, of Stroud. I had been to the theatre, and didn't turn into our private sitting-room at "The George" till about twelve o'clock, and was surprised to find it occupied by a party of nap-players, composed of Frost, Knee, Joe Luckett, or, as he was called, "Black Joe," and a pale-faced, quiet young man, of irreproachably respectable appearance and good manners, whose name I did not hear, but who was introduced to me as a friend of Luckett's, from Sheffield. I was invited to join them at nap, which was then nearly a new game, and the rage everywhere. As a rule I never play cards among strangers, or in doubtful company, and as the stakes were pretty high on this occasion I hesitated a little, but as all present, except "that man fra Sheffield," were well known to me, I thought it would be safe to join in the game, which I did, with the result that when it was over I had lost fifty pounds; my friend Frost, who, with the others, had been playing hours before I joined them, had done in several hundreds, and poor Billy Knee perhaps as much. The only winners were Black Joe and the stranger—the stranger not so much—but the cards which the black one had held the whole of the night had been something wonderful, so he had won nearly all the money.

The following day I was standing near Turner Wilson, the Sheffield bookmaker, when the pale-faced young stranger came by. Pointing him out to Wilson, I said:

"That's a townsman of yours, is it not, Turner?"

"Wat's t' want ter noo for?" asked he. "Tho'st not bin takin' you on wi' t' broads, hast teo, lad?"

"Well, I was playing a quiet game of nap in his company last night with three others whom I knew well," I replied.

"But wha rung yon in to play?" he asked.

"Well, Joe Luckett introduced him," I answered.

"And I can tell th'r what happened," said he. "Yon fellow an' t' black 'un won all t' stuff. Why, lad, yon's Jemmy Nary, t' cleverest chap wat iver touched t' card."

Later on each of us who had been victimised had some quiet conversation with Mr. Luckett—as far as I was concerned, without any satisfaction. If either of the party saved any of their losings it was Billy Knee; rumour, at the time, said as much.

Travelling about from one race-meeting to another, I have seen a good deal of card-playing in railway carriages, and have myself frequently whiled away the tedium of a long journey with a rubber of whist; but as I am not abnormally clever with the "broads," I was always careful not to take on strangers, especially when they wanted to play for high stakes. Neither my old friend, Matt Collinson, nor Dodger Luckett were so particular in this respect, because both had been "pros" at cards, and there were few men in England who could teach them anything; but I remember on one occasion seeing old Matt fairly done at his own game. We had a long journey before us, and, as usual, the cards were introduced. We were one short of a set of four, and a quiet-looking stranger who sat in the corner was invited to make it up. Professing a disinclination to play, after some pressing he came in. Before the game had been long in progress he began to grumble at his partner, and pitching down the cards, declared he hated four-handed games, but would play anybody in the company for any amount, and at any game, single-handed. This nettled Matt, and it was easy to see awoke the old evil Adam in him; so he took up the challenge, and eventually a match was made for £25 a side, and Matt named "put" as the game. The cards were well shuffled, cut, and dealt, and Matt led off with a tray. To this the stranger replied by another tray. Matt, nothing daunted, led a second tray, and was almost electrified when the stranger coolly paired that also.

"Now, what do you think of that, my friend?" asked Matt, as he played a fifth tray.

"Why, I pair that as well," was his reply, dashing down a sixth.

There was no quarrelling. They only looked hard at each other, and then they burst out laughing, evidently neither being anxious to enlighten the company as to how it came to pass that there happened to be six trays in that pack of cards.

* * * * * *

George Timson, of Birmingham, was, when I first knew him, a ready-money betting man in the outer rings. He died many years ago, but some of my readers will remember him in his later years, when he did a considerable trade as a bookmaker in Tattersall's enclosure. At one of the Liverpool meetings, "Timmy," as we used to call him, was staying at the Adelphi Hotel. After dinner, it being a wretchedly wet night, he "lighted up" and sauntered into the billiard-room. He was an enthusiast at the game, but a shocking bad player, and fancied himself a good deal better than he was. He found nobody in the room but old Tom Green, the veteran trainer.

"Will you play a game, Tom?" asked Timson.

"Ay, lad, if thee don't play much of a game," was the ready answer.

So they commenced a fifty game, at even points, for a sovereign.

Tom only just won, and by an apparent fluke, so that when he remarked, "I don't think there's much in it between us, Mr. Timson, so I'll play thee a hundred up for a fiver," Timmy jumped at the offer.

The second game Tom won, but by about 10 only, so they continued to monopolise the table till the marker was obliged to close the room, at which time they were playing for a "pony" a game, and the old trainer's play had so gradually improved that he was now conceding the bookmaker 80 in a game of 200; and what is more, Tom had won something over £200. Timson, who, of course, had had all the bad luck, and his opponent all the flukes, wanted to go on, but the rules forbade it.

"Never mind, lad," said the winner consolingly, "I'll gie thee another chance to-morrow night."

Timson determined to be revenged, was early on the spot

the following night, but no Tom Green turned up, nor on any other night during the week.

The bookie, still burning for revenge, made up his mind that he would prepare a trap for the wily Thomas at the following Liverpool meeting.

. . . .

Now there resided at that time, in Birmingham, an aristocratic-looking young gent, in slightly reduced circumstances, who would not be above earning a trifle in furthering Mr. Timson's purposes, and the bookie knew this was just the man for the job, because he was undoubtedly one of the very best amateur cueists outside London; and in consideration of all his expenses being paid, as well as a commission on the winnings, he agreed to accompany Timson to Liverpool on this expedition. So they found themselves at the Adelphi Hotel at the next Liverpool race-meeting, lying in wait for poor old Green; intending so craftily to manipulate matters there that the whole previous losses, and a good margin to boot, should be squeezed out of him.

The young gent was to pose as a "toff" who had just come into a large property, and to look as much as possible like soon going out of it again; and Tom was to be made believe he had a real good thing on. But the quarry was not at home. Again Tom didn't turn up. It became necessary, therefore, to look for some other game, as the week's expenses for the couple would be heavy.

Early on the second day fate threw this game in their way. As hunting men say, they "found." And what a find it was, to be sure! It was a tall, handsome young fellow, who evidently had plenty of cash, as well as the biggest dog of the St. Bernard breed they had ever seen. After a little managing, he agreed to play our young gent for a sovereign. Timson, who had adopted, for the nonce, the character of a high-class commercial, ventured to remark how much he would like to have a little interest in the game; the young swell, being of an affable disposition, obliged him also with a bet of a sovereign.

It was arranged that the stranger should be allowed to win the first game, and so lured on to play for higher stakes, and although he only just got home by the skin of his teeth, he evinced no hesitation to increase the stakes, and so he bet them a fiver each on the next game, which, to their amazement, he just managed to win. They played another game for still higher stakes, with the same results, and so on, again and again, till the Birmingham player and his principal, had lost over £300; the stranger proving himself one of the best players they had ever seen—certainly the best amateur. The most amusing part of the whole business was to watch Timmy's face when, about the middle of the evening's proceedings, the swell ordered his supper. "A nice large cold chicken," said the stranger. This was immediately served up, and scarcely touching it himself, he passed it on to his huge St. Bernard, quietly remarking, "I always feed my dog on chicken." And so once more we see how

> "The best laid schemes
> O' mice and men
> Gang aft a-gley."

For years after poor George had to stand a lot of chaff respecting this abortive "plant," and any time, when losing heavily at billiards, somebody was sure to ask him if this man also "fed his dog on chicken."

A capital story is told of "Chippy Norton." I think I may vouch for its truth, as I had it from one of Chippy's most intimate friends, and who was, indeed, one of the principal actors in it. It appears that a good many years ago, before he had been able to struggle out of the painful position he once occupied on the turf, he had one day, by the exercise of much ingenuity and perseverance, become possessed of thirty pounds, which he carefully stowed away in his inside vest pocket, depositing the said vest under his pillow ere he fell into the sound slumber which is the portion of the virtuous. Several of "the boys" were occupying the same bedroom. When he awoke the following morning the boys had gone for a stroll before breakfast. On examination of his "poke," Chippy found that his three ten-pound notes, by some mysterious means, had been transformed into three fivers. He went in pursuit of his pals and charged them with it, but of course they stoutly denied all knowledge of the change, and when he found there was no chance of getting his money back, he said good-temperedly:

"Well, Jarge, let me be *in* at the job and I won't grumble; but, dang it all! I must have my carner."

One of the hottest bits of sharp practice I ever saw was at a small country town. If my memory serves me, it was at Hungerford. I was staying with Matt Collinson and a houseful of racing people at an hotel there. It was a lovely evening, and after dinner a number of us strolled on to the bridge to smoke our cigars, and watch some countrymen fishing. Now the year previously the same thing had happened, and as betting men must needs bet about anything and everything, a good deal of money had changed hands on the exploits of the various anglers; and what made the business the more exciting was the fact that the current of the river took the floats a little out of sight, under the bridge. On this occasion, also, somebody proposed wagering, and very soon a lot of betting was going on, and Master Matt, who was particularly busy, in half an hour had landed a considerable sum. The man he backed was such a piscatorial adept he seldom lost; indeed, so phenomenal was his luck, or judgment, or something else, that people grew suspicious, and even went so far as to make an excursion into the meadow below, where the mystery was solved in an unpleasant fashion, for there was seen a fellow in the river, under the bridge, who was rendering material assistance to the lucky angler, who, on seeing himself detected, dropped his can of "readied" fish in the river and made off. His pal on the bridge got notice something was wrong; he also bolted, and was out of sight in a second, leaving his tackle behind him.

Of course, there was no end of a rumpus, all the losers declaring Matt, who had won the bulk of the money, was in it, if he had not really put the job up. He, however, declared his innocence in the most emphatic manner, and with a virtuous indignation he was so well able to assume, so, as nothing could be proved, the losers had to grin and bear it; but I am sure there were few among us who believed in Mr. M.'s innocence.

I remember on one occasion a remarkable case of besting a welsher. The late lamented and beloved member for the Stroud Division of Gloucestershire, Mr. George Holloway, as everybody knows, was not much of a racing man, but he was fond of all sorts of sport, and he went to one or two of the principal races every year, rarely missing Ascot. And, mind you, he was no mere looker-on when he did go; he had his fiver, or pony, or more down if he thought he had a good thing. He was generally accompanied by his brother Henry and the brothers Smith, from the Vale of Chalford, one a lawyer and the other a brewer, both of them very tall gentlemen, long in reach, and awkward-looking customers to tackle. Well, it happened that while the friends were hunting about the big ring at Ascot to get the best price, "a cert" in the shape of a 3 to 1 on chance, they got separated, and George found himself alone; but hearing a substantial-looking bookie offering to take 50 to 20, he straightway closed with the gentleman's offer, and posted his fifty pounds.

Scarcely, however, had he done so, when he ran against his friends.

"What have you done?" asked Ted Smith.

"I've laid fifty to twenty on the favourite," was the reply; "but what have you been doing?"

"Oh, we've been obliged to lay three to one on to that

bloated, aristocratic-looking bookmaker, Walter Shakeshaft," his friend answered.

The Smiths, knowing a little more of racing matters than Mr. Holloway, and knowing also that a long price is not always the sign of a sound investment, felt doubtful, and demanded to be made acquainted with the bookie who had taken the short odds; and when they saw him their doubt was by no means dissipated, so it was thereupon determined to keep an eye—indeed, a number of eyes—on the said bookmaker.

"They're off!" and the favourite got a flying start, and the nearer they got to the winning-post the more he increased his lead, which fact Mr. Holloway's bookie was aware of, and the circumstance had an evidently disturbing influence upon him, for he and his clerk were making tracks for the exit gate. Suddenly he feels a grip as of iron on his collar, and he is confronted with Mr. Holloway and the two awkward-looking brothers.

"Oh, I'll give you your money back!" groaned the craven scoundrel, fearful lest other of his clients should see how matters stood.

"My friend wants seventy pounds, and not a penny less," said Mr. Smith; and the seventy pounds were immediately forthcoming, and the welsher bolted.

While all this was taking place, the race was being finished, and it appeared that when the favourite came to tackle the stiff bit of finish he stopped to nothing, and something got up and beat him by a head.

"Oh, dear me!" said Mr. Holloway, "why, I've lost the money after all." And he seemed positively distressed because he couldn't find the welsher to return him—at least—his own £20.

Before that of 1879, and since, I have seen many more important Lincolnshire Handicaps than the one won by Lord Rosebery's moderate five-year-old. Many better races, and fields composed of horses of a very much superior quality, for although Touchet, dividing the honour of top weight with old Telescope, managed to get home with 8 st. 4 lb., it is impossible to form any exalted opinion of him on this form.

True, it was a big field—there were twenty-seven runners—but it was made up for the most part of aged and otherwise damaged goods, old crocks who had been hurdling and steeple-chasing, and there was nothing at all behind him one might call decently good.

The reasons for dragging this particular race from the storehouse of memory are to be found not so much in the race itself as in a curious incident in connection with it, which I remember very well, although it concerned me less than it did a couple of friends, one of whom, alas! has gone to

"That bourne from which no traveller returns;"

the other having since those days become a shining star in the firmament of sport, will doubtless be amused with the reminiscence. I will call my friend, the young provincial bookmaker, Sid Timbs, and the other a professional backer hailing from the same town, Fred Downey.

Everybody knew Timbs for a smart young fellow, who meant making his way on the turf. He had a keen eye for noting what the big men in the ring were doing; and he had, moreover, a wonderful scent for the goods that were going a bit "fishy" in the market. This sense, as he progressed in life, became extremely valuable to him. He was also industrious. He would be on the race-course early in the morning to see the horses do their work, and to get a chat with this jockey or that owner; and in spite of this early rising, he somehow managed to be constant in attendance at the Subscription Rooms, or other resorts of betting men, very late at nights. And in this way he managed to secure a good deal of valuable information. Was a horse to be scratched, or an unexpected one to run, or a new one to be introduced to the market, Sid would, by some means, have early information on the subject.

Now it was this inordinate appetite for information which was very near the undoing of him in that very race twenty years ago. There was only a head in it, but I sometimes wonder what Sid Timbs would be doing now but for that short head. Goodness knows! He might have recovered himself perhaps, after years of uphill work; he certainly might not have been in the year 1901 a rich and powerful man, with houses and lands, and horses and carriages.

This young man in 1879, in March weather as wretched as it could be made, had found his way to Lincoln in company with his fellow-townsman, Fred Downey. Now Fred was about as fly as his pal, and prided himself rather on being one of the very earliest of "early birds."

At that time, as now, Lincoln began on the Monday, which, however, was given up to a "leather-flapping" sort of business, none of the legitimate starting till the second day, the big handicap being set for the Wednesday. On the Tuesday morning the two friends and "fellow-countrymen" met in the ring, each, as it happened, with a separate bit of useful knowledge, with which they were ready to "take down" the common enemy, or each other, even, if the opportunity offered.

Downey had got to know that a certain outsider named Mangostan, perhaps the most extreme outsider that had been in the betting, or likely to run, was going to be backed for a heap of money, and was sure to come to a short price the following day. He didn't share this valuable information with Timbs. He didn't even try to back the horse in a straightforward way at something like 50 or 60 to 1, which anybody would have laid; that was not good enough for him.

"Here, Sid," said he, when the friends met, "I've got a few sovereigns for a rank outsider. What's your price for the greatest outsider in the race? A stumer that hasn't a thousand to one chance. But I've laid a bet against him, and must go to the insurance office."

"Well, as you're an old pal, Fred, I'll lay you a hundred to one I give you a loser."

"Done!" said Fred. "I take you five hundred to five," feeling quite certain he would give him Mangostan.

"Any more?" asked Sid coolly, trying to draw him on.

"Yes, I'll have seven hundred to seven."

"Better have one thousand to ten while you are about it," said Sid.

"Very well, book it!" the punter cried.

"Have the place money?" asked the cunning layer of long odds.

"No."

"Now, I'll tell you what I'll do," said Timbs, "I will lay you one thousand to eight more, and two hundred and fifty to eight for a place."

This knocked Downey back; he knew perfectly well that his friend could have nothing like a book of the size which would allow him to make bets of this character, because Timbs was betting in those days to small money, and hadn't the Bank of England behind him, so he declined to go any farther.

"What horse do you give me?" he growled.

"I give you Mars," was the answer, "and I've laid you one thousand to ten against him."

"Mars be d—d!" roared Fred. "No bet! Of course I must have a runner."

"Of course you must," said the aggravating bookie. "Mars is in the race, and if he does not run the bet is off."

Of course, there was no get out for Downey, and the bet had to stand. So far it looked like a case of the biter being bitten; for while Mr. Downey had been industriously gathering information regarding Mangostan, Timbs had been doing the same in regard to Mars, whom he had got to know was a certain runner. But the knowledge was of no avail unless he could find somebody to fall into the very trap his pal had dropped into, because it would be impossible to get a shilling out of such a wretch by any other means, and if he had offered 200 to 1 then or after his number was up, there would not have been a taker. In his trial Mars had been beaten out of sight by an old hurdle racer, who was also a certain starter for this race.

"Well, Master Sid," said Downey, as he turned away with anything but an angelic expression on his face, "I daresay you think it very clever to take me down for a tenner; but you look out I don't get my own back with you, *and* a bit more."

Sid Timbs had good reason to remember that threat before that season was gone; but that is another story.

The Lincolnshire Handicap of 1879 is not ancient history, and I have no doubt many of my readers will be able to recall that extraordinary finish as vividly as I do.

On the eventful day, as soon as the ring began to assemble, and in the intervals of the three races which preceded the big event, there was some heavy betting. The outsider, Mangostan, came with a rattle from 50 to 1 to a quarter the price, and the mysteriously managed Stanton horse, Cradle, fairly ousted Touchet from the post of honour, and started the actual favourite. Adventurer, Sir Joseph, Balbriggan, and Thunderstone were all strong orders; but, of course, there was no money for the despised Mars. In vain Fred Downey tempted his friends to stand a bit with him in the big bet his friend Sid had bustled him into. Nobody would look at him, and I suppose there never was a more thoroughly despised outsider for an important race.

Sid considered he had won the tenner the moment he had booked the bet, and therefore didn't trouble any more about it. He had only a small book, and must have been standing to lose £800 Mars, which was certainly more than he could, at that time, afford to lose; and, although he could have covered the amount for £4 or £5, such a certainty did it seem for Mars to be beaten, he declined to do so. It is singular that the only horse to give the starter much trouble was this brute, named after the god of war. He lashed out in all directions, tried to savage everybody and everything that came near him, and for a time no amount of coaxing or force could get him to take his place at the post. When he did, however, the start was as nearly a perfect one as possible, and, for nearly a quarter of a mile, the field was all "in a ruck," nothing in front and nothing far behind. The heavily-backed Mangostan was the first to show prominently, and he held a clear lead for about four hundred yards, being closely followed by Tallos, Telescope, Cradle, Touchet, Sir Joseph, and several others on the one side of him, and by Admiral Byng, Tentergate, St. Augustine, and Drumhead on the other. Before they had gone half a mile little Gallon asked Cradle a question, and Lord Wilton's lightly-weighted six-year-old seemed easily to wrest the lead from Mangostan. Tallos and Telescope, who had so far made a bold show, suddenly went to the rear, and joined the beaten lot. Two furlongs from home Cradle had had pretty well enough of it, and was headed by Touchet and Sir Joseph, the latter for a little distance having a slight lead. Constable now set to work with vigour on Touchet, and in a few strides he had not only deprived Sir Joseph of the lead, but appeared to have the race won for Lord Rosebery. Half way up the distance there was nothing near him but Sir Joseph, Cradle, St. Augustine and Drumhead, and as they neared the post it looked as though there might be a race for second place, but the race for first place was practically over. Suddenly there is a cry of fear from the backers, and a yell of delight from the fielders.

"What is this?" they cry, as we see flying, like lightning, through the field a strange horse and his jockey, passing all but Touchet in rapid succession; and open-mouthed with amazement, we stand and watch the struggle—short, it is true,

SHARPERS

but terrible—between this stranger and the whilom favourite. I stood within sight of Sid Timbs, and when some frantic bookmaker yelled out " Mars ! Mars ! Mars ! " knowing all the circumstances of the bet, I turned instinctively to look at him, and I shall never forget the ghastly sight his face presented. It was convulsed with fear, and running down with an unnatural perspiration, and it would be impossible to describe the colour of it. I should say it was something of a yellowy-greenish tinge. The nearest approach to it I have ever seen was the complexion of some of the passengers on a pleasure boat, caught in a gale of wind.

Timbs thought the impossible had come to pass, and Mars had won. Timbs was not alone in that matter. A good many of us thought Mars had won, and money was betted on it after they had passed the post. The judge, however, said Lord Rosebery's horse had won by a short head.

So Fred Downey did not win the thousand pounds he for a few seconds thought he had won—*on paper*. And friend Timbs had a painful time while it lasted, and not a happy time for years after, for, while Downey lived he never neglected an opportunity of rubbing salt into the little sore which the matter had left in the character of Mr. Timbs.

CHAPTER XXIX

WONDERFUL DREAMS

La Merveille's Cambridgeshire—Archer and Master Kildare—Bend Or's Derby—Common's Two Thousand Guineas.

I AM about to relate a series of veritable facts, but I am quite sure my readers, on arriving at the end of the chapter, will be prepared to pass me the medal, or show by some other gentle method their sense of my fitness for the presidency of a certain notable society. Nevertheless, in the strange facts I shall narrate, I assure my readers I will adhere most strictly and literally to the simple truth, of which I am willing to make solemn affidavit; and more than this, I can produce unimpeachable witnesses who will attest the truth of most of my statements—gentlemen well known on the turf.

I must tell you, to begin with, that in one particular I am exceedingly singular, for all my life long I have very seldom been either troubled or pleased by dreams; that is, during sleep. Almost all mine have been "day dreams." In this, perhaps, I have been more than compensated for my loss in the other respect. I say I have seldom had dreams; perhaps I ought to qualify this remark by saying that my dreams, if I have had them, have left no impression on my memory—they passed away with the sleep. I say this because I have occasionally awoke with a dim consciousness of having had dreams, but rarely have I been able to remember anything of them. This makes the circumstances I am about to relate the more remarkable, because after each of these four dreams I

WONDERFUL DREAMS

awoke with the clear and intensely vivid impression of particulars belonging to actual and striking events, immediately transpiring within one's sight, rather than to doings in the shadowy realms of dreamland. I was at Newmarket during the Cambridgeshire in 1879, and was lodging with my brother and two other gentlemen, well known in "Tattersall's," when my first remarkable dream occurred. During the night previous to the Cambridgeshire Day, I dreamt that I stood upon the Heath waiting for the big race to be run. Presently I heard the well-known cry, "They're off!" and then I watched the race, and saw the finish as clearly as ever I saw it in real life. When I met my friends at the breakfast table next morning, I told them my dream. I could not tell them the name of the horse I had seen win the race. All I knew was that I saw it very distinctly, and that a horse, whose rider bore Lord Rosebery's primrose and rose hoops, had gone first past the post. One of my friends at once declared that Lord Rosebery had no horse in the race, and as there had been, as far as I knew, no horse of his in the betting, I thought this must be so. The matter therefore dropped, and I thought no more of it. Later in the day I was standing on the Heath, among the carriages, about fifty yards below the winning-post while the finish for the Cambridgeshire took place, and, as the horses rushed past us, I put my hand on the shoulder of one of my friends, a well-known bookmaker named Horsley, crying out:

"Look, Ted! there goes my dream!"

And sure enough there was Lord Rosebery's colours going first past the post on an outsider, whose very name was, even then, unknown to me. Of course, I and my friends decided that it was a very remarkable coincidence, and as it was my first experience of the kind, I thought but little of it at the time.

A few months after this I was staying for the Epsom Spring Meeting with good old Dame Luce, at the King's Arms, Hampton Court, and among our party, which was now a much larger one than that at Newmarket, were two gentlemen who were my companions on the previous occasion. I remember that on the night before the City and Sub. we had a right jolly time of it. Most of us had backed Leolinus—a big horse which had been placed in the Leger—to win, amongst us, a large sum, and from the knowledge we possessed we were bound to feel sanguine about the result, consequently we were taking a little jollity on account. When I got to bed I was soon asleep, and slept all night soundly; but I was visited in that sleep by one of the most vivid and realistic of dreams. No regular dreamer ever had such a dream. I was rather late at the breakfast table that morning, and my friends were all there—"the flag was down, and they were making the pace."

"What's the matter with you?" asked one, as I took my place with rather a rueful visage.

"My lads," I replied, "we are done; that confounded Archer has stolen the race from us, and beaten us by the shortest of heads on Master Kildare."

Then I told them my dream. Of course, they laughed at me, and it neither affected their appetite nor damped their hopes with regard to the race. Yet, for myself, I felt an uneasy misgiving, and I could not help wishing just then that there was no such jockey as Archer in the world, and no such horse as Master Kildare, and perhaps I may have put up a little inaudible prayer that something might happen to keep them both at home to-day. Well, we drove off to Epsom, and I was restless and fidgety all the time preceding the big race, so that when the fateful moment arrived I had worked myself up to a fit of intense anxiety, which was not a usual circumstance with me; and while I know you will not credit a word I say, I solemnly assure you I saw the exact counterpart of my dream—the ding-dong finish, the terrible slogging which the Demon Jockey inflicted on poor Master Kildare, the uncertainty and suspense pending the hoisting of the numbers, the eager up-turned faces waiting for the verdict, that strange silence which

WONDERFUL DREAMS 315

at this moment is always so remarkable—all, all were reproduced with an exact fidelity. My friends, when we talked the matter over in the evening, were obliged to confess that it was really very wonderful.

I have been on the turf for nearly forty years, and during that time I have done a fair amount of backing, mixing it, I must confess, with very considerable experience as "a layer," and like all regular turf men, I have been *in* at some "good things." Unfortunately for me, as my readers are aware, the good things have not always come off; on the contrary, they have generally been disastrous. In the year 1880, like a few other clever people, I got to know all about Bend Or for the Derby. I had it on reliable authority that he was a proper crock; was, in fact, lame, and had no more chance of winning that classic event than a costermonger's donkey. Indeed, so exact was my information, and from such an excellent source, I had not the slightest doubt of it. To confirm this opinion, I received a wire quite early on the Monday morning preceding the day of the race, informing me that the horse had had his leg in a bucket all night, and it was not at all likely he could be got to the post by the following Wednesday, and utterly impossible he could win, under any circumstances. A letter followed, not only recommending me to get a bit out of the favourite, but to put it all down on Robert the Devil. This advice, I may say, was in accord with my own opinion and desires. I had already backed Robert to win me a considerable stake, so I immediately went to my club and increased my investments on him. But knowing that backing horses, after all, and however good your information, must of necessity partake somewhat of the nature of speculation, I concluded it would be wise to make a certainty of not losing on the race, by laying all I could against Bend Or. So well did I succeed, and with such industry employ the metallic, that on a careful scrutiny of my little volume I found, in case of the remote and absurdly unlikely contingency of the favourite winning, I stood to lose as much as I could afford. Indeed, it looked like getting a gentle "knock." However, any unpleasant thoughts which may, for the moment, have occurred to me were instantly dispelled. My information was of such a reliable character as to make this unpleasant contingency in the highest degree improbable, if not impossible.

I was staying at Barratt's, in Cecil Street, a quiet, old-fashioned private hotel, well known, in those days, as the London quarters of many provincial racing men, but now, alas! absorbed by the big Hotel Cecil. It was here, then, my third dream took place, during the night before the great race. I dreamt I stood on the sloping turf of Tattersall's enclosure, watching that marvellous scene, Epsom Downs on the Derby Day, than which there is, on this earth, nothing more wonderful to be seen in the way of human gatherings. I heard the babel of voices all around me, and once again the familiar cry, "They're off!" Thousands—ay, hundreds of thousands—of eyes are eagerly following the troop of gallant horses now breasting the hill, on the opposite side of the Downs. On they come along the top, and as they turn Tattenham Corner and come streaming down the hill, thousands are searching among them for the colours they desire to see in front. As they come into the straight, and are nearing home, I see, with vivid distinctness, two horses single themselves out from the rest, and, in a moment, it was evident the battle was between these two. For an instant it seemed the dark horse must win. I saw the lad who rode him just turn his head, as though to see how far he was winning. Oh, fatal indiscretion! The chestnut horse was close upon him, his rider making almost superhuman efforts, and both horses, as though they knew the interests at stake, straining every fibre in their bodies for a last effort. And so they passed the winning-post, locked together, and no man excepting the judge could tell which had won. With painful intensity my eyes were riveted on the number board. Up went No. 8, and I awoke, the remarkable thing being that I

WONDERFUL DREAMS

was utterly in the dark as to the name of either of the two first horses.

When I appeared at the breakfast table I told my friends of this dream also.

"I don't believe," I said, "anything can win but Robert the Devil; but I will have a bit on No. 8 on the card, whatever it may be, just to save myself, and for the sake of my dream."

"How about Bend Or?" asked my brother. "Suppose he should be No. 8 on the card?"

"Well, I can't back him," I replied; "still, I hope that will not happen."

The bare thought of it, however, made me feel singularly uncomfortable, and immediately breakfast was over I sallied out in search of a card. It was too early for them, so I hung about the corner of Waterloo Place, on the Strand, for a time; then a little fat woman came puffing along, with her hands full of "k'rect cards." I fairly trembled with excitement as I took one from her hands, opened it eagerly, and at once saw the fatal line, "8, Bend Or." I went down to Epsom with a foreboding heart. I had gone too far to retrace my steps. It would have cost too much, at the price the favourite had now reached, to back him in again; I dared not do it, so I determined to stand it out. Just as they started I was standing alongside poor Walter Gregory, and it occurred to me that I had said I would have a bit on No. 8, whatever it might be. I had a £20 note in my pocket. I took it out, and handing it to Gregory, who was even now offering 7 to 4 on the field, I said:

"I will have twenty pounds' worth 'ready,' Walter, for the sake of a foolish dream. Not that I hope or expect him to win."

The horses were now on the way, and in a few moments there was repeated in my sight the very struggle I had witnessed in my dream, and after they had passed the post it was not until the dreadful No. 8 was hoisted that I knew how much a poorer man I was, and oh! how much poorer than I should have been had only Robert the Devil's number gone up instead. If I had only had a modest tenner on La Merveille and played it up on "the main of three," I should have won several thousands of pounds.

I must now take my readers back once more to the famous little Cambridgeshire town, dear, quaint Newmarket, the dearly beloved of its habitual visitors, and the delight of all good sportsmen. It was here I was favoured with the last of this series of remarkable dreams, and it occurred in the night before "the Guineas," in 1891, after eleven years of dreamless nights. In this dream I saw the big race run; I saw its finish, and, as on two previous occasions, I could not make out the name of the winner. Yet I saw most distinctly the colours of Sir Frederick Johnson borne triumphantly past the post.

I did not wait till after the race to proclaim my dream. I told it to the gentlemen who were staying in the house with me, and when I went up to the course I spoke of it openly in the ring. I remember just before the decision of the race, as I stood against the rails dividing Tattersall's enclosure from that belonging to the Jockey Club, I publicly gave those standing near me the tip to back Common, and I told them upon what ground I gave the tip. Among those about me were three or four of the largest and best-known "fielders," a member of the Jockey Club, who owned horses in Jennings' stable, where Gouverneur, the favourite for this very race, was trained, and a gentleman very eminent in the musical world; then Mr. Arthur Sullivan. Naturally, some of them laughed at the idea of backing a horse on such unreasonable grounds; on the other hand, several who were present, knowing something of my previous exploits in this direction, were actually weak enough to take some notice of it, and backed Common on this singular tip. For myself, I had heard a little bird whisper something to the disparagement of the favourite, a trouble of the teeth, or something of the kind—not much, perhaps, but enough to prevent him doing as well as could be wished for two or three days previous to the race, and I believe some pains were taken to keep the matter quiet. Still, not having taken advantage of the preceding three dreams which had been fulfilled, and moreover, having burnt my fingers a time or two over these good things to lay against, I felt shy, and afraid to plunge. Nevertheless, I performed on this occasion what is known as "the doll trick"; that is, I laid £50 against the favourite, and put the £50 on Common, and as he was at the remunerative odds of 9 to 1, I won a nice sum on him without standing to lose much more than £100 if Gouverneur won, while if both were beaten I came out quits. Well, the race was run, and again, with striking exactness, all that I had seen in my dream was reproduced. The moment they had passed the post the great composer, to whom I have referred, ran up to me, declaring it was truly wonderful. He assured me he was not fool enough to reject all dreams as airy nothingnesses. "I know," he said, quoting Hamlet,

"'There are more things in heaven and earth, Horatio,
Than are dreamt of in your philosophy.'"

And further, he made me promise that if ever I had such another dream, I would endeavour to make him acquainted with it.

This is more than twelve years ago, and I have had no more such mysterious tips; nor do I expect any, for—

"There is a tide in the affairs of men
Which, taken at the flood, leads on to fortune."

Evidently I missed my chance, several times repeated, and I have no right to expect more of this sort. Seriously, however, what does it all mean? I am not prepared to assert positively that there is something supernatural in it, and yet it seems scarcely possible they were merely a series of coincidences. The theory of coincidence would do if it were a case of one, or two even, among the thousands of an habitual dreamer's dreams coming true. But here the wonder of it is I am no dreamer, and these four most vivid dreams are almost the only ones I have had in all these years. I leave it here with my readers to laugh at, if they choose, or to solve according to their varied fancies, only again reiterating the assertion that all I have here set down is absolutely true.

CHAPTER XXX

PUTTING "THE DOUBLE" ON A CHEAT

A remarkable Bookmaker—A false Friend—The Bookie's Revenge.

THE hero of this chapter has been dead more than a quarter of a century, and he had retired from the turf a good many years before he died; I suppose, therefore, few of my readers will remember him, or know anything of the strange circumstances narrated here.

That, however, is of small consequence, as my readers will see my purpose in introducing the story here, and will readily recognise the particular phase of turf life which it serves to illustrate.

Mr. Swift, the great bookmaker, had, I suppose, ancestors, and, for aught I know, he may have been a descendant of quite a different kind of bookmaker—a certain notable Dean of that ilk—and he may have been named Jonathan, after the witty clergyman; but I never knew him by any other name than "Boney" Swift, and this was usually abbreviated to simple Boney. His friends so named him on account of his extremely gaunt appearance and total freedom from anything in the nature of adipose tissue. The first thing about him which an observant person remarked was his boniness, and after that his remarkable eyes; in fact, he seemed all bones and optics. When he shook hands, one got the impression your hand was in the grip of the devil or a skeleton, and it imparted a cold and creepy sort of sensation which lasted for an hour or two. When his wonderful eyes rested upon you, there was an uneasy feeling that he was looking through you. Those eyes were jet black and intensely piercing. His bony face had never grown any hair, or else he had taken great pains to keep it clean-shaven. The hair on the top of his head, if he had any, was cropped short and entirely hidden under a tight-fitting cap, which, as far as I know, was never removed. These characteristics made his bony face anything but "a thing of beauty," even when in repose. If he laughed, which was not often, he exposed two rows of immense teeth, white as pearls, which somehow only seemed to add hideousness to his looks; but when exasperated, or moved by any violent passion, which was only too often, his face was perfectly diabolical.

Under this harsh and forbidding exterior lay a nature capable of great extremes; a heart governed at times by the most generous impulses, yet capable of bitterest hate. Everybody knew him as a good hater, but, at the same time, he was a staunch and loyal friend.

Boney had been for many years a bookmaker, and was reputed very rich. It was generally understood, also, that he owned a number of good horses, running in other people's names; for in those days there was no law against this kind of thing, therefore it would be impossible to tell who were the *bond-fide* owners of half the horses in training. One thing is certain, several nominal owners were mere puppets in his hands; however they might jig and sputter in the face of the public, Boney, behind the scenes, was quietly working the strings.

He was not of a trustful nature; in fact, he looked upon his fellow-man, generally, as his natural enemy, whose chief business in life it was to attempt to plunder and outwit him. In one or two exceptions where, as he thought, he had proved the honesty of an individual, there was no limit to his trustfulness, and his generosity was equal to his faith.

Jack Wivell was one of the few trusted ones. A few

years before, while keeping a small public-house in a town which Boney visited once a year, at its race-meeting, he had made the acquaintance of the great bookmaker, with whom Mrs. Wivell claimed some sort of distant relationship, so that it came to pass, while sojourning in those parts, Boney made his home among these good people at the Wheatsheaf. It was a poor little inn, with scarcely a living in it for Jack and his wife and four youngsters, and was altogether unworthy of the brilliant abilities, and soaring ambitions of Mr. Wivell. These facts were pressed upon the attention of cousin Swift with such force and assiduity that the result was, Jack one day found himself the host, and nominally the owner, of the George, which was the principal hotel in the little market town.

It is true that after a time, when Jack began to drive a fast-stepping trotter to the local races, and Mrs. Jack put on her newly-found fine airs, their envious neighbours, who hadn't rich and useful cousins, wickedly insinuated all sorts of things. The bookmaker entrusted Jack with a few trifling commissions, and these being done with care and honesty, led to more important matters, until at last Jack Wivell had become Swift's confidential and most trusted agent; and although he continued host of the George Hotel, he was too important a man to devote much personal attention to its affairs; he had other and more profitable fish to fry; so the George and its concerns were left to Mrs. Wivell, a good-looking young man whom they called manager, and several smart barmaids. The manager was not only good-looking; he was a singularly cool-headed and clever young fellow, and it was clear from the beginning that he intended making himself as agreeable as possible to Mrs. Wivell, which, of course, was no more than his duty.

Nearly the whole of Mr. Wivell's time was spent in attending Boney at the various race-meetings, and in jigging to whatever tune the worthy puppet-master chose to call. He had earned by these means a considerable amount of money, but as he had, unfortunately, contracted some expensive habits, he was not at present rich; but he intended to be so, and he thought he saw the means by which that praiseworthy intention would be realised. He had running in his name a three-year-old belonging to Boney called Flash Girl, which had been very bad as a two-year-old. She had run a good many times, and always badly, although her trainer had tried her, at home, to be more than useful. During the winter she appeared to have improved in her temper, and she had certainly grown into a lovely mare, and the trainer had tried her to be as good as her looks; but so cunningly had she been handled that this fact was known only to Boney, his trusty agent, Wivell, and the trainer. The lads in the stable, and even the jockey who rode her in the trial, knew nothing of the weights she carried, and, consequently, were ignorant of her merits. She was bottom-weight in three small handicaps, so Boney decided that in the first race, which looked like being a poor field, both as regarded quantity and quality, it would be well to back her for a fair amount, and then get her well beaten, knowing that whatever he lost on this race was money well invested, for the ring would be sure to follow the owner, and perhaps, with this outlay and her good looks, she might even be favourite, which would give her running a genuine look, and the money might be got back with good interest in the next race, and there, with a better field, Flash Girl would probably be an outsider.

The morning of the first race found the nominal owner of Flash Girl closeted with the real owner, Boney Swift.

"Well, Jack, how's the mare this morning?" inquired Boney.

"Oh, she's first-rate—fit as a fiddle," replied Jack, "and I only wish she was going for the money to-day."

"Don't you be in a hurry," said Boney, "but do exactly as I tell you; and whatever you do, don't breathe a word to anybody. You back her for me with six or eight of the principal layers for two hundred pounds among them, and I'll back her

"THE DOUBLE" ON A CHEAT

for a bit also, and if it's done properly, I have no doubt the punters will bite, and we may have her a good favourite. You can leave the rest to me."

The numbers went up for the race. There were five runners, and it was clear either the public knew more than the confederates bargained for, or the mare's good looks had impressed them, for she was made favourite before a bet was made by Boney or his agent. This appeared to delight the worthy couple immensely. When the punters saw the reputed owner, and also the astute Boney Swift, begin to back her, they tumbled over one another to take even money. But somehow the rage for Flash Girl cooled down in an unaccountable manner, for it was evident to Boney's clear eyes that no large commission was being worked for either of the others, and every minute the mare got a worse favourite, although it was certain she had been backed for a great deal more money than all the others put together. To an old hand like Mr. Swift, there was only one possible explanation for this state of things. There was treachery in the camp. He was doubly sure of this when he found a noted "dead meat" man like Smiler Kirk not missing a shilling Flash Girl, and always offering a shade over the odds. He was standing by Jack as the horses were at the post, the start being delayed by one which was fractious.

"If that brute keeps them at the post much longer, the mare will be the outsider of the party," said Boney; and then looking at him with those keen black eyes, he asked: "Can *you* explain it, Jack?"

"No, that I can't," answered Wivell. "I put all the money on, and never cracked a lay."

"I can explain it for you, Mr. Wivell," said a punter, who stood by, and had evidently overheard the conversation.

"What do you know about it?" snapped out Jack, looking, however, nervously at the man, who answered:

"Well, I had five pounds to four ready with Sim Lunt,

which was half a point over the price, and when Flash Girl had gone back to two to one, I found old Sim still laying over the odds. I got a peep at his volume, and I found it was a one-horse book; he'd laid nothing else, so I knew somebody had laying orders, and I took the liberty of getting my fiver back by laying over the odds, and I don't think I shall be sorry for it either."

The horses being off stopped any further talk. Flash Girl was last; in fact, she walked in with the crowd. The jockey declared she had "rolled all over the course." Some of the newspapers the following day said that the mare was "good-looking, but a gay deceiver—" "a jade that wouldn't try," etc. and others that she ran "*green*." Mr. Swift thought a good deal, and said nothing. He knew that the trainer, or his bosom pal, Wivell, had put one or two in to lay against the mare, and had, at the same time, put him " in the cart." With a great effort of will he composed the awful twitching of the yellow parchment which covered his bony face, and his wild black eyes became placid as those of a little child, and he walked away with his friend as quietly as though nothing was amiss, and no raging hell-fire of the direst sort burning at his heart.

Before Swift left the course he found an opportunity of having a few words in private with an eminent Scotland Yard detective, to whom he was well known.

"I want you, Tanner, to get two men watched to-night," said Boney. "I want to know where they go, how long they stop at any place they visit, and their every movement till they go to bed. Can you manage it for me?"

"Yes, sir, if the men have no suspicion they are being watched," replied Tanner. " Who are they?"

"One is my friend Wivell, the other Phil Blunt, the trainer," answered Boney. "You know me, Tanner; do this job well, and it shall be made worth your while. Report to me, at my hotel, at eight o'clock to-morrow morning; I'll arrange they are both out of the way."

After dinner that night Blunt proposed the usual game at whist, which Boney readily agreed to; Wivell said he'd a bad headache, and would prefer a good long walk through the neighbouring park, but the set was easily made up, and they played till bed-time.

At eight o'clock next morning Mr. Tanner was shown into Swift's bedroom, where that gentleman impatiently awaited him. The detective was so admirably disguised as a farm labourer that, until he spoke, Boney did not recognise him.

"Your report, Tanner," was the laconic demand of the fierce old bookie.

"The trainer, as you are aware, sir, didn't leave the house," began Tanner; "Wivell I'd a fancy for taking on myself, in this disguise."

And then he gave a long account of his tracking Jack through the wood and into the park, where he met Smiler Kirk; the pair evidently having met by appointment, had important business to transact. He told also of his following him when it was quite dark to a private house in the town, where Sim Lunt was lodging, and where he remained for an hour. The report left no room to doubt who was the traitor. Boney handed the detective a twenty-pound note for his night's work.

"There will be another pony for you," he said, "in a fortnight's time, if this matter is kept perfectly secret between us."

The following week Flash Girl was in her second race at Warwick, and Boney was in high spirits, intending, as he told Wivell, to bring off a good *coup* with the mare. Jack didn't say as much, but all the same he had made up his mind that he wouldn't be far behind his principal in this matter. Swift *said* he had made elaborate arrangements in London and in most of the large towns to send trusty agents to skin the ready-money lists, in addition to wiring to his usual agents. Jack *said* nothing, but really did take this course unknown to his friend, as he supposed. He had received three or four hundred pounds as his share of the secret laying order to Messrs. Kirk & Lunt. This, and as much more ready money as he could put his hands on, had gone in this way. When the numbers went up, he backed her for as much money as he possibly could without attracting the attention of Boney. He had also several people doing commissions for him. For the mare having a couple of stone in hand, why should he not take advantage of his knowledge and win a stake at one *coup* which would place him beyond the caprice of his employer and make him independent? This would have happened if the mare had won, but, unfortunately for him, the crafty Boney was even now at his old game of pulling the strings, and this time with terrible purpose—indeed, tragically—for poor Wivell. In making the bend for home, when well in front and going great guns, she bolted out of the course. The jockey declared she must have gone mad, as he lost all control of her. However that may have been, the result didn't seem to distress Boney. On the contrary, he was overpowered with a sense of satisfaction and pleasure. The strings had worked smoothly and well, and the puppets had danced exactly as he desired. Within a month Jack Wivell was not only a posted defaulter, he was a ruined outcast. The George had passed into other hands, his good-looking wife had gone, no one knew where, leaving him nothing but four young children to remind him of her. The smart young manager also had disappeared, whither was also a mystery. The uncharitable neighbours, of course, again said uncharitable things.

CHAPTER XXXI

RINGING IN A WRONG 'UN

How Maurice Felton became a Punter—What came of it.

Bookmakers have earned the character of being more than commonly clever, and there is no doubt the majority of them have done something to deserve the character. Clever as they are, however, they are frequently victimised by people quite as clever and less scrupulous than themselves. There are many methods by which bookmakers are swindled. One of the commonest, years ago, and one they had least chance of guarding against, was known as " ringing in a wrong 'un "; that is, introducing to the ring a well-got-up young man of good appearance but no means, who will be unprincipled enough to lend himself for the purpose. Occasionally these swindles have been so successful that they have not only succeeded in robbing the fielders of large sums of money, but the " wrong 'un " has eventually established a position, and become quite a respectable member of the ring. The mode of operation will be fully explained in the history of a young man whom I knew, although in this case neither bookmakers nor others ultimately suffered by the fraud.

Maurice Felton was a fine, dashing young fellow, with a really very aristocratic appearance, without being an aristocrat by birth. His grandfather had been a successful manufacturer of brass buttons and buckles in the good old town of Birmingham, where he worked hard all his long life, most of which had been passed, day and night, at his cosy home on the manufacturing premises, as was the custom in those old-fashioned days among successful men in the famous hardware town.

Young Maurice had come of age some two years before my story opens, and, having gone through the usual course of a gentleman's education at Cambridge, he was now busy sowing wild oats in the beautifully rich soil of London town, making all haste, there and elsewhere, to get rid of that portion of the old button-maker's wealth which, in the course of nature, and forty years after the old man's death, had come to be his share. His father and mother, who had been a sadly unfortunate, or, shall we rather say, a sadly improvident, couple, were dead, and, as far as he knew, the only relatives he had in the world were his father's elder brother, a gay old bachelor of some sixty-five summers, who, with a spinster sister, ten years older than himself, lived a few miles from the big town at a fine old house, with an estate, and rent-roll of something like five thousand pounds a year, which estate the old buttonmaker had bought in his later days, and being tainted with that vulgar weakness, a desire to found a county family, he had settled the same in male-tail, etc., on his heirs for ever, which was a fortunate thing, I was going to say, for young Maurice; but that would not be so true, perhaps, as saying it was a fortunate thing for a certain notorious moneylender and a shrewd, if not too scrupulous, bookmaker. And it came about in this way. At present our young friend had had but slight acquaintance with bookmakers or betting, but with Mr. Jacob Jones, the money-lender, he had enjoyed the luxury of a constant intercourse for several years—had, indeed, done very considerable business with him, and in this direction had now come pretty near to the end of his tether. In fact, Mr. Jones was just declaring, in the bluntest possible manner, that he had already nearly ruined himself by advancing such a large amount of money on such a dreadfully poor security and wretched interest, which had hitherto been merely at the rate of about eighty-five per cent.

"Why don't you go down to Button Hall again," he inquired, "and try to touch your old uncle for a bit?"

"You know why I don't go," replied Maurice; "my old aunt has been very good to me, and she, as well as the old man, is pretty warm, I know, and when they die—supposing I behave myself—I shall come into whatever they leave, as well as the entailed property. I have told you that they both declared, in the most solemn manner, when they settled my last batch of college bills—yours among them—that if I got into any further scrapes they wouldn't leave me a shilling of their savings to squander—and their savings, I'm thinking, are worth a good deal more than the property; so that's why I won't go to them. I would rather go abroad and lose myself for a few years."

"Look here, my boy," says the tempter, "why don't you go on the turf?"

"Go on the turf! What have I to go on the turf with?" asked Maurice, who had had some very little experience, while at college, running over from Cambridge to Newmarket Heath occasionally. "I have now barely enough oof left to settle my overdue bill at the hotel."

"I'll show you how to do it," said the money-lender. "You are a fine, handsome-looking young swell, and the bookies would jump at catching you. I can get you introduced, and supply you also with some fine goods to back. Bet moderately for the first few weeks; then, when your credit is well established, I can supply yon with commissions which might get you out of all your difficulties and be useful to me also, and in the meantime I will see your account is settled regularly—that is, if you act on my advice, and don't get plunging out of your depth."

So after details were carefully gone into, and the undertaking made to look plausible, nay, even pretty sure of success, our young swell was accommodated with some further advances to cover immediate wants, and all was arranged to start him in his new career the following day at Sandown Park. Thither he went, having his mentor at his elbow. He more than held his own the first day; indeed, he won a nice little parcel for himself, and considerably more for the mentor, who, as our sporting readers will perceive, was standing it "all to nothing." On the following Monday he had his first account settled at Tattersall's by a gentleman provided for that purpose by Mr. Jones. Several weeks passed with varying fortunes, but generally with a balance to the good, the larger part of which, however, he had won for the money-lender, so that, after deducting expenses, he was but little the richer for these winnings. One good result, anyhow, had accrued—his credit was established beyond dispute.

He had settled so consistently—having nearly always won, he could scarcely have done other—so the bookies almost fought for his patronage, and now the wily Jones saw his time had come to try to land a big *coup*.

It was the first day at Epsom. Mr. Jones knew of what he thought *a cert*.

"Now, Maurice, my boy," he said, "I have at last secured a pinch, and I want you to put a 'monkey' on for me, and would advise you to have two or three hundreds on for yourself. There will be eight or ten runners, and we ought to get a good price and land a pretty *coup*."

The young punter thought this a dreadfully large sum to risk all at once, and didn't quite relish the job; but being reassured by the confident manner of his clever companion, immediately the numbers were hoisted he set to work in earnest to "put on" the five hundred pounds for his friend, and nearly as much for himself, the price averaging four to one.

"This is a snip," said Jones, as they stood watching the horses about to start, and he really thought so, for he knew it had been "kept" for this little handicap, and that all connected with it believed the horse had ten pounds in hand, at least. Unfortunately, as the result proved, this was one of those little handicaps wherein there was a party with another snip, which had been even better kept, and had just a little more in hand; hence our snip was beaten by the length of a walking-stick. Maurice was dreadfully excited when it was all over, and Mr. Jones had that yellowy-greenish tint on the parchment of his cadaverous face.

On the following races our hero, with the advice of his mentor, made desperate plunges, trying to retrieve himself, but without avail, so that at the end of the day he had lost twelve hundred pounds on the balance.

"Never mind," said Jones, patting him affectionately on the back as they parted at Waterloo Station on their return to town. "We must get it all back to-morrow on the second favourite for the Derby."

And the morrow found Maurice once more in Tattersall's enclosure, eager for the fray. Instead, however, of finding his friend the money-lender, he found a telegram from him, regretting to say he was taken suddenly ill, and would not be there, but urging him to get it all back on the horse he had named for the Derby, and if it won, recommending him to return home at once and bet no more that week. This advice he acted upon, as far as fate permitted; but, alas! he was again defeated, and at the end of that day had made his liabilities £2,000. On the Thursday he was at his post, betting away with the recklessness of despair, again losing heavily. On Friday he was there again. Many of the old hands among the "fielders" knew what it all meant. They saw it was a case of "going for the gloves," and fought shy of him, what little they were obliged to bet him going to the "back of the book." Young hands, however, took him on eagerly, with the result that he managed this day to make his total loss on the week £4,000. After the races were over he made his way to the residence of Mr. Jones, anxious to know how provision was going to be made for the settling on Monday. That worthy greeted him quite effusively, and before Maurice could get a word in edgeways, cried out:

"Oh, Mr. Felton, what a dreadful day that was for me on Tuesday! And then to be taken ill, with no chance to get it back again. Five hundred pounds! five hundred pounds, Mr. Felton! And I don't know how I can raise five hundred to settle on Monday; but I hope you have done better, my boy, and got yours back, and a bit beside, so you may be able to help your old friend."

All this, and much more like it, with such well-feigned excitement and volubility, and before he could get a word in, made poor Maurice sick at heart; and when at last he was able to explain the true state of things, with the frightful amount of his losses, Mr. Jones threw up both his hands in horror, declaring they were both ruined. The young man was not quite green enough to believe this, consequently began to wheedle and coax the old money-lender, hoping to induce him to help through the settling on Monday. Need we say with what result? As well might he, with soft words, have tried to coax Cleopatra's Needle off its solid base.

Through the lonely hours of that night he walked to and fro in his room at the hotel, ruminating on what was to be done. Should he go down to the Embankment there, and throw himself into the black waters which had hidden for ever so many sad secrets? ought he get out his revolver and shoot himself? or should he pack up, take the first steamer for New York, and leave all the future to chance? After long consideration of these alternatives, he suddenly decided to adopt neither. He reminded himself that the only man he had won of during the week was the notable Dodger Luckett of Birmingham, who was his debtor for about four hundred pounds. Surely he, coming from his own town, knowing his family, and all about his expectations, and having this four hundred pounds in hand, might perhaps be induced to settle for him, on promise of liberal interest, and such security on the reversion of the Button Hall estate as was now possible. So he took an early train, and was whisked off more than a hundred miles, and was on the worthy Dodger's doorstep before that gentleman had left his snug little villa in the fashionable suburb of the great town.

The burly betting man looked a little surprised to see the young heir of Button Hall ushered into his sanctum, and politely inquired to what the honour was due. A long explanation followed, which need not be detailed here. Now Mr. Luckett was not only extremely cute, but was also very off-hand in his manner, not being troubled, either, with any inconvenient delicacy of feeling; so when the young man had finished his pitiful story, he quietly pulled down the lower lid of his right eye.

"Do you see any green there, Mr. Felton?" he inquired.

Mr Felton couldn't say he did; in fact, he couldn't say anything at all for some time, so knocked out was he with this reception. When he was able to speak, he ventured to say very meekly:

"Then you don't consider the security good enough, Mr. Luckett?"

"Good be blowed!" replied that amiable gentleman. "What's the security worth if your Uncle George should take it into his head to marry some nice young woman who would be certain to manage somehow to produce, in due time, a son and heir, who would put your nose out?"

Now this serious view of possibilities had never once occurred to Maurice Felton, and now it was disclosed to him he simply laughed an unearthly sort of laugh, and began to argue the utter impossibility of the thing.

"Don't tell me about the impossibility," said the burly one. "Why, there's old Snipe, within a mile of your uncle's house—he was nearly eighty when he married one of those meek-looking trained nurses who had been attending him for gout in the stomach, and in less than a year she provided the old man with an heir, one of the bonniest little kids you ever saw."

Having finished, he laughed so long and so violently at his own story that Maurice was quite alarmed, and thought it would be a case of an apoplectic fit.

When he had quite recovered himself he assured the young man that he was very sorry for him, but it would be quite out of the question to think of raising a quarter of the amount on the security of such expectations. How sorry he was might have been inferred had one watched his merry little eyes twinkling in their bed of fat, when, after the young man had gone, the Dodger sat down to erase Mr. Felton's name from his account, where he was down to be paid £400, knowing for a certainty that Mr. Felton's account would not be there next Monday, nor for many Mondays.

The hapless young man turned away from the house with a heavy heart, but resolved swiftly what he would do. He chartered a cab, and was soon on his way through the pleasant lanes of Warwickshire, making for the big house of his Uncle George. He determined to tell the old people none of his trouble, but of his resolve to get away to America, and right across that continent to Australia, and New Zealand, trusting to chance for the means to keep him going. He found the kind old couple concerned for his haggard and woe-begone appearance, and fully sympathising with him; they were sure—dear old souls—they knew what ailed the lad.

"Poor boy," said the sympathetic old lady, "you have met with a disappointment, I know you have," wiping a tear from her old eye, and thinking, maybe, of some far-away chapter in her own history.

"I have indeed, dear auntie," replied the smug young hypocrite, "but don't let us talk about it," and the old people had too much feeling not to see the force of this request. Agreeing that the young man showed rare good sense in deciding to travel for a time, they set about preparing an outfit for him. In a few days, with this, and a couple of hundred pounds to go on with, and with many tearful blessings, also, they set him on his way.

In the meantime, Mr. Jones' friend, the member of Tattersalls', who had settled each of the young man's winning accounts, had but a roughish time of it with the bookies, who were mostly busy calling our young hero bad names, varying this by comparing with one another the amounts they had paid the young swindler during the past month, little dreaming into whose pocket the larger part of it had gone. One of their number had received a short note from Maurice, regretting his inability to cash up at present, and stating that he was proceeding abroad at once, concluding with the comforting assurance that he hoped to come back *some day* and pay them all.

The Dodger, who was present, and in the happy position of owing, four hundred pounds he, most likely, would never be called upon to pay, exasperated them still more by quietly remarking that he would go to the Insurance Society with his four hundred pounds, and wouldn't mind giving any of them two shillings in the pound for their debts. One or two of the more needy ones, who thought a certain bird in hand worth more than five in the bush—or, worse still, flying in space over far-away countries—offered to close with him if he would double his price and make it four shillings in the pound. These terms for the present he declined, feeling pretty confident that Felton's account could not be settled within the 365 days of grace, after which, under such circumstances, no claim could be made against him. At the same time, knowing so much more of the prospects of the knocked-out punter than any of these, and seeing possibility of profit looming in the future, he makes up his mind to keep his mouth closed and his eyes open, particularly down Button Hall way; so should anything look like diminishing the old uncle's prospect of marriage, he would be ready to buy up the nephew's debts.

Ten months after this, while Maurice Felton was still on his travels, and, we will hope, getting useful experience, a sad event happened at Button Hall—Uncle George was suddenly stricken down with paralysis of the brain, and the doctors declared that, although he might linger a sort of life in death for months, he would never speak again, or recover consciousness.

With this "straight tip," knowing that no cunningest trained nurse whatsoever could have any further chance with the old man, who was now beyond the possibility of new wills, the burly Luckett, like a busy man and a cute one, went forthwith to London. There was no undue haste with him as he lay there in wait for his victims; cunningly and quietly he contrived the business, succeeding in the end in buying nearly the whole of these £4,000 worth of debts for less than £1,000, which was not a bad stroke of business from the Dodger's standpoint, and according to his limited—and I am afraid I must say somewhat oblique—range of moral vision.

Within three months of his seizure the old man died, whereupon Maurice returned home, coming into the estate and a large sum in cash and shares. The account was duly settled, and even the wicked old money-lender got his pound of flesh.

CHAPTER XXXII

CASES OF MISTAKEN IDENTITY

Sir John Astley's Claim—Lord Marcus Beresford—A fistic Preacher—
Taking a Liberty.

SIR JOHN ASTLEY was a frequent customer of mine, and a more agreeable man to do business with one could not desire. A true English gentleman, in the true sense of the word, was the bluff and jolly Sir John. There were no airs of the superior creature about him, such as belonged to many of the swells I knew so well, and whom, in too many cases, I have powerful reasons to remember—the sort of people who condescend to do business with you, making you feel the while that you must belong to another order of humanity, and that they only submit to the contact because it suits their purpose, and often, I verily believe, they consider themselves conferring an honour upon you by getting into your debt, and remaining there.

Sir John was not only the most genial of sportsmen, he was the soul of honour, and I am sure he would have been the last man in the world to make an unjust claim. Yet he was mortal, and therefore fallible; and on one occasion he made a claim upon me for £500 which I did not owe. The claim was made on behalf of Sir John by the gentleman who did his settling for many years, Mr. Henry Emmerson, otherwise known as "Black Harry." Now Master Harry, although, I believe, as straight as a gun-barrel, and a good sort of fellow at bottom, was by no means a meek-and-mild sort of person, and was apt, occasionally, to use English of an extremely forcible and not altogether classical description. He knocked me almost senseless, and entirely upset my equilibrium, one Monday at the Victoria Club by demanding, in his usual stentorian voice and peremptory manner, the trifle of £500 for Sir John Astley.

"I don't owe Sir John five hundred, or any other sum," I replied.

"Don't you," retorted my *fair* friend; "he says you do, so make haste and pull it out."

"But what is it for?" I asked. "I have had no bet with Sir John, I assure you."

"I don't know nor care what it's for; he's got you down for five hundred, and you'll have to part."

"I don't owe it," I repeated passionately; "and what is more, whatever the consequences, I will never pay it."

After more hot words on both sides, it was decided to defer the dispute until we reached Tattersall's in the afternoon; and in the meantime he would send to Sir John for particulars of the bet. I had been for months past having a very bad time, and the last week had added considerably to my misfortunes; and now, on the top of it all, to have an unjust claim made upon me for what was, at the time, a very large amount, filled me with dismay, and I am sure, could even Emmerson have known my feelings at the moment, he would have exercised a little more gentleness. At Tattersall's the argument was reopened. Unquestionably Sir John had got the bet down in his book to me clear enough and just as clearly my book showed no transaction; and, as I had but a very small book on that one particular race, one certainly of not more than £100, I could not possibly have laid £500 against any horse. I was aware this argument would avail me little if Sir John still believed I was the man he had betted with. I promised to see him the following day, my only hope now being that I might be able to convince him that the mistake was his, and if I really could not convince him, I made up my mind that I would, under no circumstances, pay it, so strongly did I feel the injustice of it, although I was aware that the consequences would be, in all probability, a "warning-off" order against me.

The next day I saw Sir John, produced my book, and tried to impress him with the improbability of my laying such a bet under the circumstances, using the most forcible language I could command, for, apart from the seriousness of the matter to myself, I felt really anxious not to quarrel with one whom I so entirely respected, and whom I knew had simply mistaken me for another. I felt he was incapable of saying the thing he did not believe; but, alas! all my eloquence was wasted upon him.

"Damn it all, Dyke!" he said; "how the devil could I mistake you for anybody else? You were standing on the rails between Tubby Waterhouse and little Jimmy O'Connor, and I have the most distinct recollection of every particular of the transaction."

And this had really been my position on the rails, which made the affair the more mysterious and awkward for me, for I was obliged to admit this fact, which served to confirm the worthy Baronet in his illusion, for an illusion I knew it was. I perceived that nothing now would move him, so I left him, and went back to my place in the ring, where a very agreeable surprise awaited me, and a revelation made which I have often thought of since those days, and one which I have always considered reflected infinite credit on Messrs. Shakeshaft & Clowes. To make a short story of it, it appeared that this firm had laid Sir John the bet in question, and had honourably come forward the moment they learned of the claim being made upon me. I have always considered Walter Shakeshaft a rather good-looking fellow, and I felt flattered to be occasionally mistaken for him. In make and shape there was, *in those days*, some resemblance, and Sir John had evidently got us mixed up. However, he afterwards frankly admitted the error, and expressed his sorrow for the trouble he had given me.

"Still, it's a devilish good job for you, Dyke," he said, "you found the pea, for I could have sworn you laid me that bet."

Some months after, this was followed by a remarkable coincidence. During another settling, a claim was made upon me for £100 on behalf of Lord Marcus Beresford. I knew I had had no transaction with his lordship during the week, and at once told his agent so. Again I was assured I should have to pay, as it would, no doubt, be an error of mine, or of my clerk's, Lord Beresford being too careful a man to make such a blunder. I felt very much annoyed and sorry; and while I felt certain it was his lordship's mistake, as I had no remembrance of even seeing him during the previous week, I knew that he was not only careful, but one of the most upright of all the swells I did business with, and, like jolly Sir John, he had a genial manner and a kindly word for everybody; and for one in my position it was most disagreeable to have disputes with such people.

It was agreed that the matter should stand over until I had an opportunity of speaking with his lordship, which opportunity came, a few days after, at Kempton Park.

"What the dickens do you mean, Master Dyke, by disputing that bet of mine?" his lordship inquired, as he came up to me between the races.

"I simply mean, my lord, that it was someone else you had that bet with; it certainly was not with me," I replied.

"Not you!" he answered, with more sternness than I thought it possible his pleasant face could assume. "Why, I have as clear a recollection of the matter as though it had occurred two minutes ago. I was on the stand alongside Sir George Chetwynd, who had his glasses watching the start. He saw my horse had got a flying start; you shouted out the name of the horse, and were loudly offering to lay a hundred to ten against him. I shouted down to you : 'I'll take that !' You looked up at me, and replied : 'All right'; and then I saw you turn round to your clerk, who appeared to be putting the bet down. This I will swear to."

"I can only repeat, my lord, that it was not with me you had that bet," I said; and then a happy thought struck me.

"Will your lordship oblige me by walking down the side of the rails, and have a good look at everyone of the fielders?" I asked.

"Certainly, if that will be any satisfaction to you," he answered.

And away we marched, Lord Beresford carefully scrutinising everyone. When he came to Walter Shakeshaft, he made a long pause, and I saw a puzzled look creep into his face.

"By Jove! I begin to think you'll be right, my boy," he said; then turning to Shakeshaft, inquired: "Did I have a hundred to ten, a winner, of you last week, Shakeshaft?"

"Yes, you did, my lord, and Clowes has just been telling me it was not claimed on Monday."

"Well, I'll never be certain about anything else," said his lordship, " for I would have gone upon my oath I had that bet with Master Dyke;" and turning to me, like the gentleman he is, he apologised for the trouble he had given me. So happily ended another incident which had looked, for a time, like being a very awkward one for me.

The frankness of his lordship, and the jovial baronet's acknowledgment of their error, contrasts forcibly with a similar case which occurred at Stockbridge about the same time, in which case, if I remember rightly, one of the Collins & Christy were concerned. Here a wrong claim was made by a swell of quite another sort, and on being referred to the committee of Tattersall's, was promptly decided in favour of the swell, Collins being ordered to pay the Captain forthwith, which he did, while smarting under the certainty that he was being robbed of the money. Now in this case also, Mr. Christy, who had laid the bet, was discovered, and refunded the amount to Collins. This fact was brought to the knowledge of the Captain in the hope that he might be a gentleman as well as a captain, and be made to unsay some of the hard words he had used, and possibly, in a mild sort of way, apologise for the wrong he had done. Nothing of the sort, however, happened; indeed, quite the contrary. The Captain more than insinuated that it was a got-up job among them to square themselves. This he could not really have believed. The fact was, his was one of those spiteful little natures which could never forgive one he had wronged, or one who had proved his fallibility. There are a good many of this sort to be met with on the turf; but as a rule they do not belong to the blue-blooded aristocracy, but rather to shoddy specimens of it—the sons of men who have made their money in trade, and who are never guilty of referring to their grandfathers.

Before I close this chapter I must relate a very curious and, for the lookers-on, a most amusing case, which I think may also be called one of mistaken identity. It must be thirty years ago, perhaps more, I was returning from a Midland race-meeting in a third-class carriage, with about half-a-dozen other turfites. In one corner of the carriage sat a thick-set, bullet-headed individual, the very type of a Brummagem bruiser, which one might easily have taken him to be, were it not for his clerical dress, the black broad-cloth suit of the regulation cut, and the orthodox white choker. He had quietly ensconced himself in one of the corners, taking not the slightest notice of any of his fellow-travellers, excepting, perhaps, just to turn up the whites of his rather striking eyes when, occasionally, the language of two of the travellers became very violent and unnecessarily indecent, for the presence of the clergyman, so far from acting as a restraint upon these gentlemen, only seemed to increase their bad behaviour. After a little time the reverend gentleman fell into a gentle dose, or he feigned to do so. And then the fun began. Now these two men were in a fairly good position in the town they hailed from, and they would have considered themselves insulted to have been classed with the common rough, one being a prosperous shopkeeper, and the other a well-known malster. The latter was known also as a terrible bully, especially when it happened, as on the present occasion, he was exhilarated with an extra glass or two; and he had the reputation, moreover, of being useful with his fists. No sooner was the clergyman asleep, or apparently so, than they began playing practical jokes on him. One, getting his pipe into a welding heat, blew clouds of smoke into his face, and the other untied his choker. The parson seemed to sleep through these and similar jokes, perfectly oblivious to all his surroundings. The two ruffians, seeing these mild jokes had so little effect, proceeded to some of a more violent and indecent character. Whereupon, suddenly, the reverend gentleman opened his remarkable eyes, and at the same time tightly closed his immense fists, and like a flash of lightning his left went straight for the nose of the green-grocer, and at the same instant his right seriously disfigured a useful, but too prominent, organ of the malster. Then followed a perfect storm of blows. To defend themselves was out of the question; they were no sooner on their feet than they were sent sprawling again as with a sledge hammer; and in the space of about five minutes the two cowardly bullies got a well-deserved, dreadful thrashing from the sturdy little parson. My travelling companions seemed struck with amazement, but to me the catastrophe caused no surprise; indeed, I felt certain I knew what would happen when those practical jokes commenced, for I had recognised, in the clergyman, my old friend, the invincible Birmingham pugilist, Morris Roberts, who at that time had one of his preaching fits on.

This story of Morris Roberts reminds me of another, also concerning one of the best known of the old Brummagem "fancy."

George Giles, better known as "Fat 'Un," was not one of

Birmingham's most distinguished, or most polished exponents of the noble art, but he was known, far and wide, as a terrible slogger, who could give and take as much punishment as any of his townsmen. I remember him well, and knew him in his palmiest days. A roly-poly sort of young fellow, thick-set, with a fat face, and an evident predisposition to adiposity. I remember when he gave over fighting, instead of taking a public-house and drinking himself to death, as so many of them do, he got himself converted by the Methodists, went into business on his own account as a gasfitter, and settled down a really quiet, harmless, and respectable member of society. His natural love of sport took the form of angling, and he became a devoted follower of the "Gentle Izaak." One day three Brummagem roughs were spending a day in the country, and, after their kind, were ready for any bit of devilment. In this frame of mind they came across a respectable-looking gentleman, rather stout, with a benevolent, florid face, and middle-aged, on the bank of the river, fishing. Here, evidently, was safe game for three sportive young men. One of them had the small branch of a tree in his hand; he commenced the proceedings by shying it at the line, and so successfully, the fat gentleman was left with the rod in his hands, but line and float had gone. The fisherman mildly remonstrated.

"Why should you take such a liberty with me, young man?" he asked. "I have done no harm to you, but it would serve you right to pitch you into the river after my line."

I dare say Mr. Giles—for he it was—had some idea what the effect of this threat would be, and, gentle as he was, would be prepared for it. Rough No 1, using very bad language, threatened to throw the fat man after his line if he did not keep a civil tongue in his head, and came menacingly close up to him. Like a shot from a gun-barrel and straight from the shoulder, Mr. Giles let him have one of the old sort, and the young man was flat on his back, and considerably dazed. Almost at the same instant Rough No. 2 met with the same fate, while No. 3, realising that there had been a mistake somewhere, made off with all speed, leaving the local preacher and sometime pugilist, master of the field, and with an excellent opportunity of " improving the occasion," which, I believe, he did not neglect.

CHAPTER XXXIII

SETTLING RACING ACCOUNTS

How some Noblemen settle—"A Lady on Horseback"—A Trifle overlooked—Sharping a Sharper—Trying it on—Welshing a Lady.

FOR many years I attended Tattersall's, and the Victoria Club, every Monday for the purpose of settling my own and other people's accounts. While so occupied I often came across amusing as well as serious experiences. The public generally, and the vast majority of racing men, who have lacked the privilege of belonging to "The Vic.," or the more exclusive "Tatt.'s," would find it difficult to realise the immensity of the business transacted during the afternoon of every Monday during the racing season. And on the Monday after every great meeting the money which changes hands is simply enormous.

To me the surprising part of the thing has always been that a business of such magnitude should be done in the space of a few hours, with mistakes and disputes so rare. Smith settles with Jones, for, possibly, a dozen different gentlemen, receives large sums on some of the accounts, and pays heavily on others. When the balance is struck, the actual money changing hands between these two agents may be a few pounds only, or it may be ten thousand pounds; in any case, no receipt or acknowledgment, of any kind, is given. They simply write a cross against each of their client's names in their own book, and there the matter ends.

It says a good deal for the integrity of these agents that such a thing as disputing a payment is scarcely known. And these agents are largely composed of that much maligned and abused class, the bookmakers.

A few professional backers and commission agents also act as "settlers." And there are men who have made settling a profession, and have done little else, and a fairly good thing some of them made of it. Reporters for sporting newspapers, and some few quite high-class sporting writers, have always had a fair share of this lucrative employment.

It often happens that these agents have a good deal more to do for their clients than merely settling their accounts.

Some great men who mix with their statesmanship, and other public duties, a bit of racing, are notably careless with their betting accounts. Some of them keep no books, but scribble each day's transactions all over their cards, and even where books are kept some of them find it too difficult to unravel the particulars, so send these cards or books, as the case may be, at the end of the meeting to the bookmaker or other agent who settles for them. On him devolves the duty of finding out what the noble lord has won or lost on the week. I know at least one Cabinet Minister of to-day who, years ago, was in the habit of doing this. Now, I don't want anybody to suppose that I am insinuating that the gentlemen lose anything by this carelessness; the probability is that they get their accounts done much more correctly this way than they would if done by themselves. To begin with, and to place the matter on very low moral grounds, it does not pay these agents to go in the slightest degree crooked; and on the other hand, they are, as a rule, a class of men as likely to be actuated by higher and better principles as would be found in any walk in life.

Having said this much in favour of this deserving class, "as a rule," I feel bound to say I have come across a few exceptions in my time. I knew one settler in particular, a very rich man, who for many years occupied one of the foremost, if not the very front place, among them, a man who had contrived to impress certain great nobleman, whose accounts he settled, with an idea that his character was above reproach. This gentleman was a veritable scorcher. There was nothing too hot or too heavy for him, as the saying is, and this was perfectly well known to every one of us who had occasion to do business with him every Monday at Wellington Street, or at "the Corner," yet, to the day of his death, among the swells, he was looked upon as a paragon of virtue.

In his day this gentleman, whose identity will be readily recognised, did some very large "coms" for a certain stable, and it is somewhere about thirty years ago that he made that famous *mistake* which put £10,000 into his own pocket. The facts, briefly stated, are these. Mr. Blank had the working of an immense commission for a great horse in one of the big races on behalf of the owner, known to be of the careless and confiding class. This big order was successful, and Mr. Blank produced for his principal's perusal an enormous list of the bets he had made on his behalf, with columns upon columns of figures, which totalled up to a win of over £70,000. The swell was too delighted with the result to be over-critical, too careless to take the trouble to wade through this mass of figures, and too confiding to employ an accountant to do it for him, consequently during the owner's lifetime it was never discovered that Mr. Blank had made a trifling *mistake*, in adding up the columns which made £10,000 difference to the total, and it was not until many years after the event that the matter oozed out.

An old friend of mine, who, until his quite recent retirement, was perhaps the oldest fielder in England, used to settle a good many accounts, and was, "take him for all in all," a very estimable man. He has been blessed with a good many useful punters, during his long career, and were he so disposed, could tell some amusing tales anent the same. He once had among his *clientèle* a gentleman for whom he also acted as agent or settler; and he was a very good sort, for however diminutive the account, he never forgot to include the £1 which is the usual fee for settling this kind of account, and as he did nearly the whole of his betting with one man, and that one man my friend, whom I will call Mr. Thomas, it was generally an easily-earned sovereign. And, in fact, on one occasion he carried his punctiliousness to an almost ludicrous excess. He had been out for a few days' racing, and, as was nearly the invariable custom, he had a losing account; but he had confined the whole of his business, on this occasion, to my friend Thomas, who was a good deal amused on his arrival at "The Vic." to find not only a cheque for the amount he had lost to Mr. Thomas, but included in it was the usual fee for settling his account.

On another occasion this same punter was racing a whole week, and was betting with unusual recklessness, but still, mostly, with friend Thomas. After he got back home the bookmaker received a telegram: "Have not the slightest idea how I stand with you. Let me know."

Now it so happened that the punter had this week blundered on to several long-priced winners, and Mr. Thomas made out himself indebted £340 to the punter, so he simply wired in return: "I make the difference between us £340." You may imagine my old friend's amazement when he found himself in the punter's account to *receive*, instead of to pay, £340.

All betting men will know what is meant here by "a lady"; but as many of my readers do not, I will explain. "A lady," or, as it was called originally, "a lady on horseback"—derived, I think, from *Punch*—is any unexpected amount made in the course of settling.

There is a saying that tactics of questionable character, under ordinary circumstances, would be considered "fair in love or war." There can be no doubt, also, that practices which would justify the appellation of "sharp," or the use even of a harsher adjective—if exercised in the regular business of life—would yet be perfectly allowable on the turf, and properly so. Hence, if I am settling an account for betting transactions, for myself or for another, and I have on my list to pay to Mr. Brown £100, I am not expected straightway to hand to Mr. Brown £100. I have to ask what he claims. If he claims £100, I pay him; if £50, I pay him £50. I am not bound to tell him I have him down for £100; but the ethics of the turf are most emphatic in insisting that I shall tell him he has made an incorrect claim, so giving him an opportunity of searching it out for himself, and finding, if possible, where the error is. And it were easy to prove that, in strictest justice, he has no right to more.

I will illustrate this by the statement of an incident in my own experience which occurred many years ago.

I was settling at "The Vic."; a well-known member of that club came up to me hurriedly, and, before I could ask him a question, he thrust into my hand £25 in notes.

"There, Mr. Dyke," said he, "I owe you a pony," and immediately turned away.

I knew there was a mistake, somewhere. Looking at my book, I found I had to pay him £200 instead of receiving £25. I called after him, giving him the customary warning.

"I am quite satisfied. I had one bet only with you on the week; it was twenty-five to two hundred." Naming a certain horse, this was all he replied.

On careful inquiry, I found that the horse he had named ran in the race, and, moreover, that the race was won by a horse with a name which might easily have been mistaken for the one my friend had backed.

In the hurly-burly of the betting, it was probable my clerk had entered the name of the wrong horse. So, had the other horse won, instead of receiving £25, which I should have claimed, I should certainly have been compelled to pay £200, as doubtless the gentleman would have been able to prove he

SETTLING RACING ACCOUNTS

had backed the winner. In the many thousands of transactions compressed into the space of a few minutes, and amid the hurry and excitement, immediately preceding a race, it would be more than marvellous if mistakes were not occasionally made; the wonder of it is that they are so rare.

Racing men who remember the unpolished and eccentric Billy Nicholls, the once great Nottingham bookmaker, will not need to be told that an undeviating honesty was the strongest characteristic of this man of violent speech, and rugged exterior. The other day, while strolling through the gardens at Bournemouth, I chanced to meet my very old racing pal, Mr. William—otherwise remembered as "Spectacle"—Collins.

The conversation naturally turned to the old times and old men of the turf. Billy Nicholls, among others, was introduced.

"Ah, he was a downright honest fellow, was old Billy!" said Collins, "and nobody has better reason to know it than I have, for I once backed a horse with him, in the way of covering, to win a monkey, which was a serious amount for me, in those days, and if I couldn't have received it there might have been some trouble; and he need not have paid me, and if he hadn't been an honest man he wouldn't, either. Poor old Harry Mitchell, who booked for him for so many years, had made a mistake, putting the wrong horse down, so when I went to claim the five hundred pounds he swore they didn't owe it, but that they wanted fifty of me; and there was no doubt he believed it, too; and as that was what their book said, and I had no witness, it looked an awkward job for me. You may perhaps imagine, then, what my feelings were when good old Billy turned round to his clerk, and said:

"'Thee pay the mon the money, Harry. I remember the bet. It's thy mistake, lad.'"

Sometimes bets may get wrongly entered, or omitted altogether, through excitement arising from other causes than racing. Tom Russell of Walsall, an old friend of mine, was in the habit of betting heavily on coursing events, and had for many years a £1,000 book on the Waterloo Cup; a few nights previous to the decision of which he was staying at the Adelphi Hotel, Liverpool, where, I may remark, most of the betting on the Cup was done. The regular business of the evening being over, my friend and some boon companions over their glasses were *set* for an hour's enjoyment, among these being good old Tom Coleman, one of the shrewdest of punters, racing or coursing. In the early hours of the morning, when really every man of them ought to have been in bed, Tom began to manifest a high degree of excitement, worked upon, I suppose, by his convivial surroundings, flow of soul, etc. He began offering to take all sorts of leviathan bets on the Cup, among which was an offer to take £1,000 to £20 a certain outsider.

"I'll lay you half that," said Russell.

"All right," replied Tom, and 500 to 10 was booked, forthwith, at least by the layer.

Now, this outsider won the Cup, and, on the following Monday, I had my friend's account to settle at the Victoria Club, and had got in it, of course, to pay Coleman £500. I had been paying and receiving for an hour or more, and was standing with a great pile of notes before me, certainly several hundreds of pounds, when I observed Coleman, for the first time, coming towards me. Without waiting to see if he was going to speak to me, with an unpardonable impetuosity, I cried out:

"I'll pay you later on, Tom; I've scarcely enough in hand to settle with you."

Tom opened wide his bright black eyes, looking for an instant struck with amazement, and I knew then what a blunder I had perpetrated.

"*You* have no claim, I can see; Sam Coleman of Liverpool is probably my man," I said quickly.

He made no remark, but passed away with a puzzled look.

I saw him no more that day. There was little doubt he had gone to think about it, and to work. I decided I would, if possible, prevent any of the men I had yet to settle with getting a look at my book, taking, as I fondly imagined, every necessary precaution. I got to Tattersall's, and towards the close of the afternoon I had occasion to do some settling with Mr. Tom Collins, and had my book open at the C's, when, to my dismay, I caught a long-necked wretch, over my shoulder, having a fair good inspection of that page. I knew in a moment I was done. I went home, and during the next day I received—not unexpectedly—a telegram from old Tom asking me to kindly send him a cheque for £500, which trifle had been overlooked the day before. True, very true, old Tom, overlooked indeed! Of course, the money had to be paid; but Coleman told me years after, in the frankest manner possible, that he had not the remotest recollection of making any such bet, and he was quite certain my friend, Mr. Russell, was drunk at the time, and had imagined it.

Dodger Luckett enjoyed nothing so much as getting about him a company of betting men, and holding forth on the iniquity of "the toffs," as he called them, betting, and not settling.

One Monday morning he was in the breakfast-room at "The Vic.," before the settling commenced. He had a congenial audience, so he pulled out his big settling book, and proceeded to read out the names of swells who were in default to him.

"Look here, George," said a bookie who was present, "I often have a gamble when I've little chance to win. Put up a few of your bad items, and perhaps I may speculate. To begin, what does Lord Blank owe you?"

"Two hundred and eighty," replies Dodger.

"How much for that lot?" asked the bookie.

"You can have it for the odd one hundred and eighty," was the reply.

"I'll give you eighty."

"I'll see you —— first," said Luckett.

"Who's the next about the same figure?" asked the would-be buyer.

Amongst the various items came one against the name of A. Jones for a similar amount. Now, you would never guess that this gentleman with the uncommon name hailed from Wales, and yet it was so; and, moreover, he was one of the very best ever sent from that splendid little principality.

Now, it happened that this gentleman occasionally overran the constable, and we had to wait a little; but some of us had known him many years before Luckett became acquainted with him, and we knew, also, that, given life and a little time, he was sure to come again.

"How much did you say Jones owes you?" queried the bookie. "And what Jones is it?"

"I don't know who he is," answered Dodger. "I only know his name's Jones, and he's got into my book for exactly the same amount as Lord Blank, and you can buy him at the same price I offered the lord—one hundred and eighty."

"Well, I'll buy either at my price, and you can give me whichever you like, Taffy or the lord, and my price is one hundred for the two hundred and eighty; but I'll only buy one just at present."

"Done!" says Luckett. "Let me touch the stuff. I'll give you Jones."

The cash was immediately paid, and A. Jones became thereupon indebted to ——, bookmaker, instead of to Luckett, in the sum of £280.

You may have some inkling of the fury of Dodger, but unless you have been highly educated in the classic language of the turf, you can form no idea of the powerful kind of speech the Dodger delivered when he came into the settling room, an hour later, and found the following notice posted on the blackboard provided for that purpose: "*Charles Head has Mr. A. Jones' account for last year.*"

It was months after when Luckett made the discovery that the lucky purchaser knew, before he entered the breakfast-room, that Head had received a cheque on Coutts' Bank for Jones' full account, which cheque had already been converted into cash, and that it was actually with one of Head's clean £100 notes that he had been paid.

During the partnership of my brother and George Collins, which extended over many years, there were few fielders more regular in attendance at the various race-meetings; indeed, it was a very rare occurrence for them to be absent a single day, from any of the principal meetings. On one occasion, however, a day's absence came near costing them two hundred pounds. During the first three days of a Newmarket Meeting they had been betting with a gent, whom I'll call Mr. White. On the Thursday night an urgent matter took them home, so they saw no more of Mr. White, who owed them about a couple of hundred pounds. The account was returned on the following Monday unsettled. Nobody knew anything of Mr. White.

Two or three years passed, and they looked on the account as gone. They were betting at Sandown, when George Collins cried out suddenly:

"Why, there's that White who owes us two hundred!" and thereupon he was confronted, by the pair, and charged with it.

"I don't owe you a penny," said the gentleman. "You were not there on the last day of the meeting—I remember it all distinctly; so I went to your friend, Mr. Percival, who was betting next you, and asked for you; and as you weren't there, I had some bets with him, and won a trifle on the day, and when I had done, I gave him the balance, and told him to pay you the two hundred, as I was going to sail for China the following day, and might be away for years."

Immediately the bookies made tracks for Jack Percival.

"What the devil do you mean by drawing two hundred pounds of a Mr. White for us, two years ago, and never parting?" asked one of the partners.

"It's all right, my boy," replied Jack, laughing. "It's quite safe; the money's here, my lads, waiting for you," handing the amount to them.

They threatened him with all sorts of dreadful things, but the good-tempered rosy one laughed them out of it.

There are few better-known members of the metallic pencil fraternity than my friend, this same Jack Percival. He was, indeed, quite a striking personality in the ring; one by no manner of means to be overlooked when you are taking stock of the aforesaid fraternity. You could swear to him as he comes round the corner, even before you get a fair look at his face, one feature of it having such remarkable prominence. And when you do get a real good look at it, what a face it is—clean-shaven, keen, and rubicund; eyes as an eagle's, piercing and bright, which look, too, like having the gift of seeing many things duller folks would altogether miss; lips dropping a little, and too heavy; these also indicating—to the observant—something. A nose, not only prominent, as I have already intimated, but well set on, and full of character. The whole face, in fact, is full of character, depth, and meaning, alert, keen, sagacious, and the whole topped with a well-shaped crown, close-cropped, and white as the snows of winter. See him as he takes his place on the rails, bright, brisk, and gay; carrying his sixty-eight summers, or more, as lightly as a youth of twenty.

Of him, his doings and his sayings, for the forty years or thereabout he has been known to the turf, there are curious stories afloat, many of them as well worth recording as is a great deal appearing in the biographies of your great men, and certainly more interesting, if not more sensational, than much

SETTLING RACING ACCOUNTS

emanating from the imaginations of our modern novelists; with this advantage, that our stories shall be true, or, anyway, founded on that sublime virtue.

Jack did a large trade in his way of business, and many of his customers were found among the rich and titled ones of the earth; one of these same being the late Earl of Dudley, who, while not being an habitually heavy bettor, it was well known did periodically indulge in a very large bet, which I am given to understand was generally lost, and always promptly settled. Sometimes one of the leviathan fielders, and sometimes another, had the pleasure of accommodating his lordship with his big bet. On the occasion I am to speak of it was the fate of Percival to lay his lordship five thousand pounds against a certain horse for the Derby, and although this horse won the race, it was, nevertheless, a fine bet for our bookie, because there was no difficulty in covering at a large profit, which our friend, J. P., was far too astute a practitioner to neglect. In fact, it was the making of his book; this one good big bet enabled him to be " over round " on the race, and although the horse won, he was himself a considerable winner. On the Monday following, Jack takes his smiling rubicund visage to the Victoria Club in the first place, to meet the settling over this important race, and he takes also along with him five irreproachably clean, crisp, and quite brand new thousand-pound notes, wherewith to liquidate in prompt and satisfactory manner the claim of my Lord Dudley, the moment it shall be made. He comes across his lordship's accredited agent; does business with him in other accounts, but no mention is made of this matter of the five thousand pounds. He softly inquires of the worthy agent the names of the clients for whom he is settling this morning, discovers that among others he is settling for Lord Dudley, discovers also with inexpressible pleasure, and some amazement, that his lordship makes no claim against him in respect to this five thousand pounds, or any other sum. However, not a muscle of this sagacious man's face is moved, as indicating pleasure or amazement; clearly a mistake somewhere. Perhaps his lordship had forgotten or had not understood that the bet was really laid, but he will not hug himself, too much, at present. Perhaps his lordship, being a generous man, and considerate, was giving him a few hours to collect his own accounts before he put in his claim, and this being an unusually large amount to draw, he would be up at "The Corner" himself, later on. In the meantime, hoping and dreading, yet silent as the grave.

At the usual time he drives off to complete the settling at Tattersall's; does business with many, among them, once again, with his lordship's agent. Still no claim made, and no lordship turning up. Business being all done at "The Corner," see how nimbly he jumps into his hansom, and is whisked away to his snug little house in the West End, hugging himself enough, now, and hugging also the five crisp notes, folded neatly and stowed away, in his inside vest pocket, so near his heart were they. I fancy I can see him as he bounces into his elegant little dining-room, where waits for him his wife and a dinner fit for a king.

I must tell my readers that Percival was under a promise to divide with his wife all unclaimed trifles, or whatever amounts he might make at the settling, which items are known as "ladies," and Jack *said* he had done so for many years. She, knowing all his moods, and every atom of his character, as could no other human being, and having eyes, she watched him frisking about, looked at his bright, shining rubicund face, and saw sitting there something more than satisfaction, knew, at once, that some great good luck had befallen him, and, like a woman, thereupon became possessed of the desire, nay, rather say with the determination, to share it with him. She struggles to know his secret, but this he will in nowise allow, but he does admit to the great good luck, and declares that she shall, *as usual*, share that with him ; say, sundry new dresses, etc. etc., and, above all, a nice little carriage and a pair of ponies, which Mrs. Jack herself can drive. So the struggle is over, and Jack goes on his way rejoicing.

Many Mondays come and go, and much settling is done, and still no claim for these five useful bits of paper, which meanwhile are still lying, snugly, inside the great safe at his West End house, ready at a moment's notice, if such unlikely and untoward event should occur as that they should be required by their rightful owner. This faint fear was becoming more and more faint—had, indeed, well-nigh gone altogether—and he decided it was now time to add these notes to the pile already in the care of his banker. And now, behold! The rosy J. P. returned once more from a satisfactory day's settling; his rubicund face shining; self-satisfaction, and an untroubled conscience, beaming, as it were, through every pore of him. He is in the act of sitting down to the customary little dinner with Mrs. Jack. Suddenly is heard the roll of carriage-wheels in his quiet street, and, in fact, a carriage does actually pull up at his very door. Rather startled, J. P. jumps up from the table, gets a hasty look through the window, and sees, at once, what gives him a shock, and drives the blood from his rubicund face. Two gentlemen are alighting from the carriage, one his Lordship of Dudley, and the other a well-known sporting baronet, his intimate friend. Jack grows hot and cold, blue, red, white, all sorts of colours in the space of one minute, while they stand at the door inquiring for him. They are shown into a room, and Jack makes a mighty effort to compose himself. And such a perfect master of arts is he, that in two minutes he has joined his visitors, and no one could have recognised him for the man who was looking through the window just two minutes ago. He was perfectly himself again, only, as the saying goes, rather more so; his face once more blazing with fun and good temper, his whole manner jolly, even to hilarity. Conversation ensues on all sorts of subjects —health, the weather, business, and the prospects of the coming glorious Goodwood Meeting; glasses were filled and emptied, and the visitors were evidently preparing for departure, and still no mention of the five thousand pounds; till Jack began to breathe a little freer—to feel even a little hope, as, indeed, why should he not? Great folks had called upon him often enough, before now, to get a little chat; this same great lord, even. Alas, for human hopes! just as the nobleman was putting on his first glove, he turns his head quietly toward our hero, saying:

"Well, Jack, I thought I wouldn't trouble you about my Derby bet just at the time, but if it's quite convenient, I should like to draw it now."

A great lump rushed to Jack's throat, and I have heard him describe his own feeling, of that moment, by the aid of his own powerful vocabulary; but no language I could command would do justice to the subject, so I'll not attempt it. Let it suffice, Jack instantly swallowed the lump and his feelings, and turning to his lordship, with perfect composure, replied:

"All right, my lord! Why didn't you claim it before? I've been expecting you every day. It's all right, my lord; it's in the safe, here, waiting for you, and I shall only be too glad to have it out of my hands and off my mind."

So the visitors departed, carrying with them the five crisp bits of paper, and, I am afraid, had they known it, something else, which Jack could not help burdening them with at that unhappy moment.

I shall not attempt to describe the change in him, once again, when he rejoined his wife in the dining-room, where his dinner was getting cold, and where his wife waited with impatient curiosity. Nor shall I tell what became of that dinner, and the valuable utensils which contained it. I shall draw a veil, also,

SETTLING RACING ACCOUNTS 363

over the scene which took place when the true facts of Jack's great good luck became known to the lady.

"Nice share of five thousand pounds! A paltry little pony turn-out, new dresses, etc., etc. Serve you right, Jack; it's a judgment on you for trying to welsh a lady."

CHAPTER XXXIV

PLUNGERS

The Marquis of Hastings—Old Will Roberts—George Gomm—" Little Hill "—An American Plunger—Benzon, the Jubilee Plunger.

I HAVE already dealt with Riley, my earliest acquaintance among plungers, and the one best known to me; so I need not include him with the few I shall now briefly deal with.

There never was a time, as far as my memory goes, when the turf was without its plunger, and I have seen the rise and fall of a good many of them. Until quite recent years there never was a rise which was not followed, sooner or later, by a fall; and generally speaking, there was no long spell of time between the one and the other. The most famous of them all, and, in all respects, the best of a foolish lot, was the good-hearted but hapless young Marquis of Hastings, and his was, with a vengeance, "a short and merry life."

There are two kinds of plunger: one comes on to the turf loaded with this world's goods, and goes empty away; the other comes empty-handed, and runs quickly into a huge pile. Both are afflicted with the same sort of madness, for surely only a madman could do what they do; and Hastings is the type of one, and Riley of the other.

I know it will be said that certain men, in very recent days, have plunged as heavily as either, who enjoy vast wealth at the present time, and look like finishing with it. These gentlemen, the intelligent, up-to-date reader with knowledge of turf matters will readily recognise; but these I do not count among my plungers, any more than I should Hill, Padwick, or the celebrated Freddy Swindells. If I mistake not, when these gentlemen plunge they do so on very solid grounds; and when we read of them having laid against any particular horse, or backed one for an immense stake, depend upon it they have excellent reasons for it—reasons which you and I, gentle reader, know nothing of.

The Marquis of Hastings, as I remember him on my first acquaintance with him at Stockbridge, was a delicate-looking, slim, pale-faced youth, with an exceedingly amiable expression, and generally a gentle smile on his pale face; and of all the notable names associated with Stockbridge during the eventful sixties, none stand out with more prominence than that of this hapless young lord. If I am not mistaken, he made his first appearance there in 1863, on the first day, which was devoted to the Bibury Club, and he won the very first race, a Handicap Plate of £100, with his three-year-old colt Tippler, ridden by Deacon.

Liston, belonging to Lord Uxbridge, and the mount of that little demon, Jimmy Grimshaw, who was just then approaching the summit of his popularity, was also among the half-dozen runners. Lord Uxbridge and the followers of Grimshaw were sweet on their chance, and the other noble lord rarely ran anything without having a plunge, so that between the two parties there was a battle royal, in the market, before the actual fight began. And as another big gambler was in the field in the person of the famous old American plunger, Ten Broeck, who was running a filly named Tornado, things were indeed lively. In the betting the Marquis finished best man, as usual, 7 to 4 being Tippler's price, while Liston finished at 9 to 4, and Mr. Ten Broeck's filly about twice that price. In the race only Tippler and Tornado were in the hunt, and between them it was a terrific finish, the Marquis having the best of it by a head.

After such a race it would appear scarcely likely that either of the two would be fit to race again for a day or so; yet an hour, or so, later in the day Tippler was pulled out again, and in the Bibury Stakes he opposed the greatly fancied even-money chance, Rubicon, ridden by that nailing good horseman, Mr. Thompson; General Hess, with Captain Little up, and a couple more. The finish of the race was a perfect replica of the previous one; after another punishing struggle, Mr. Wombwell got the game Tippler's nose in front, on the post.

The following year the Marquis made his second appearance at Stockbridge, bringing with him a "*dark*" two-year-old, who was destined to become one of the sensational horses of the century. The Duke made his first appearance, before the public, in the hands of Judd; and although Jem Goater's mount, Wild Boy, was looked upon as a nailer, and backed like one, too, the private reputation of The Duke, and the usual heavy metal of his noble owner, made him a long way the better favourite. Nothing else was backed, and nothing else was near the two at the finish; but The Duke opened the eyes of the onlookers, and gave them a taste of his quality, winning very easily; La Fortune, a chestnut filly belonging to Count Lagrange, ridden by poor Harry Grimshaw, was a very bad third. Wells weighed out for Sydmonton, but got himself unshipped on the way to the post. The horse bolted, and was not caught in time to be included among the starters.

For the Stockbridge Cup, at the same meeting, the Marquis ran no less than three, Tippler, Attraction, and The Grinder, of whom the last-named did best; but the best was a very bad third to old Jimmy Barber's The Clown and Lord Westmoreland's Birch Broom, both then three-year-olds, and both hereafter to play no mean parts on the turf. It was a big field; but some distance from home these two singled themselves out, and a memorable and artistic finish between two of the most accomplished horsemen of the day, resulted in Fordham squeezing The Clown home, a short head in front of Jem Goater, on Birch Broom.

PLUNGERS

Nobody who happened to be at Stockbridge in '65 will have forgotten the senstional meeting of Lord Portsmouth's Robin Hood with the Marquis of Hastings' King Hal, or the big plunge which the noble Marquis had on that occasion. The race was one of the old-fashioned biennials, and thirteen two-year-olds went to the post; but there was little interest in anything but the two I have named. Robin Hood had shown himself, at home and in public, a real good horse, and his owner, trainer, and a good deal of the talent were extremely confident, and the fact of having the redoubtable Tiny Wells in the saddle added no little to the feeling. And so they put the money down in lumps. But they had for an opponent a man who knew no fear, and who, when he believed he had something good to bet on, was too strong for a whole army of ordinary betting men. King Hal, who had up that consummate jockey, George Fordham, had made his *début* in a large field at Newmarket First Spring Meeting; the Marquis had backed him then to win a big stake, and he landed it easily, and now he thought it impossible to be beaten, and he soon stalled off all opposition, filling everybody's book, and ultimately laying considerable odds on. The Portsmouth party stuck manfully to their guns, but they had no chance with the reckless young plunger, and about Robin Hood 4 to 1 and more was obtainable up to the finish. Nothing else was backed for a shilling, and it might have been a match, so entirely did the two absorb the interest of the public, and all parties. Indeed, at the start it had become quite painful. The suspense was, however, very soon over, and the great superiority of Robin Hood was quickly manifest, for he won all the way, securing a three lengths' verdict.

Those were, indeed, merry times when the ring had the young Marquis for a punter. He bet thousands as though he was playing at marbles "for love"; and while he lasted, he was a wonderfully good-tempered loser. I never knew his equal. Mr Stephenson, the fielder, better known as "Old Stevey," once laid him an even ten thousand pounds against a horse in a fifty pounds selling plate, where neither of the wretched "screws" engaged was worth fifty, and he watched the race with as much concern as though he had a fiver depending; and when he had lost—which he did, you know—he looked quite cheerful. Probably the heaviest blow he got during his brief career was when Hermit won the Derby; yet when the little chestnut came into the saddling paddock he was one of the first down and patting him on the neck quite affectionately; an on-looker, who did not know, might well have judged him a winner on the race—alas! when he had lost a very large fortune on it.

With the private life of the Marquis, with the tragic and romantic episodes connected with this sensational Derby, I do not propose to meddle. A veil—perhaps wisely—has been drawn over much of it, and it is not for me to raise it.

During his short and meteoric career he was one of the most generous supporters of Stockbridge. He entered horses in nearly all the races, and, in fact, there were but few of them where his popular colours were not sported. In 1868 they were seen but once there, and then not in the front. The brilliant career was dimmed, and life itself nearing the end. Another five months gone, "life's fitful fever" was over, and he was sleeping quietly at Kensal Green. I knew him through nearly the whole of his racing life, and saw a good deal of him. I believe he was a gentle, large-hearted, foolish young fellow. He was himself, doubtless, blamable for many things, but what blame belongs to others for the huge misfortunes of his later days, and for his all too early and tragic ending, no human being can tell. Just the fringe of the cloud of mystery which enveloped The Earl was once lifted a little. We should stand aghast could it be entirely raised. Thirty-five years have passed since those days, and perhaps it is too much to expect that a true account of M Henry Padwick's connection with this horse of mystery, and this unfortunate young nobleman, will ever get itself properly written.

The next plunger I shall have to introduce to my readers was, in almost all respects, a totally different man to the noble Marquis, but he will admirably suit my purpose as a type of the second sort of plunger.

A very familiar figure in the ring, for many years, was old Bill Roberts, and in many respects he was a notable character, deserving a place in my collection of plungers; although a plunger, he managed to remain on the scene through a long course of years, chequered with strangest vicissitudes. But Roberts was something more than a plunger. As I have said, a plunger generally has quite an ephemeral existence, but he had a knack of turning his hand to all sorts of jobs. When he was "stony broke" as a backer, which was not infrequently the case, he would swear to back no more horses as long as he lived, and would actually take book and pencil in hand, put on the satchel, and join the ranks of his natural enemies, "the bloated bookmakers," as he was wont to call them. As a rule, these fits didn't last long; so soon as, by any means, he became possessed of a bank, he went back to the ranks of the punter.

I remember him coming up to me at the opening race at one Warwick Meeting. I was offering 5 to 1 against anything, bar the favourite. Handing me a sovereign he said: "That's the only quid I have in the world, Dykey. I'm going to have the lot on the winner of this first race, and I'll show you at the end of the day what I run it into." The horse he backed won, and he came and drew six pounds. I saw him several times during the day, apparently very busy, but thought no more of his remark, and had no business with him again till the very last race of the day, when he backed another horse which turned out the winner, and this time for a large amount, so that he had to draw, I believe, a hundred and fifty pounds; and when he came for it he had a great bundle of notes in his hands, which I presume he had been drawing elsewhere.

"Well, Master Billy," I observed, as I paid him my contribution, "you've made the poor fielders sit up with your quid to-day."

"I have, my lad," he replied, "and I wish I'd broken every one of them. I promised I'd show you what I'd run the quid into. Here it is." And he pulled out of his inside vest pocket another roll of notes, totalling up, as he told me, altogether, to upwards of nine hundred pounds.

Roberts was betting very heavily during the remainder of the week, having occasionally as much as a monkey down on one race, and it was said he won nearly four thousand pounds on the week. In less than a month it had all vanished, and he was scrambling along as best he could. Some men would have lost heart, and given the business up as a bad job. Not so poor old Bill; he came up to the scratch again, fresh as paint, prepared for another battle. And, defeated or victorious, he took it all as a matter of course; hence he lasted so much longer than the ordinary plunger.

I have witnessed many wonderful feats performed by these plungers, but a friend of Roberts', and a man remarkably like him, in many respects, was the hero of one of the most startling. Old Bill Page was an inveterate gambler and plunger, who went through as many vicissitudes as any of his class. He was backing horses at Newmarket, at a five days' meeting; he bet on pretty well every race during the four first days, and didn't win a single bet, and on the morning of the last day he found himself "stony," so taking a rather valuable pin out of his scarf, he visited his avuncular relative and raised two sovereigns. Before closing time that evening he had redeemed his pin, and had upwards of two thousand pounds—*ready*—in his pocket.

Mr. George Gomm, the owner of Fraulein, Pageant, Congress, and many other real good horses, was a great plunger. By business he was a corn merchant, with a very large business in Birmingham, and residing in the delightful village of Moseley, from whence I, and my party, hailed. Hence I knew him intimately, and had many transactions with him, but I am certain if it were possible to strike a balance between us, it would be found that I had had none of the best of our business relations; but when the crash in his affairs came, and I happened to become the owner of his beautiful house and grounds at Moseley, some ill-informed newspapers circulated the stupid report that I had won them off him, which was grossly untrue.

Watching the career of Mr. Gomm on the turf, from the first day of it until its close, it was a constant source of wonder to me how he could play the game as long as he did, so utterly reckless and void of method was his style of betting. He was not content to plunge heavily on his own horses, but betting had such a fascination for him, he found it impossible to stand by and see the most paltry race without betting on it, and betting with Mr. Gomm meant plunging. He would have a thousand pounds, or more, on a wretched race in which he had no interest, and ought not have meddled with, because some half-shoeless, vagabond hanger-on to the turf had told him it was "a snip." It is an astounding assertion to make, but I believe it is a fact that this disreputable class of tout contributed more to his downfall than anything else. His ear was ever at their service, and so was his purse, and if by an accident one of them blundered on to a winner for him, they expected, and, indeed, generally received, no small share of his winnings. In private life Mr. Gomm was a gentleman, and a real good sort; the statements I have made regarding him will show what sort of chance he possessed with the "square-heads" of the turf, as they will indicate my opinion of his mental fitness for the job he had undertaken.

The plunger who, I think, succeeded Mr. Gomm was

known as "Little Hill," a smart, dapper little chap, something under five feet high; hailing from whence nobody knew, and no one knew what became of him when his brief flash-in-the-pan was over.

He was a quiet, smiling, pleasant little fellow, who would never be taken for a betting man, much less for a sensational plunger. He was exceptionally spruce and particular in his dress, which, from his shiny patent leather boots to his glossy silk hat, was irreproachable for style, and, I should think, bran new about once a week. In fact, it used to be said he came out in a new silk hat every morning.

I don't think Mr. Hill bet so persistently on every race as did my friend Gomm, but, like him, when he once began to pencil his bets down he rarely stopped till the flag fell; down they went as fast as he could write. Bets of all sorts and sizes with anyone who would lay him, sometimes winning immense sums, and, of course, frequently losing as heavily; and I need not say he did not last long, and there came a day when we missed the little man, and his shiny top-hat and patent leather boots, altogether.

Later on there came from America a plunger of quite a different species—one Mr. Walton—a thick-set, bull-headed gentleman, with no gentle smiles for anybody. An alert, keen, determined man, who quickly won a reputation for methods not over-scrupulous, mixing a good deal with certain jockeys, and, it was more than hinted, having many of them in his pay. For a time he gave the bookmakers a terrible shaking, and people said: "Here, surely, is the man who will break the ring!" But the gentlemen who compose that magic circle require a lot of breaking, and Mr. Walton, with all his cunning and pluck, was not destined to accomplish that feat.

If Walton was keen as the blade of a knife, some of his antagonists were sharp as razors; and the battle between these contending forces was an interesting study for the observant looker-on. At times the cute Yankee got information from sources which only lumps of gold could tap—ah! how he would bet then! Yet, if the truth must be told, this valuable information was frequently worth less than nothing to him—was, in fact, a snare artfully prepared for him.

Walton was a man not easily snared, and more than once his natural shrewdness and clear sight enabled him to see the trap which was laid for him, and the adroitness with which he avoided it, letting somebody else, perhaps, drop in, was amusing. I recall one which illustrates my meaning. A well-known ex-jockey and trainer, with great secrecy, one day handed the plunger a hundred pounds, begging him to invest it for him on a certain horse of his in the next race; but in his anxiety that the hundred pounds should not be thrown away he spoilt the game.

"You try Charley Blank, Mr. Walton," he said; "he will be sure to lay you a good price."

"Right you are," replied Walton, walking away, as the trainer fondly hoped, to put his hundred on with Charley Blank, and then, probably, two or three thousand of his own.

Instead of this, however, the wily American proceeded to turn matters over in his mind. He knew Mr. Blank was not only a large bookmaker, and an owner of horses, but that he had close relations with this same trainer and his stable. The outcome of these cogitations appeared when Walton and the trainer met immediately after the race, which, I suppose I need not say, Mr. Blank's horse did not win.

The trainer was surprised to see an unusual smile on the face of the Yankee.

"Sorry we got beaten," began the trainer; "I hope, however, you didn't have a bad race?"

"Oh no; on the contrary, I had a very good race," said Walton. "You see, I didn't fancy yours, so I took the liberty of putting your hundred pounds in my own book, and of laying against him as much as I could."

With a view of throwing dust in the handicapper's eyes, and

other contingencies relating to future races, it was very desirable that our trainer's horse should have been a good favourite for this race, and equally so that he should be well beaten when, apparently, backed for such genuine money; and there is no doubt it was intended that Mr. Walton's heavy investments should bring about this desirable result. Besides this, the conspirators had no doubt that a considerable part of Mr. Walton's investments, as well as those of his numerous followers, would go into the right channels.

Mr. Walton, himself always digging pits and laying snares, with all his cleverness, was unable to steer clear of the deep holes which were dug for himself, and ultimately he had the misfortune to get into one too deep for him. Consequently, toward the end of one season, he went suddenly back to America, leaving a heavy account unsettled, and a good many people mourning for him. He left word he would return early in the following season, and settle with everybody. A good many seasons have come and gone since then, but the bookies are still waiting his return.

In 1887 there burst upon the turf-world another phenomenon in the shape of a very youthful plunger, named Benzon, who was perhaps the most foolish and reckless of all who had gone before him, and as he had a very handsome fortune to begin with, he was a little gold-mine to the bookies while he lasted, which, of course, was a very short time. "The Jubilee Plunger," as he was called, was a handsome, well-built young fellow, merry as a cricket, open as the day, and generous to a fault, with a disposition as innocent and unsuspicious as a child's. It was said he had a quarter of a million in ready money, and by the way in which he squandered it—not only on horse-racing, but on every conceivable form of folly—it looked as though he really was intent on trying how quickly he could get through such a pile. He allowed worthless horses to be foisted upon him at big prices; then he trained them, and raced them, and backed them for ten times as much as they were worth. He was not satisfied with betting huge sums with straight men who would pay him when, occasionally, he did back a winner, but he bet with thieves and welshers, who drew from him when he lost, and owed it him when he won.

Of course, for him the end came very soon. I think he was one of the most short-lived plungers I have known. When his money was done he wrote a book—or someone wrote it for him—to show what astounding folly he had been capable of in running through a magnificent fortune in record time.

CHAPTER XXXV

LAYING AGAINST "SAFE 'UNS"

Pilgrimage's One Thousand Guineas—O'Connor and his "Safe 'Uns"—The True Story of the Fraulein Case—The Disqualification of Pattern.

I HAVE told my readers already how disastrously some of my early efforts at finding "safe 'uns" to lay against turned out, and have made frank confession of a weakness in that respect, the like of which has, I believe, afflicted every layer I have known, with one solitary exception.

After I had improved my position, and was betting to a large amount of money, I felt no less disposed to lay a bit extra against a horse I knew, *or thought I knew*, had no chance. All this I know, as well as you, dear reader, is dreadfully immoral, and I ought to be ashamed of myself for such an unblushing confession. But before you begin flinging big stones, pray ask yourself a question or two. Consider if the same thing, under other names, is not common enough in this highly moral world among all grades and conditions of men, and in all trades and professions? It is not on the turf alone where sharp men, with a little more knowledge than their fellows, take advantage of it to get the best of a deal. The same thing is going on in every pathway of commerce, and in every walk of life; always excepting, of course, those paths of virtue round about Threadneedle Street, in this virtuous city of London.

I shall open this batch of "safe 'uns" with the reminiscence of a race which is anything but pleasurable, and, I am afraid,

LAYING AGAINST "SAFE 'UNS" 377

some of my readers also will have memories stirred which were better sleeping.

There was always a certain amount of dickiness about Pilgrimage's legs, and when she pulled up for the Two Thousand Guineas, there were not wanting critics who declared she was lame. My old friend, Bill Collins, was very intimate with George Fordham, who had told him that it was not only impossible the mare could win the "One Thou.," but utterly out of the question that they should even get her to the post, although it was certain the stable was very anxious to keep the matter quiet. Collins knew George was a man he could rely on, and consequently took the liberty of laying a considerable amount against her—I believe it was to lose a couple of thousand pounds. Of course, I and my brother, being a part of what was known as the Brummagem division, were in the good thing, and also helped ourselves, freely. The evening before the race Collins dined with Fordham and old Chris Fenning, and again the famous jockey assured him the mare was lame, and went so far as to declare that if they got the cripple to the post, he would never throw his leg over another horse.

My brother and George Collins, who were partners, had already laid very heavily against Pilgrimage. At the breakfast table, before going on to the Heath, there was some comparing of volume, and each member of the party was reckoning up what he had been able to get out of her, all looking upon that as so much already won.

"Let me see," said old Bill to his brother George, "you have just bought that nice little freehold at Yardley Wood, have you not?"

The younger brother replied in the affirmative.

"Well, then, as soon as you get in the ring," went on the old man, "you have an extra dash for a thousand or two more, just to pay for it, and build yourself a nice house upon it; you'd never get another chance like it."

And this we all firmly believed, because we had got to know

that the astute gentleman who controlled the stable had been up with the mare the whole of the preceding two nights, having ice brought into her box by the bucketful; and our information was that he had had her leg in it up to the knee. After events, however, threw a good deal of doubt on this story.

Captain Machell came into the ring just before the race, and, standing by Charley Hibbert, said: "I'll take ten thousand to eight, in a bet, that Pilgrimage wins."

"Wouldn't you like to lay that wager yourself, Captain?' asked Hibbert. As she was then being freely backed by the public at evens, nobody ventured to accommodate the redoubtable Captain.

Of course, the cripple's number went up among the starters.

"Now, what do you think of the Pusher's information?" asked my brother, who had all along been a little suspicious that Pilgrimage would be got to the post. "Now, I'll secure a good pitch to see the race, and if she's with them when they have travelled half a mile, you can reckon up the book, George, and tell me what we have lost, for if she can gallop at all she is sure to beat this lot."

That this opinion was largely shared by the public the betting made manifest, for she became, before the fall of the flag, an odds-on chance. There were nine runners. Clementine and Strathfleet, at 5 or 6 to 1 each, had friends, but scarcely any price would tempt backers to invest on any of the others; 25 to 1 was on offer. Jannette was unquestionably the best mare of the party, but as she had been seriously amiss, her friends had little hope of her. The result of this race, and her clever defeat of Pilgrimage in the Oaks a month later, proves that she must just then have been coming round again.

There was an excellent start, without delay, and Blue Ridge made the running. We, however, were horrified to see Pilgrimage lying comfortably at her girths, and going without any evidence of lameness. At the Bushes the favourite took the lead, and now Jannette, who had begun worse than anything, was seen running through her field, and had passed everything but the favourite and Clementine; the latter, however, was almost immediately beaten, and Archer lay down to his work on Jannette in his own determined fashion; but in Tom Cannon he met a foeman as determined, and as able, as himself. And although Lord Falmouth's mare struggled in the gamest possible manner, and Archer left nothing undone that human skill and energy could accomplish, to our dismay we saw Jannette succumb to the favourite by three parts of a length, and I think some of us got a lesson we shall never forget.

The late Mr. James O'Connor was for many years a friend of mine; and a notable layer against "safe 'uns" was Master Jimmy. And I might tell of more than one occasion when he went out of his way to save me from falling into a trap. His kindliness toward myself is shown in the ancedote which follows.

I often observed how badly some of the horses went when he took the liberty of laying a little over the market odds; it wasn't at all a good sign for the horses, or for those who backed them. I remember once having a job to put £500 on a prominent favourite for one of the classic races; the first portion of this money I invested with my old friend James.

"I suppose ye've more money for this animal, Friend Dyke?" said he.

"Oh, yes, a goodish bit," I replied.

"Then put it in your own book, my bhoy," said he; "onyway, kape it a few days, indade, it'll do you no harm."

I didn't like acting on this well-meant advice, my commission being for a gentleman who ought to have been quite as well informed as Master James; but before going any farther, I told my client I feared there must be a screw loose somewhere, begging him make more inquiry before the commission went any farther. Of course, I didn't let him know the source of my fears. The upshot of the matter was I received orders not to proceed with the commission. And it was made abundantly clear to me that my old friend James was better posted in the concerns of that particular stable than was my client, who was one of its chief patrons.

I always considered him a nice little fellow, but he was now and again a regular "take down," and I have known him on more than one occasion earn for himself the soundest cursing I ever heard a man get; but he rather enjoyed taking a rise out of the "sharps," and he did it in a style so quietly unconscious and innocent as to deceive all but those who knew him intimately. I should think he made a good deal of the £121,000 which he has left behind him in the days when ante-post betting was all the rage, for he was in the habit of making large books on future events.

And strange as it may appear, he bet most money, and *apparently* more recklessly, when he was "three sheets in the wind"; and stranger still, at such times, it was usually found that if anybody had suffered by this recklessness it wasn't Jimmy. I remember the first time I witnessed one of these performances I left the room with a feeling of pity that the nice little man should be making such a fool of himself; and rather disgusted with the sharps who were taking advantage of him, I happened to run against O'Connor's friend and compatriot, George Silke, and hastily explained the circumstances.

"For God's sake, George," I said, "go in and get him away; he's laying a ton of money against the favourite for the Ebor, and I'm sure he doesn't know what he is doing."

"Don't he now," was Mr. Silke's reply; "then, begorra, I'll not be able to tache him. Never fear for Jimmy, me bhoy; he'll be taking no harm. Sure, it's the gintlemen he's playing with who'll have the dirty end of the stick."

The favourite for the Ebor was scratched the following day.

At the present time, when ante-post betting is of a very limited character, and, I may say, in a moribund condition, laying against "safe 'uns" is no longer the profitable business it was in the good old times, when, in all our great races, horses were backed for an immense amount of money months before they were to be decided, with the result that, where there was any "milking" to be done, the opportunities were not only much greater, but the danger of being discovered at the work greatly minimised. A quarter of a century ago the Liverpool Cup was one of the races about which there was considerable ante-post betting. The Summer Cup of 1875 produced a "safe 'un" of the safest sort I have ever known, and furnished the racing world with a sensation and a scandal which is remembered with bitterness to the present day. Years ago I was urged to tell the world what I knew about it, and have been offered inducements to do so; but, so far, I have resisted the temptation. And it is with the greatest reluctance, and only after a trying wrangle with myself on the subject, that I have arrived at the conclusion it would be impossible for me to publish these reminiscences of my turf life without some reference to this notorious case, wherein I and my brothers, and other near friends, were at the time, and frequently since, charged with complicity. For, for years after the Fraulein scandal, I and my friends were compelled to submit to pretty constant abuse on the subject, and it was quite a common thing, when we were driving away from a race-course, to be assailed with "There goes the Fraulein mob," with occasionally a very much more violent assortment of epithets; and yet it is a fact that neither myself, my brother, or either of the three younger of the quartette of Collins', had the slightest bit to do with the inception or carrying out of this big "job." In fact, not until the very day of the race, and about an hour before it, did either of us suspect anything was wrong with the mare. The truth is, I was on the point of backing her—although, I must confess, I had been told not to do so until I got definite orders—when I received my first intimation that she would probably not be found among the runners, although she was on the ground—her trainer very confident; and, as I had reason to know, he and his friends had backed her to win a good stake.

Fraulein had been a good favourite, but, in the language of the turf, she had just begun to smell a bit "fishy"; and when I settled down to my business of making a book on the race, I found it a difficult matter to lay a fair share of it against this mare.

Among others of my regular clients, good old George Payne came up.

"Now, Mr. Dyke," said he, "what will you lay me your Brummagem horse?" meaning, of course, Fraulein.

"I'll bet *you* four ponies, Mr. Payne," I replied.

"Put it down," he answered.

"Make it four fifties, Mr. Payne."

"I'll see you —— first, Master Dykey," was his answer; and as he turned away, added: "She oughtn't to be half the price if she's a right one."

In a few minutes Mr. Payne returned.

"Your friend Gomm's mare goes badly," said he. "I suppose I've thrown my pony away, eh, Mr. Dyke? You ought to know something about it, eh?"

Well, I could not tell him what I knew, or rather what I had reason to suspect; but having the greatest respect for this grand old sportsman, I could not refrain from dropping a hint of it.

"I'd have a pony on Tam o' Shanter if I was you, Mr. Payne," I answered.

"Well, what will you lay me him?" he asked.

"As you have backed what you consider a 'wrong 'un,' sir, I'll lay you the same price—four ponies, Mr. Payne."

"Done! I'll have four fifties," he replied quickly.

"No, sir; I'll only lay the odds to twenty-five pounds," I

answered; and as that horse was at the time a better favourite than Fraulein, I thought I was treating him liberally.

So the two transactions I had with him on the race cost me seventy-five pounds. But, although I would lay him no more myself, I saw him busy among the bookies; and I fancy he took advantage of the hint I had dropped to a considerable extent.

As far as my memory serves me, it was about twenty minutes before the time set for the race, when a friend of Mr. Gomm's walked into the weighing-room, and delivered into the proper hands that famous letter, signed by the owner of Fraulein, and which ordered his mare to be scratched for the Liverpool Cup. That gentleman's own trainer protested; everybody present was indignant, and cried, "Shame!" But it was all useless. Fraulein's number did not go up, and some three or four people won a big sum of money, which the public, which did not even get a run for it, lost. The fact of leaving the mare in the race up to almost the last moment, and squeezing out of the public the last shilling, intensified the indignation of the whole racing community, which the sporting press of the country voiced in language more vigorous than polite toward the authors of the scandal. A very old and dear friend of my own came in for the biggest share of it, while Mr. Gomm himself was not spared. Gomm long since departed this life, in more senses than one a broken man; but how much of the blame he got was really deserved, there is, I believe, but one man living who could tell.

The following facts, however, will, I know, stand uncontradicted.

Some time before the Liverpool Races, Mr. Gomm gave this old friend of mine an order to back Fraulein for a large amount, limiting him to a price which any sane man should have known it would be impossible to obtain. With this big order he handed my friend the letter authorising the scratching of the mare—in the event of this tremendous order not being carried out—at what time he should think most opportune. The hour my ancient friend thought most opportune was some twenty minutes before the time the public was expecting the mare's number to go up for the race.

In the meantime, a notable bookmaker in Manchester, still alive, another in Newcastle-on-Tyne, another in London, Dan Lawrence in the Midlands, Timson & Carr in Birmingham, and others, elsewhere, had been busy laying against her. This much I know for a fact; and I have always held an opinion that the long-headed Staffordshire collier was the prime mover in the whole business. That Fraulein would have won her backers' money had she been permitted to run was amply demonstrated, when, two days later, she cantered away with a race almost as important as the Cup; and again when, a few months later, she won the Doncaster Cup with nearly 9 st on her back.

And so ends, for ever, as far as I am concerned, this painful episode; which, if I could, I would gladly have left untouched.

I come now to another highly sensational case—the disqualification of Pattern, wherein, I suppose, I must consider myself the chief actor; for the disqualification of that horse for all the races he had ever won was brought about by myself. The case, at the time, caused a great sensation, and brought me, from certain people who happened to suffer by it, a plentiful crop of abuse and ill-will; the amusing part of the business was, however, that those who howled loudest, being a little hurt, were all such as would only too gladly have assisted at it, if they had known as much as I did anent this matter. In fact, I question if the sting of being left out of such a good thing was not, with some of them, more painful than losing their money.

In the year 1885, Pattern ran twelve times, winning six races. It was, I think, in the spring of that year when I got my first inkling of the fact that those responsible for entering him for all these races were getting an unfair advantage over all their opponents, to the extent of some pounds in every race he ran in; the fact being he was a year older than they claimed him to be. And now, before I proceed any farther, let me frankly admit that I do not believe—what I have more than once heard insinuated—that there was anything like a fraud intended. I am quite certain Mr. Young Graham, who bred the horse, and who was, I believe, all through, his actual owner, would never have countenanced such a thing, nor have I any reason to suppose that Dr. Dougall, who managed him under a lease, had the slightest idea that he was wrongly describing him when he entered him as a five-year-old, while he was really a six-year-old.

Up to the present time the whole of the facts of the case have never been published, and that is what I now propose doing. For my own share in these transactions, whatever blame belongs to me I am willing to bear; and, judged by the general standard of morality, I am aware I shall be considered blamable, but judged by the ethics of the turf, and its common practice, I must be acquitted. I am certain I did nothing that any ordinary followers of racing would not have done in similar circumstances.

I do not intend to disclose the exact means by which I received the first hint of the fraud which was being perpetrated, and which, for all I knew at the time, might not have been so innocent as I now believe it to have been; to do so would possibly do an injury to a person still actively engaged on the turf.

I need not tell the brotherhood of bookmakers, or indeed any human being acquainted with the turf and its practices, that the moment I became possessed of the valuable asset contained in this knowledge I did not share it with everybody I met. According to ordinary morals, that is, of course, what I ought to have done; instead of which, however, I carefully locked up the knowledge until such time as it might be of use to myself, and the friends whom I might see fit to enlighten.

The thing I set myself to do was to wait patiently until I should find Pattern a red-hot favourite, then lay my little pile against him. He ran a good many times, but never, when I was present, was he such a favourite as would make it worth my while acting against him.

At the Shrewbury Meeting he was in a Hunters' Flat Race, when I thought the time had surely come, and I went there prepared to bring off the good thing. On the book it appeared good for him to beat all the known performers, but there arrived on the scene a certain unknown candidate, a grand-looking black horse belonging to Mr. Fowler, and trained by Sam Darling. Just before the race, Mr. Best, one of the principal patrons of the stable, and one of the most astute men I have met on the turf, took me into a quiet corner.

"I want you to put a bit of money for the stable," he said, "on one of ours, in the next race."

"With pleasure, Mr. Best," I replied. "Bloodstone is the horse, I presume; how much do you want on?"

"Well, I cannot tell you the exact amount," he answered; "but get *all* the long prices you can, and go on till I tell you to stop. I'll be near you."

I could see this was a big job, and coming from such a quarter, no doubt an absolute "cert." So I ventured to remind my astute friend that he should not expect too much; as Shrewsbury was no longer the Shrewsbury of John Frail and the old times, when you could have put two or three thousand on a horse, and then not make him a favourite; the market now was poor and weak, and the big black horse was sure to be a good favourite when three or four hundred pounds had been invested, and I then added:

"He is in at Derby next week, you say, Mr. Best; why not keep him till then? You may win as many thousands there as hundreds here, and perhaps with no greater outlay." This advice, however, was of no avail.

"The horse is here," he said, "and must take his chance,"

LAYING AGAINST "SAFE 'UNS"

I saw it was all over with any possibility of seeing Pattern a favourite, so I made up my mind to "field" on the race for Bloodstone, and allow Pattern to wait for another day. Of course, with the knowledge I had of Bloodstone, I may have laid something extra against Pattern, but with no idea of getting him disqualified, as was, in after days, more than once asserted by my old and esteemed friend, "Toney" Benjamin, who happened, on that occasion, to subscribe to my book, I believe, a matter of five-and-twenty pounds.

Well, Bloodstone won very easily, as he was bound to do, considering he was receiving a lump of weight from horses to whom he could readily have conceded as much.

So we arrive at December, 1885, and unless the *coup* can be brought off before the end of the month, all my knowledge and patient waiting will have been thrown away, for on the first day of another month he will be, according to the book, an aged horse, and he will therefore, thenceforth, be carrying his correct weight.

I saw he was entered at Kempton Park, and I fervently hoped Dr. Dougall would run him; for it was not only, in all probability, the last opportunity I should have, but his opponents in this race were but a middling lot, with old Beckhampton, perhaps, the best of them; so if the field should not be too numerous, it might be a case of odds on; and with this, given a good market, what possibilities loomed before me!

When the day arrived, it seemed as though all the forces of nature were arrayed against me, and that after all I should be baulked of my prey. It hailed, rained, and snowed, and there had been a sharp frost during the night. "No racing to-day," I said to myself, "and perhaps not for many days, and so ends my golden hopes in this direction."

However, I went down to Waterloo Station to try to ascertain whether there would be racing. There were very few people there, and among them great diversity of opinion on the subject. No authoritive message arrived, so some went home again. I, and a mere handful of others, went down to Kempton on the off-chance. We found there a very miserable attendance, with still a doubt as to whether there would be any racing.

At last the stewards decided to give it a trial, and, with danger and difficulty, the first three races were brought off; and then the numbers were hoisted for Pattern's race, and my eyes were gladdened to see that animal's number among them, accompanied by Beckhampton, Maid of the Mill, and Quite Too Too; so I was satisfied that Pattern would be a strong favourite, and one of the right sort of "safe 'uns" to lay against; but the unfortunate condition of the market was not promising for anything big being done.

I tried, hurriedly, to find Tom Leader, so as to impress upon him the necessity of his jockey persevering with his old horse, so as to make sure of being in front of the two outsiders—which I knew he would be certain to do, unless he should be pulled up in the event of Pattern appearing to have the race in hand—my intention being to back Beckhampton heavily instead of laying against Pattern, which would come to much the same thing, without exposing me to quite so much notice. In this, however, I was foiled, as Mr. Leader was not to be found; so I commenced to make a one-horse book, laying all I could against Pattern.

The gentlemanly element of the turf was almost entirely absent, and I could see that all my customers would be the hard-headed sharps of the ring. My clerk not being with me, I begged the genial Tom Collins to wield the pencil for me on this one race. The clever division rushed to lay the odds on Pattern, and I accommodated them as fast as they came; and when Mr. Fry, and some others of the few fielders present, began to hold out for increased odds, I continued to accommodate them at about the old rate, and friend Tom looked aghast.

"Do you know what you're doing?" he asked, with

dismay. "You'll lose a heap of money if Pattern wins."

"No, I shan't," was my reply. "You go on writing all I lay, and ask no questions."

Of course, he then understood I had a reason for what I was doing.

They are off! Up the straight the four horses come! Pattern, as my friends afterwards told me, leading many a length. I had no care for the horses; I did not see them; nor did I want to see them. My back was turned to them, and my face toward the hard-heads on the stand, who thought they were besting me, while still my cry rang out:

"I'll take two to one!"

"Me a pony!" "Me a pony!" and "Me fifty!" shouts out excitedly, and at the same instant, such innocents as Arthur Cooper, Teddy Hobson, and John O'Neill. And down went these amounts, with many others.

The race is over, and Pattern is acclaimed the winner. I rushed instantly to the weighing-room, arranged with Leader for an objection, and then the fun began again—this time in the paddock.

The doctor himself came up.

"What do you suppose you know about my horse?" he asked, through his clenched teeth.

"I know enough to take you three ponies you don't get the race," I answered.

"Done!" said he.

And "Done!" "Done!" "Done!" came again from the same old set, who might be excused for believing that the doctor knew more of his own horse than I could possibly know. So there was ultimately almost as much money betted after the race as before it.

Well, the objection, on the question of wrong age, and therefore carrying short weight, was duly gone into by the stewards, and Pattern promptly disqualified.

This decision was more disastrous and far-reaching, in its results, than I had intended or dreamt of, for it necessitated the horse's disqualification for every one of the six races he had won throughout the year. The second horse in all these races was declared the winner; stakes and bets were ordered to be refunded. Law-suits and trouble of other sort, for which I was sincerely sorry, ensued, and there was any quantity of excitement about the case in racing circles. Losers on the race refused to pay up; those who had won by Pattern on previous races protested against having to disgorge, and there was great difficulty in recovering the stakes which had been unjustly won. There was much printer's ink wasted 'twixt leading articles and vehement correspondence; and altogether such a stir made, that ultimately the racing authorities were compelled to so far modify the rules as to prevent future disqualifications from having such a retrospective penalty.

It was most unfortunate for Captain Middleton, Dr. Dougall, and those who suffered with them on this occasion, that Pattern's race was not later on the card, because immediately after it, the ground becoming rapidly more dangerous, the stewards ordered the racing to be discontinued.

Those who had lost most money to me declined to settle until they had consulted the highest authority on the subject; so I was summoned, at the instance of Dr. Dougall, to appear before the Committee of Tattersall. And, for the purpose of hearing the case, there was a very full meeting of that august and important body, with the Duke of Beaufort in the chair. Dr. Dougall was first called upon for his version of the affair, and then three or four of his fellow-sufferers. Finally, I was called up for my defence, and to make a short story of it, I may say I came out with flying colours, and they were ordered to pay, which, with one solitary exception, and that for a very small amount, everyone did. Prince Saltykoff, as I was about to leave the room, put the whole case in a nutshell:

"You were betting, I suppose, Dyke, on what you thought *you* knew," said the Prince.

"That was so," I replied; and then the Prince added:

"Evidently those gentlemen were betting on what *they* thought they knew, only your knowledge, on this occasion, happened to be the better."

My readers, I am sure, will be wondering how it came about that a horse could be entered in such a lot of races, run in a dozen of them, winning no less than six of the stakes, and this happening all over the country, and extending throughout one entire season, the horse all the while wrongly described in the vital matter of age, and therefore always carrying short weight—and no one of the clever people who are always on the look-out for such opportunities becoming aware of the fact.

Without a true understanding of the case, it seems impossible to exonerate from blame certain people, especially the breeder and owner, and perhaps another nearly concerned in the management of the horse.

Here, then, are the simple facts of the case. Pattern began his inglorious career, in public, almost as early as it was possible for him to do so, which was in the Cup for two-year-olds, at Lincoln, the 23rd March, 1881; poor Archie Wainright riding him. He ran again at the Newmarket Second Spring Meeting in a two-year-old plate, this time Charley Wood being his jockey. Running very badly on the two first attempts, it was decided to trust him no more till such time as the Nurseries were about; so we find him running his next race—and his last as a two-year-old—in the Loudoun Nursery at the Derby September Meeting; and here he showed no improvement on his wretched performances in the early part of the year, hence his owner, in disgust, turned him out of training, and tried to forget such a horse had been foaled—the tragic part of the business, for Dr. Dougall and many others, being that the owner forgot too much; so that when he had been thrown on one side for nearly three years, and everybody, including Mr.

Graham, had well-nigh forgotten him, some wretched groom did that gentleman the ill-turn of reminding him of the horse's existence, intimating at the same time that he looked, after all, like making a race-horse. So he was fetched up, groomed, and then put into training, and by-and-by the time arrived to enter him in a race, and then ensued the tragic part of the matter.

Time had gone, I suppose, so pleasantly with my friend young Graham that he counted the three years Pattern had been "turned up" as two, entering him as a five-year-old instead of six, neither Mr. Graham nor anybody else taking the simple precaution of testing memory by a glance at the Stud Book. So originated this hubbub, and trouble, and terrible loss for Messrs. Dougall, Graham, Middleton, and a host of others.

THE END.